D1247727

Broadcasting and Democracy
in France

Broadcasting and Democracy
in France

Ruth Thomas

BRADFORD UNIVERSITY PRESS
in association with
CROSBY LOCKWOOD STAPLES   LONDON

Granada Publishing Limited
First published in Great Britain 1976 by
Bradford University Press in association with
Crosby Lockwood Staples
Frogmore St Albans Hertfordshire AL2 2NF and
3 Upper James Street London W1R 4BP

ISBN 0 258 97006 5

Printed in Great Britain by
Cox & Wyman Ltd
London, Fakenham and Reading

❦

Broadcasting and Democracy in France

This study of French broadcasting, together with its companion volume *Broadcasting and Democracy in West Germany*, has been generously funded by the Joseph Rowntree Social Service Trust. In 1905, Joseph Rowntree made the remark that the best way of influencing public opinion was through journalism. Since that time the Trust has maintained a continuous interest in the media, of which broadcasting has achieved an importance that could scarcely have been foreseen in 1905. While, in Britain, the Annan Commission is reviewing the broadcasting arrangements here, it seemed to the authors and myself that there were some very interesting new developments taking place in both West Germany and France which should be investigated and made available to English-speaking readers.

One of the litmus tests of a healthy liberal democracy is the effectiveness of its broadcasting system. It is, however, difficult to produce successful results because here, in contrast to the press, the need is to maintain balance *within* one organization and not just overall. As France is a unitary State, the organization of broadcasting is more straightforward than in Germany. On the other hand, direct government interference in the selection and presentation of news and current affairs programmes has been much more overt and intense. It is not widely realized in Britain, moreover, that this interference had become established before de Gaulle returned to power in 1958. A spirited struggle has been waged against it, particularly from the time of the revolt of 1968. Ruth Thomas has given a fascinating account of this struggle,

[v]

including an assessment of the changes following the 1974 reforms. By abolishing the post of Minister of Information, President Giscard d'Estaing has indicated that there should be no going back to the old system.

As in the German case, the French broadcasting system constitutes one of the windows through which French society can be observed. For example, only in a country with a high degree of national consciousness would a Head of Radio and Television News be likely to make the remark that 'A journalist should be French first, objective second' (see Chapter One). While admittedly this statement is reported to have been made at a time of national crisis in 1961, it only made more explicit the attitude of the authorities for some years before and afterwards.

It is clearly vital to the health of a liberal democracy that the electorate has easy and prompt access to news objectively presented. It also needs to be able to listen to its leaders debating the great issues of public policy in a way that enables the important available choices to emerge. While all governments in liberal democracies now accept this in principle, all of them also feel resentment when in practice it involves constraints on them. As John Stuart Mill remarked in his famous essay *On Liberty*: 'While every one well knows himself to be fallible, few think it necessary to take any precautions against their own fallibility...'.

Just as the independence of broadcasting can be threatened by political pressures, so can it be threatened too by pressure from commercial interests. In this field France has had a much happier experience. In many ways she has had the best of both worlds. The presence of private stations round her frontiers like Luxembourg and Monte Carlo has meant that there was some competition for the state monopoly during the worst years of government control. On the other hand, when advertising was eventually admitted on French Television it was done by the State network. Furthermore, the most stringent controls have been imposed to protect the public from misleading statements by advertisers. This part of the story is told by Ruth Thomas in the same fascinating detail. The book will, I am sure, be of absorbing interest both to the specialist and to the informed general reader.

Stephen Holt
Professor of European Studies
University of Bradford

[vi]

Acknowledgements

I am grateful to the Joseph Rowntree Social Service Trust for
financing a year of full-time research at the University of Bradford,
and for enabling me to make several journeys to France to collect
material.

Jacques Jochum, Lecturer in Modern Languages at Bradford
University, has guided the project from its beginnings. He has
read the entire manuscript, and made invaluable suggestions at all
stages. His first-hand knowledge of France and of French politics
and institutions has saved me from a number of errors. I am very
grateful for his careful supervision and unflagging interest.
Professor S. C. Holt, of the School of European Studies, has
followed throughout the progress of our research.

In France, I would like to thank Mr Mark Mortimer, *maître de
conférences* at the *Institut d'études politiques* in Paris. A number of
people directly concerned with broadcasting kindly agreed to give
me their time, answering my questions and suggesting or sending
me material. I am especially grateful to M. Alain Duhamel,
political journalist; M. Édouard Guibert, Philippe Dominique
and Jacques Barbot, of the *Syndicat national des journalistes*; M.
Édouard Durand, of the *Syndicat national des réalisateurs de télévision-
CGT*; M. Jean-Frédéric Laignoux, of the *ORTF* Research
Service. M. William Studer, then Delegate for Public Relations at
ORTF, also sent me some valuable documentation. My thanks also
to Judith and Tim Le Goff, who obtained some material for me in
Paris.

I am grateful to Dr Jay Blumler of Leeds University for

inviting me to attend his seminars at the Centre for Television Research.

My gratitude also to the librarians at Bradford University, who facilitated my research in a number of ways; and to Michigan State University, East Lansing, Michigan, which allowed me to use its graduate library.

Mrs Paula Greenwood has very efficiently typed the manuscript.

Finally, I thank my husband, Tim Webb, not only for his financial support, but for his extraordinary tolerance, his practical help, and his invaluable encouragement at every stage.

Ruth Thomas
October 1975

Preface

The present study attempts to explore some aspects of the relationship between broadcasting as an institution and the exercise of democracy in France. Chapter One examines the history of French broadcasting from its beginnings, concentrating, however, on the period after 1959. Chapter Two describes the structures and finance of broadcasting before and after 1974 (since the 1974 reorganization has not yet had time to show its workings), and asks whether the organization itself is 'democratic'. Chapter Three examines on the one hand the relations between broadcasting and the State (government, Parliament), and on the other, between broadcasting as a State monopoly and various commercial interests. Chapter Four deals with the two central features of a democratic broadcasting system: information and citizen participation.

It may be thought that there is too much about broadcasting and too little about democracy. Unfortunately, on the former, there is very little material available in English. I have felt it necessary, therefore, to provide a considerable amount of basic information about the organization of French broadcasting. Institutions can be no more democratic than the structures on which they are based, and while personalities may make more exciting reading, mechanisms cannot be ignored. Examining how men form the structures of institutions and are then caught and formed by them in their turn has its own peculiar fascination.

R.T.

Abbreviations

Contents

[xi]

❦

CHAPTER ONE

The Weight of the Past

THE BEGINNINGS

Conditioned by war and occupation, refashioned by the idealism of the Liberation, French broadcasting can early be seen developing those traits which appear so clearly in later years. On the one hand, government control, more extensive and more political than is usual in Western Europe; and a weighty though often ineffectual bureaucracy. On the other – condition of survival – a wealth of individual talent which manages to circumvent the handicaps and pressures so frequently laid upon it.

The first regular radio programmes began in November 1921, broadcast from the military transmitter of the Eiffel Tower, under the command of General Ferrié, one of the pioneers of the new technique. Within two years, in June 1923, the French State extended its long-standing monopoly of postal and telegraphy services to cover radio communications.[1] However, this monopoly was largely nominal: the State retained ultimate control, but, like other European governments at that time, it sold permits to private companies which operated alongside the State network and were run largely by industrialists and newspaper proprietors. A decree of November 1923 stated that these concessions were to run for 10 years, during which time it was hoped the State would gradually take over the private companies.[2] In fact, the system lasted until 1939, although intervening decrees insisted on the temporary and revocable nature of the permits, and no new ones were issued after 1929. In 1935, 13 established private stations received temporary concessions.

Meanwhile, the State radio service was being gradually given some kind of official structure. On 1 June 1927, radio was made a separate and outside service of the Ministry of Posts, Telegraph and Telephones (*PTT*), and was given its own administrators. This authority ran the official 'Paris-PTT' station. It later extended State control by buying up 'Radio-Paris' in 1933, and in the following years, by setting up a regional network of stations, an enterprise too costly for any private company to consider. In 1933, a law was passed creating a tax on wireless receivers, while two years later the State radio agreed to abolish advertising. The private stations were given the monopoly of radio advertising; in exchange, they had agreed to extensions of government control.[3]

Already, then, State radio was part of the French administrative system; its personnel were Civil Servants. The figure of authority was the Minister of Posts rather than the Director of Radio, and there was a direct telephone link between ministry and radio station. In the mid-1930s, Paul Vialar, the first head of radio drama, arrived on his first day to find an office but no furniture. A telephone call to the Minister, Georges Mandel, produced the appropriate ministerial tantrum; furniture rapidly appeared. It would be a mistake to think of ministry supervision as a wholly sinister phenomenon, as the anecdote shows: ministers, and Mandel in particular, did much to encourage the development of the new art.[4] None the less, government control and bureaucratic administrative procedures became habits which have never been fully shaken off.

Not only did successive governments assert their control, but naturally enough other political groups struggled to influence radio. For example, the radio stations' management councils (*Conseils de gérance*) set up by Mandel in 1935 included a large proportion of members directly elected by listeners. Here was an opportunity for a political arena, and indeed in 1937 the election of listeners' representatives became a straight contest between the government and opposition.[5]

Mounting international tension during the immediate prewar period justified an increase of government control. The dangers of broadcast propaganda had been recognized much earlier, but after 1933 in particular, the Nazi example showed even more clearly radio's potential effect on public opinion. In October 1938 a decree set up strict surveillance of programmes dealing with economic, political or financial matters.[6] Then in July 1939, radio was virtually removed from the control of the Ministry of Posts. Recognized as a separate administrative department, it now came under the direct supervision of the Prime Minister (or President of the Council as he was then called), and, in theory at least, of the General Commissioner for Information, the playwright Jean Giraudoux. The job of the new department, the Central Administration of National Broadcasting, was to run the State network – Radio-Paris, Paris-PTT, Tour Eiffel and the colonial service, Paris-Mondial – as well as to keep a close eye on the 12 remaining private stations. In this way, the government could use radio as a 'powerful instrument of moral defence' in a situation that was now extremely grave. Furthermore, a government department provided official news bulletins for all French radio stations to transmit at fixed times. Private stations continued to broadcast during 1939–40, but were financially restricted by lack of advertising revenue.[7]

The Occupation in June 1940 created two zones in France. In the north, the Germans requisitioned all radio installations whether public or private, while in the south, the Vichy government created a public organization, National Broadcasting (*Radiodiffusion nationale*), which exercized a monopoly in that zone and which formed a vital part of its propaganda services.[8]

The prewar extension of government control over radio in general and radio news in particular meant that the Vichy régime already had a framework to build on. National and private radio in the southern zone could continue to be controlled – with German permission – by the various acting heads of government under Pétain. Unlike the Third Republic, which had shown considerable reluctance to use any form of overt action on public opinion, for Vichy, propaganda was an indispensable method of government, and radio one of its most important media. For this reason, radio now became one of the main pieces of the power game within the régime, and reflected the vagaries of the latter. Thus, confusion as to responsibilities for radio in 1939 and 1940–41 corresponded to the instability of government itself, while Pierre Laval as head of government in 1942 kept his own hand firmly on all the information and propaganda services. Similarly, in 1943, when various totalitarian movements tried to take over the government, radio propaganda gave the impression of a multiplicity of 'voices' each with its own message. The final phase shows the process even more clearly: the SS-backed *Milice* (Militia) took over all State propaganda services in 1944, and Philippe Henriot, the Secretary of State for Information and Propaganda, later assassinated by the Resistance, not only used radio for daily, personal, propaganda broadcasts, but had the law changed in order to make himself, by virtue of his office, the rightful president of the Higher Broadcasting Council.

Private radio stations which continued to broadcast in the southern zone were likewise dependent on the government, not only because of legal controls but also by the economic fact that in the absence of advertising revenue they needed government subsidies to survive at all. Their docility to the régime and its needs in terms of propaganda was in any case guaranteed by the political allegiance of their owners: Pierre Laval himself had owned 'Radio-Lyon' since 1929, and had shares in 'Radio-Nîmes'. A further means of State control, however, and one that was to outlast the Vichy régime, was financial. The law of 7 November 1942 gave national radio the opportunity to acquire shares in private stations. In early 1943, the State bought up the *Société financière de radiodiffusion* (*SOFIRAD*), which in turn, as a State company, bought 50 per cent of shares in the new *Société Radio-Monte Carlo* (the other 50 per cent being controlled by German and Italian interests).

While the Vichy government used radio blatantly as part of its propaganda machinery, it also reorganized radio's administrative structures, giving them a theoretical flexibility which might have proved fertile under a different régime. The State monopoly was confirmed by law in late 1941, but in the following year more detailed legislation removed radio from the usual framework of public administration and set up management methods more appropriate to its character as an industrial and commercial enterprise. For example, most of the personnel, hitherto officially Civil Servants, were put on contract.[9] Meanwhile, the National Council of the Resistance prepared its own blueprint for radio.

This, then, was the situation facing France at the end of the war. After the Liberation, all private station licences were officially revoked,[10] driving commercial companies to start all over again but this time from outside France's borders. The radio network as a whole had suffered enormous damage at the hands of the

Germans, and, as in other sectors of the economy, only the government had the money and organizational structures available for large-scale reconstruction. Both popular feeling and economic necessity favoured widespread nationalization of services and industry. In the case of broadcasting in particular, it was felt that State supervision, far from being repressive, was the only way to guarantee freedom from the more dangerous control of commercial interests.

After some hesitation, the Vichy laws on radio, revoked *en bloc* by the blanket ordinance which nullified all that government's legislation, were nevertheless reinstalled and finally cannibalized. With solemn assertions of its temporary nature, *Radiodiffusion-télévision française* (RTF) was created by decree on 8 November 1945. The new organization (the official inclusion of television was one of its main novelties) was a State monopoly and public service, directly attached to the Prime Minister (President of the Council) and his Minister of Information, and financed by a government subsidy subject to annual review. (The licence fee revenue went directly into the Treasury.) The alternative plan drawn up by the Resistance Committee for the Liberation of Radio formed the basis for a projected statute submitted to the government in December 1945. This, like many of its successors, never reached parliamentary debate.[11]

By early 1946, a pattern seemed to be establishing itself. Further 'temporary' legislation set up a Higher Broadcasting Council, and a Central Council whose task it was to draw up a definitive statute for broadcasting. The latter's proposals, again largely inspired by the Resistance project, were sent to the Ministry of Information, but never saw the light of day thereafter. More than a dozen statutes were to meet a similar fate between then and 1958. The Ministry of Information, itself originally a temporary measure and a response to the extraordinary circumstances of the war, also proved remarkably persistent. Claude Bourdet, the Director of Radio from October 1945 (under Malraux's Ministry) resigned in February 1946 as a protest against the interventionist attitudes of the new Secretary of State for Information, the Socialist Gaston Defferre. The war had shown the political power of radio for good or evil: few European States were to let control of broadcasting slip entirely from their hands after such a lesson.

While radio was already highly developed, television in France was still largely experimental. There were about 300 sets in France in 1939, as compared to about 25,000 in Britain.[12] Research had continued during the war, with results being as far as possible withheld from the Germans, who set up their own studios in a Paris cinema. Regular television programmes did not begin on any reasonable scale until 1947–48, and it was not until the late 1950s that television, by virtue of the number of viewers, became a major social or political force in French life.

As far as broadcasting is concerned, the years between the Liberation and the fall of the Fourth Republic were marked by growing dissatisfaction in France. The state of television is symptomatic. While radio, well-established, had administrative and political problems, television, rapidly expanding in other countries, was struggling in France against a variety of circumstances which combined to stunt its growth. As a product of the laboratory, French television was second to none; as part of the social fabric, it was comparatively backward. Annual figures for TV set ownership show that in 1950 there were fewer than 4,000 sets in use. By January 1954 the figure had jumped to 60,000, but this must be set against 3 million in Britain. In 1958, the figure eventually reached over 1 million.[13] Throughout the 1950s, then, television remained the privilege of a wealthy minority.

Coverage of the territory was similarly a slow process, not helped by France's difficult terrain. The first transmitter outside Paris was Lille (1950), followed by Strasbourg (1953) and Lyons and Marseilles (1954): political and military considerations probably influenced the choice of location. More or less complete coverage was only achieved in 1961. However, a number of factors combined to encourage a certain expansion both in the transmission network and in set-ownership after 1954. On the one hand, sets became cheaper, and credit facilities more flexible.[14] On the other hand, the television transmission of the coronation of Queen Elizabeth II to a number of European countries provided enormous stimulation by the interest awakened in the public. It has also been suggested that the discovery in 1953 that the population of Strasbourg and the Alsace region in general were regularly watching German television finally prodded the government into providing the funds needed for a national expansion of the network.[15]

Some of the reasons for France's backwardness in the late

1940s and 1950s are easy to find. It was, after all, natural that in the immediate postwar years scarce resources should be used first of all to reconstruct more essential services such as education and transport. The Monnet Plan, in other respects farsighted, gave little space to the new medium, an indication perhaps of a long-lasting indifference – or even scorn – on the part of the French intellectual and political élite. The press, too, contributed, at times by misinforming the public, at others by announcing technical improvements so far in advance that prospective set-owners were encouraged to 'wait and see'.[16] But the heaviest responsibility lay with governments and with broadcasting's links with government. Political instability meant constant changes of those responsible for policy. Little wonder that there was no dynamic campaign to persuade the public to become viewers. (In 1947, for example, television programmes shut down at weekends.)[17] Furthermore, a well-meaning protectionist policy towards the French electronics industry resulted in 1948 in a government decision to adopt an 819-line picture definition. This meant not only that France was temporarily cut off from the rest of Europe (until the invention of a transforming device in 1952), but also that in order to satisfy the numerous owners of older, 441-line sets, for several years two separate cameras had to work simultaneously to transmit each programme. The effect on the public was unfortunate: who knew whether the government might not change its mind again in the near future (especially since it was likely to be a different govern-ment)? Buying a set became an expensive gamble.[18] Finally, government control of the finances of broadcasting meant cheese-paring and bureaucratic delay to those in charge of production.[19] For example, out of 1,100 new posts demanded in early 1958, 80 were authorized, including 60 technicians, to be paid at rates far below those in private enterprise.[20] Expansion was difficult, in such circumstances.

A further cause of widespread malaise within and without RTF was the latter's organization – or lack of it. Frequent strikes (over 80 between 1944 and 1959) not only aimed at salary increases, but were symptoms of a general feeling that the present structures were inappropriate to the tasks and methods of broadcasting. RTF's legal framework was that of a Civil Service department, responsible ultimately to the President of the Council but in practice to his delegate, the Minister or Secretary of State for

Information. The Director General was nominated by the Cabinet (*conseil des ministres*) and responsible to the Minister for Information, while the Director of Radio News was appointed directly by the latter. A Higher Advisory Council, its members nominated by government decree, had had its powers considerably reduced since its creation in 1942, and by 1957 hardly existed except on paper. A 16-member programme committee was likewise appointed in the main by the President of the Council or his Minister.[21]

Some of the administrative problems resulted from the division of responsibilities for broadcasting: Ministry of Information, Ministry of Finance, and Ministry of Posts, Telegraph and Telephones (the last-named for technical services). All of the ministers, moreover, were temporary members of some very temporary governments. While their insecurity reduced the possibility of long-term political 'colonization' of RTF, it also diminished their zeal for reform.

RTF's status as a Civil Service department meant financial as well as political dependence. Its annual budget was voted and controlled by Parliament, although from 1949 it was at least spending its own revenue (from licence fees and payment for services rendered). In practical terms, all financial operations within RTF required prior consent of the Ministry of Finance, accounting had to conform to Civil Service rules laid down in 1862,[22] while salaries were held down to levels current throughout the State sector.

At the same time, there was a multiplicity of different contracts applicable to different kinds of employee. People felt confused, hard done by, isolated into 'categories', and frustrated by the heavy administrative machinery. According to Étienne Lalou, speaking from some years of personal experience, every achievement took ten times the normal amount of effort.[23] On top of all this, the organization was hampered by the presence of numerous employees who were only there because they had influential friends in a present or previous government.[24]

All attempts at reforming RTF's statute proved vain during the Fourth Republic, though attempts themselves were not lacking. Some Bills proposed greater independence, others, such as the one accepted by the Cabinet in 1956, would have led to a considerable increase of State control.[25] However, the fragility of governments and the delaying tactics of those who hoped to reinstall commercial broadcasting in France combined to frustrate all efforts.

The insecurity of Fourth Republic governments, as we have said, helped to slow down the growth of political control over broadcasting. However, the legal framework of RTF described above offered unlimited opportunities for interference, and in more ways than one radio and television tended to be considered as a government department. The ideal of state control as guarantee, in a democratic country, of objectivity and public service generally, put forward by the Resistants in good faith as the alternative to a system ruled by selfish, commercial interests, easily degenerated in practice into the abuse of broadcasting by the party in power.

Until about 1956, government pressures were largely negative: radio would be asked, for example, not to emphasize certain news items.[26] Then in early 1957, under Guy Mollet, the Socialist Prime Minister, an unpleasant crisis at RTF led to the replacement of the Director General, Wladimir Porché (who had held office since 1946), by Gabriel Delaunay, a high-ranking Civil Servant. Political pressures became more exacting. Pierre Corval, a radio journalist, was forced to leave because of his liberal views on Algeria. Jacques Sallebert was under threat of dismissal for having interviewed political personalities in opposition to Mollet. Ministerial instructions to radio news on 29 March 1957 are said to have included requests not to mention certain demonstrations nor the fact that a French general had asked to be relieved of his command in North Africa. In April, a broadcast declaration against nuclear weapons by Frédéric Joliot-Curie was suppressed.[27]

The date most frequently suggested for the beginnings of government interference with television is 1956. The Algerian situation and the realization that the television audience was no longer a negligible minority of the public combined to bring it to government attention. Television news was removed from the control of the director of television programmes and placed under the head of radio news, who, as we have seen, was directly responsible to the Minister of Information. No precise mechanisms for control were openly set up, though it has been suggested that daily conferences between RTF and Ministry on the shape and limits of the day's TV news date back to that period.[28] Not only news programmes suffered; serious discussion programmes were not encouraged. In late 1956 the 'Tribune des journalistes parlementaires' was suppressed. Early in 1958 Max-Pol Fouchet refused to continue producing his programme 'Le Fil de la Vie' because of attempts at censorship. The most important problem facing France, the Algerian crisis, was not dealt with specifically until 1959 with Pierre Lazareff's 'Cinq colonnes à la une.'[29]

Broadcasting was evidently not adequately fulfilling its duty as an information medium. Alfred Sauvy remarked in 1951 that the public was being treated like an imbecile, and that since the Liberation the radio had contributed even more than the press to widening the gulf between citizens and State.[30] A rough analysis of the content of television programmes in late 1953 tends to confirm the criticism: out of a weekly 36 hours, $14\frac{1}{2}$ were devoted to light entertainment (*variétés*) and 6 to commercial films, while news and magazine programmes together only added up to about $3\frac{1}{2}$.[31] This state of affairs was, of course, due to a number of factors, among them the need to attract a wider public to become viewers, as well as technical problems concerning visual news coverage. If radio and television programmes were generally felt to be of high quality, often lively and original,[32] this was to the credit of the men involved in production, and certainly in spite of rather than because of *RTF*'s political and administrative structures.

The legacy of the Fourth Republic was hardly, then, an enviable one. On the positive side, professional broadcasters of considerable talent and devotion; on the negative side, an unsuitable legal and administrative framework, a pile of wasted reform projects and some unfortunate precedents for political interference with broadcasting. The first step, therefore, was to provide a charter or 'statute'. In the early months of the new régime, Christian Chavanon, the new Director General of *RTF* (and former General Secretary for Information), proposed a formula which would have given that body a considerable degree of independence. The Minister of Information would not have 'authority' but merely 'guardianship' (*tutelle*) over broadcasting. No information could be withheld by him except in the 'national interest', while government communiqués would be clearly announced as such. Moreover – an important point – *RTF* was to enjoy 'financial autonomy'. At about the same time, a second, commercial TV channel was proposed by a well-known advertising agent: the press reacted with hostility. De Gaulle rejected both projects. But the special powers period, during which the government could act by decree, and which had been granted for the Algerian crisis, was coming to an end. Chavanon's project was taken up again and carefully emasculated. 'Financial autonomy' was replaced by 'budgetary autonomy', 'guardianship' once more became 'authority'.[33] Even so, many observers considered the new legislation to be a genuine attempt at a liberal statute for broadcasting.[34]

The main points of the ordinance of 4 February 1959 were to prove the hopeful wrong.[35] On the one hand, the reaffirmation of RTF's monopoly and its financing primarily by licence-fee revenue was reassuring for those who feared a commercial formula. Again, the definition in law of RTF as a 'State public establishment, of an industrial and commercial character, and with an autonomous budget' was in theory a considerable step towards independence (Article 1). However, the opening phrase of the ordinance was an unequivocal statement of government control: 'French radio and television are placed under the authority of the Minister responsible for Information.' Article 5, which gave the Cabinet power to nominate by decree the Director General, his second-in-command and the other directors, confirmed this control within the basic structures of the organization. No Administrative Council was set up, though it was usual for a French 'public establishment' to have such an organ. Instead (though these were not part of the 1959 ordinance) there were two committees to assist the Director General: the Higher Advisory Council, composed of delegates from ministries and heads of specialized programme committees; and the Watchdog Committee, which included Members of Parliament, Civil Servants and various personalities and which met by convocation of the Minister for Information to discuss the running of the establishment. Obviously, neither of these was any guarantee of independence.[36]

The new ordinance was indeed a sort of legal bastard; as such, it could satisfy nobody. From the financial as well as the political point of view, RTF's relations with the government were theoretically contradictory. As a 'public establishment of industrial

and commercial character', it was *ipso facto* entitled to a considerable degree of financial independence, but the very terms of the
ordinance subjected it to the control of the Ministry of Finance
just as before (Articles 7 and 11). All the government had succeeded in doing, whether consciously or not, was to maintain its
own powers of control and reduce those of Parliament. In practice,
the results were, according to a senator and former Director
General of radio, 'financial anarchy'.[37]

There were serious anomalies too, as far as internal administration was concerned. The recognition of the 'industrial and
commercial' nature of RTF should in theory have led to a new
flexibility, more suited to the particular aims of the enterprise.
The lack of any wide-ranging administrative reform, together
with the continuation of strict *a priori* control from above for all
major spending, meant that in practice nothing had changed
since before the ordinance. In 1963, an employee could describe
the 17 separate administrative steps to be taken to obtain a new
glue-pot.[38] Sometimes, there were more serious results amounting
almost to failure to fulfil RTF's essential mission: during the
Congo crisis, for example, French journalists arrived two days
late at Leopoldville and had to buy newsreel from an American
company.[39] To many people, the wonder was not that RTF
functioned badly, but that it functioned at all.

The major failure of the 1959 ordinance, however, lay in its
lack of any guarantees for political independence; indeed, in its
legalization of government control. Under the Fourth Republic,
no one party had been in power long enough to make much
impact in that domain; now, with a strong President and a large
stable parliamentary majority, things were to be very different.
It would be naïve, of course, to see de Gaulle and his government
as the only villains. For one thing, the early years of the Fifth
Republic happened to coincide with the expansion of the TV
audience. Whatever the party in power, once the new medium
reached a sufficiently large proportion of the population it would
automatically become a political force, and, particularly at election
times, a subject of political debate. For another, one must re-
member that the new régime had its beginnings in the Algerian
crisis, when it was at least more understandable that a tight rein
should be kept on broadcasting. (Though even then, the government seems to have gone to extremes: for example, signatories

of the manifesto of 121 artists, teachers and intellectuals support-
ing revolt in Algeria were banned from all radio and television
broadcasts.[40] The list included Jean-Paul Sartre, Simone de
Beauvoir, André Breton, Alain Robbe-Grillet, Vercors and
Simone Signoret.)[41] None the less, well after the crisis that brought
him to power had ended, de Gaulle abused his legal control of
broadcasting, making radio and television into instruments of
propaganda for his régime. In 1958, Gaullists or sympathizers
were moved into almost every key post affecting public opinion.[42]
The trend was continued in the following years. It was, furthermore, during this period that Alain Peyrefitte as Minister of
Information set up the Interministerial Information Liaison
Service (SLII), at whose daily meetings representatives from
government ministries and men from RTF planned together the
shape and content of news programmes.

Election campaigns, from the autumn of 1962 onwards, were a
natural focus for discontent. While candidates were given strictly
allocated TV time during official campaign periods, no one could
fail to notice the omnipresent figures of the head of government
and his ministers, and the virtual absence of any opposition
politicians the rest of the time.[43] Other measures were only a little
less obvious: within RTF, unorthodox journalists were replaced
by loyal ones or suspended if they protested about government
interference. After the strike at RTF in October 1962, some of the
best journalists – Georges Penchenier, Joseph Pasteur, Michel
Péricard – had to leave.[44] While new magazine programmes
flourished (as compared to before 1959), TV news became more
and more orthodox.[45] Even before the setting up of SLII, André
Gérard, head of radio and TV news, was in direct contact with the
Prime Minister, Michel Debré. Gérard's conception of his duties
may be illustrated by his remark during the Bizerta crisis in 1961:
'A journalist should be French first, objective second.'[46] Not only
news programmes were affected by RTF's links with government.
For example, when the latter concluded a Franco-German treaty,
it felt obliged to cancel at the last minute a programme on the
twentieth anniversary of the battle of Stalingrad.[47]

Television in particular was more than a medium for propaganda: it became an instrument of government. Observers noted
de Gaulle's command of the new art, and some claimed he had
taken elocution lessons and professional advice on how to appear

at his best.[48] Certainly during the early election campaigns of his régime, his opponents were forced to appear live on screen, usually to their disadvantage. He frequently used broadcasts to make the first announcements of vital policy statements.[49] By 1964, a minister could announce the national budget to the television audience before announcing it in the Assembly.[50] It has been pointed out that de Gaulle's frequent personal use of television fitted in with the underlying tendencies of his régime: the personalization of power, the direct appeal to the nation, with the corresponding decline in intermediary bodies such as Parliament. The nation-TV-audience was given the impression that it was being taken directly into de Gaulle's confidence and into the heart of the decision-making process. It did not always realize that it could not answer back.

ORTF

To be fair to the new régime, it had more urgent problems to deal with than the reform of broadcasting. Already in 1960, a parliamentary finance committee suggested a number of internal reforms – administrative and financial changes – which would have made *RTF* closer in reality to the 'public establishment of an industrial and commercial character' it already was in law. These changes included a more flexible application of *a priori* controls by the Finance Ministry.[51] But it was not until the Algerian crisis had faded to some extent from public and government attention that broadcasting became a focus for political discussion.

By 1962, public opinion was aroused. André Diligent, a young deputy, whose party, the *MRP*, had recently broken away from de Gaulle, proposed a new, liberal statute, and published an official report which a popular weekly condensed for the general public.[52] The statute, which included provisions for an Administrative Council and a President-Director General responsible to the Council, was adopted unanimously by the Cultural and Social Affairs Committee, but got no further.[53] On 4 October, Georges Pompidou, Prime Minister, promised Parliament that a new statute would be prepared by the government as soon as possible.[54] The use of television in the election campaigns that same autumn naturally kept the issue in the forefront of public debate.

The following year, the ferment continued. Serious articles

analysed *RTF*'s political and financial problems, which were 'alarming'.[55] Frequent strikes at *RTF* irritated and confused the general public as well as the government; among the strikers' demands was the call for a new statute.[56] Furthermore, the extension of regional programmes was seen by many as a political move connected with coming local elections. The opposition called for, and obtained, a debate in the Assembly, though the Gaullist majority used its prerogative to curtail the time allotted.[57] As expected, the debate centred largely on the problems of information – the need for a greater degree of impartiality and for a better service in general – and on the long-needed administrative and financial reforms.[58]

By 1964, it was clear that action had to be taken. The government's first step was to consult the Constitutional Council on the problem of whether the reform of *RTF* fell within the domain of law or of regulations. It hoped to be allowed to act by regulations, not to avoid public debate, which it had already promised, nor defeat, which its parliamentary majority precluded, but apparently with the intention of preserving a flexible procedure for future change.[59] However, the Council ruled that five out of seven of the Bill's major points fell within the legislative domain, and the government decided to take the whole project through Parliament. The passage of the Bill, in May and June 1964, was instructive as far as the government's attitude to *RTF* was concerned. Detailed amendments of points of importance were voted by both Houses; the Senate, where the opposition was in the majority, rejected, in fact, most of the Bill's major provisions. An inter-House conference committee eventually reached a working compromise. But the government (under instructions, it was hinted, from the Elysée Palace) refused all concessions, and forced the Assembly to vote the Bill through in its original form.[60]

The law proposed was fairly broad in its outlines, and details of financial and administrative reforms did not really come within its scope. The debates, therefore – which were lively and prolonged – focused in the main on the relations between *RTF* and the government. Autonomy, it was recognized on both sides, would help to ensure impartiality and credibility. The problem was just how much independence the new body could be given.

The Minister for Information's opening speech presented serious criticisms of *RTF* as it stood, condemning not only the straitjacket of financial controls and the undynamic Civil Service attitudes of management, but also the clans and coteries within the personnel, and the linking of all these internal pressure-groups to political movements outside. The main problem, however, was the constant confusion in the public mind between *RTF* and the government; for the average citizen, French radio and television were 'the government in the dining-room'. To remedy this, autonomy was essential. It would be brought about by three main changes: a financial structure similar to that of other public enterprises of the same legal status; the replacement of government 'authority' by 'tutelage', and the setting-up of an Administrative Council with genuine powers. Two major consequences would ensue: impartiality, to be guaranteed by the Administrative Council, and the restoration of strong authority in the persons of the Director General and the President of the new Council.[61]

While the Gaullists jibed predictably that the previous régime had done nothing to reform broadcasting, and attacked the corporatism and the political affiliations of *RTF* personnel, the opposition heavily criticized the present government's record of interference and claimed that the new statute gave no substantial guarantees for improvement. In a series of amendments, they tried to change the composition of the Administrative Council and the mode of designation of the Director General, as well as to transfer the main responsibility for management from the latter to the Council. They also attempted to set up a control committee (*Comité de contrôle*) to safeguard impartiality and tried to write into the new law some provision for a right of reply.[62] All these amendments, as we have seen, came to nothing.

The new statute, which became law on 27 June 1964,[63] changed *RTF* into the *Office de radiodiffusion-télévision française* (*ORTF*), and reasserted its monopoly and its legal definition as a State public establishment of industrial and commercial character (*établissement public de l'État à caractère industriel et commercial*) (Article 1). Placed under the 'tutelage' of the Minister for Information and the Minister of Finance, the *Office* was to be run by an Administrative Council and a Director General. The former would have between 14 and 28 members. Half of these would represent the State, and the other half would be made up of representatives of viewers and listeners, of the press, and of the *ORTF* personnel, together with 'highly qualified persons'. The representative members would be chosen from short-lists drawn up by the 'most representative' organizations concerned. Members would be appointed for three years – though the State representatives could be revoked at any time – and would elect their president and vice-president from among themselves (Articles 2 and 3). The duties of the Council were: to lay down general policy lines; to deliberate on the budget and follow its workings in practice; to ensure the quality and moral acceptability of programmes; to safeguard the exactitude and impartiality of broadcast information; to make certain that the major currents of thought and opinion could be freely expressed on the air (Article 4). The government could broadcast communiqués or other messages to the public at any time, but these would be clearly announced as such (Article 5). (This clause was probably inspired by the example of the BBC.) Parliament itself would have general control over the broadcasting of parliamentary debate (ibid.).

The Director General was to be nominated by Cabinet decree, together with his second- and third-in-command. He would be the person most directly responsible for day-to-day management; he would have power to appoint to all posts except those just mentioned (Article 6). Financial and economic control was to be in line with the usual practice for public enterprise (Article 7). In this connection, a parliamentary delegation would meet the Minister for Information regularly (Article 8). Parliament as a whole would vote annually to authorize the collection of the licence fee, after consideration of a detailed breakdown of the *Office*'s budgets for the previous, current and forthcoming years (Article 9).

This legislation was completed by five decrees issued in July 1964.[64] These included a statute for the personnel, a separate statute for journalists and further details of financial control. One fixed the composition of the Administrative Council in detail, giving the Director General a consultative voice at its meetings and obliging him to submit an annual report of his management.[65] Finally, another decree set up two programme committees, one each for radio and television. Composed of 24 members, one-third of each committee represented the State public services, and the other two-thirds were made up equally of professionals competent on the one hand in social sciences, family counselling, etc., and on the other, in the arts, sciences, music and so on. These last two-thirds were proposed by the President of the Administrative Council and the Director General and appointed by the Minister for Information. The programme committees were to be largely advisory.[66]

The new statute was evidently a compromise. The major innovations – tutelage, Administrative Council, lessening of financial controls – were certainly steps towards independence. For example, the substitution of ministerial 'tutelage' or guardianship for 'authority' theoretically kept the government's power to intervene within certain legally defined limits. As the statute laid down, the Minister of Information's task would be to safeguard the monopoly, ensure that the *Office* fulfilled its duty as a public service, and, in conjunction with the Minister of Finance, to approve its budget and keep an eye on the use made of its resources (Article 2).

The new Administrative Council, on the other hand, was not such a satisfactory measure, even in theory. Half its members were direct representatives of the government, and of the other half, none were elected, even in cases such as the representatives of *ORTF* personnel, where it would have made sense to do so. Instead the government could virtually choose all the members to suit itself. The category of 'qualified persons' in particular left an easy way open to ensuring a permanent 'government' majority on the Council.

Even if the latter were independent, however, and with goodwill it could have been, the Director General and his two assistant directors were to be government appointees and could be replaced at any time. Furthermore, the balance of power between Director General and Council was ill-defined. Both had considerable legal powers and were dependent on the same source for their authority. Equilibrium – and the smooth running of the *Office* – would be left too much at the mercy of the interplay of personalities involved.

Finally, the lessening of financial controls, obviously impossible to eliminate completely, had not yet gone far enough. The *arrêté* of 31 July 1964 stipulated that prior consent should continue to apply over a large area, including recruitment, pay and promotion of all permanent staff. Administrative autonomy was still very much a mirage.

The year 1964 was in several ways the beginning of a new era. A second television channel began transmission; its audience was limited geographically, but it was at least the beginnings of choice for the public. Albert Ollivier, head of television programmes, long an inspiration to those who worked for him, died and was replaced by Claude Contamine, a staunch Gaullist from the Ministry of Information advisory team (*cabinet*), and a product of the prestigious Civil Service college, the National School of Administration. Meanwhile, Peyrefitte's 'democratic and liberal' statute was beginning to be put into practice.[67]

The government had apparently started out with the noblest of intentions. General de Gaulle, opening the impressive but already too small *Maison de la Radio* in December 1963, had proclaimed that he would make radio and television capable of responding to and reflecting without prejudice every current of news, arts, letters, science and politics, and give French broadcasting a place 'worthy of a democracy and worthy of France'.[68] However, less than two years later, Peyrefitte was making his unfortunate speech in the Assembly: since in many regions of France the press was hostile to the government, radio and television could legitimately act as a political counterweight.[69] To many people, this statement seemed closer to reality than de Gaulle's.

From the point of view of political interference, it appeared indeed as if nothing much had changed at ORTF. The personnel continued to be manipulated. Several well-known journalists were dismissed, 'exiled', or kept from important work because they displeased the government.[70] Jacques Thibau, a liberal Assistant Director of Television and left-wing Gaullist, lost his job early in 1968, under suspicion of being a Communist sympathizer.[71] A serious and very popular historical series disappeared from the screen in 1965 because of its producer's political views.[72] Programmes in general were exposed to pressures of all kinds. The most frequent came from government ministries: the Ministry of Health suppressed a programme on nurses, claiming that it would discourage recruitment; the Minister of the Interior and the Prefect of the Department concerned blocked a programme on a private mental home.[73] An unusually large number of both radio and television programmes were devoted to François Mauriac's eulogistic literary portrait of de Gaulle.[74] However, the ruling party was not the only culprit. In 1967, a programme about the Resistance was made but not screened because of objections raised by Resistants' associations.[75] Obviously, the statutory guarantees of independence and impartiality were not functioning correctly.

Just as in the years before the new statute, television news was still a major target for criticism.[76] (Radio news, in competition with commercial stations such as Radio-Luxembourg and Europe No. 1, was somehow felt to be both freer and less important.) At least half of each news bulletin was devoted to official ceremonies, without any attempt to give the public an understanding of the wider significance of such events. Ministers appeared and were 'interviewed' by ORTF journalists with kidgloves. Speeches made in the Assembly were reported tendentiously: opposition politicians were shown stumbling over their words, for example. The remaining minutes were filled with trivia: dog shows, beauty contests, suburban misadventures told with heavy humour. The whole thing was a 'mixture of government propaganda and meaningless anecdote'.[77]

Again, as in the earlier years of de Gaulle's régime, election campaigns were felt as significant landmarks in the political use of television. In particular, the television coverage of the presidential election of December 1965 was an extraordinary shock to both government and nation. The General and his political supporters had monopolized the screen for several years. Just before the official campaign, for example, the Minister for Information took advantage of a programme designed to explain the repartition of TV time between candidates in order to expound de Gaulle's political position and attack the opposition.[78] Broadcasting during the official election campaign period – the 14 days before polling day – was controlled by a special *ad hoc* committee set up by decree, on a temporary basis.[79] Each presidential candidate was allotted two hours. De Gaulle, cocksure, did not bother to use all his allotted time before the first ballot. Meanwhile, the effect on the public of seeing opposition candidates on their screens for the first time was electrifying. At the polls, de Gaulle failed to win a clear majority. Before the second ballot, both he and his opponent used all their broadcasting time and all the skill at their command.[80]

The official TV and radio campaign of 1965 had been fair to all candidates. However, programmes which fell outside the official period were sometimes manipulated. Rumour had it – and the *Diligent Report* in 1968 more or less confirmed – that for the municipal elections of 1965, the *SLII* had drawn up a list of Gaullist towns for the purposes of radio and TV journalists reporting on pre-election public opinion.[81]

Overall, the results of the experiences of 1965 were to prove salutary. The government was shocked into the realization that one-way propaganda could have the opposite effect to that intended. The following year therefore saw the creation of several new television programmes devoted to current affairs: 'Face à face', in which a politician defended his views against a number of journalists (the first guest being Guy Mollet), 'Zoom' and 'Caméra III'.[82] This was a victory for liberal Gaullists such as Jacques Thibau, Assistant Director of Television. Former Prime Minister Michel Debré himself in 1966 had advocated free and open debate as the best method of defending good government policy.[83] However, in spite of genuine improvements, the legislative elections in March 1967 showed that all was still not well. The Cabinet's decision (in November 1966) to divide broadcasting time equally between majority and opposition was met with widespread criticism: it would give the two Gaullist parties the same overall time (90 minutes) as the four main and several smaller opposition parties. Moreover, only national programmes were to show campaign broadcasts, though the elections concerned local candidates.[84] During the pre-campaign period, as usual, only majority party candidates were seen on screen. The regional news was peculiarly shameless in this respect.[85] On 4 March, the eve of the election, when the official campaign was closed, de Gaulle came on television to make a personal appeal to the nation. This abuse of privilege may have won his party the election.[86]

Political control was as usual not the only malady from which the *Office* suffered. Administrative procedures had improved in some respects, but the traditions of bureaucracy lingered on and prevented the organization from functioning at its best. Financial independence was largely illusory: the Ministry of Finance retained more powers than the statute appeared to warrant.[87] Strikers at *ORTF* tended, more and more frequently, to include the call for a new statute among more precise demands for salary increases and greater worker participation in decision-making.[88] In the autumn of 1967, *ORTF* was brought to the forefront of public attention by the government's announcement that it intended to introduce brand advertising on to the national screen. At about the same time, and quite independently, the Senate set up a special Commission of Control to report on the *Office*'s problems and to make suggestions for reform. The results of the inquiry – the '*Diligent Report*' – are worth looking at in detail, not only because of the high quality of the report itself, but also because of the timing involved. Just a few weeks after the completed report was presented to Parliament in April 1968, the *ORTF* (with the rest of France) erupted into one of the most violent crises in its short history.

The *Diligent Report* was not directly concerned with the problem of advertising except as part of the overall financial framework. Rather, it set out to look at *ORTF*'s basic missions – overseas broadcasts, information, education, culture and entertainment – and the administrative and financial organization of the *Office*. Much of the *Report* was, therefore, essentially an inquiry into the working-out in practice of the 1964 legislation. Had the statute worked? Had it even been applied fully and correctly? Accounts of broadcasting institutions in West Germany, Britain, Italy and the Netherlands were among the many appendices.

Not the least shocking of the *Report*'s contents was, right at the start, the account of the difficulties the committee encountered in carrying out its task. Both the government and the directors of *ORTF* proved reticent, even obstructionist in their dealings with the committee. For example, some Civil Servants were forbidden to testify to the committee, some *ORTF* employees were only allowed to appear in the presence of the Director General, certain documents could not be communicated. The Administrative Council refused to let its minutes be examined. The *Report* states sadly that it was often easier to obtain information abroad than in France.[89]

One of the *Report*'s main starting-points was the avowed intentions of the government as stated at the formation of the new organism in 1964. Autonomy, the cure for all *RTF*'s ills, was, it recalled, to have been achieved by three major changes: financial independence, tutelage, and the Administrative Council. While recognizing that considerable progress had indeed been made with respect to the internal workings of the *Office*, and that the personnel showed overall a professional integrity and a devotion to their establishment which did them credit, the *Report* was far from satisfied with the practical application of those three basic structural reforms.

Financial autonomy, promised by the statute and then more or less removed by the *arrêté* of 31 July 1964, had never become a reality. 'Analytical accounting' (*comptabilité analytique*), without which no realistic costing of programmes could be established, and which had been promised by the government in 1961 and again in 1964, was still nowhere near being put into practice. Its absence was used to justify the continuation of *a priori* control by the Ministry of Finance. While the government's controls had been maintained, the powers of other controlling bodies, notably Parliament and the *Cour des Comptes*,* had been reduced to the minimum, either by the statute itself or by the fact that the necessary legal texts were vague or non-existent. This incoherent system of financial controls meant constant delays in small matters and lack of supervision in large ones such as wastage of costumes, records and films. The *Office* seemed to have no precise long-term plans for expenditure or investments. Furthermore, the tax situation was completely chaotic, and the government did not seem to be in a hurry to clarify the matter.[90]

As for tutelage, that too had hardly been put into practice. The *Report* denounced political interference and in particular the role of the *SLII*. The hierarchical structure of the news services and the insufficient protection afforded to journalists by their contracts were factors which helped to perpetuate *diktat* from above. Moreover, much of the government's action was 'invisible', outside the official channels: personal contacts, the old-boy network, discreet telephone conversations between friends. Article 5 of the statute, which stipulated that government messages should be announced as such, had been applied in neither spirit nor letter.[91]

Most important of all the structural defects, however, was the much-vaunted Administrative Council. Already in 1964, *Le Monde* was pessimistic about this body of elderly Gaullists with little time to devote to their meetings or their TV screens. In 1967, the same paper commented that the *Office*'s statute had in fact given the Council 'derisory' means of action while appearing to invest it with considerable responsibility.[92] The 1968 Council included two members of the Prime Minister's advisory team

---

*Cour des Comptes: a judicial body which investigates and audits public and semi-public enterprise.

(*cabinet*), including its head, and one from the Minister for Information's team. Viewers and listeners – some 30 millions – were represented by only one person. There were no Members of Parliament, no university men, no representative of the Ministry of Culture. The representative of the press was a newspaper director not a journalist, and there were no journalists among the *ORTF* representatives either.[93] The government could always be sure of the support of at least three-quarters of the Council's members.

The 1964 statute had theoretically given extensive powers to the Administrative Council. Partly because of the parallel powers of the government-appointed Director General, partly because of the State's own interference by means of the *SLII* and other, unofficial, channels, and partly too because of the Council's own collective lack of character, the latter almost entirely failed in its role of guarantor of independence and impartiality for the *Office*. The President of the Council on several occasions admitted the difficulties he faced in this respect.[94] If any confirmation of the *Report*'s conclusions were needed, one could look at the fact that for election campaigns it was felt necessary to establish a special control committee: the Council, whose statutory task was to ensure objectivity and the free expression of all currents of thought, was thus explicitly recognized as inadequate.

The *Report* concluded by suggesting a number of reforms which would enable the *Office* better to accomplish its mission as a public service. Primarily, a new statute was needed, to replace the 'essentially paternalistic' law passed in 1964.[95] Briefly, responsibility for *ORTF* should be given to the Minister of Culture rather than the Minister for Information. The Administrative Council should be made far more representative, and the government's members should be clearly in the minority. The Director General and his assistants should be nominated by the Council, or at the least, proposed by the latter for appointment by the government (the committee was divided on this point). A 'Higher Council' (*conseil supérieur*) should be established to ensure impartiality and to protect journalists against unjustified sanctions.[96] The *Report* also put forward a large number of detailed suggestions for change in specific areas, from overseas broadcasts to internal administrative procedures. All these sensible and moderate proposals were, however, to be swallowed up, in the short term, by the explosion of May 1968. The *Report* was not in fact made public until halfway through June, when the long strike was almost over.

Though the extent of the upheaval which paralysed *ORTF* in May and June 1968 may have been unpredictable, the revolt itself could hardly be called a surprise. As the *Diligent Report* showed, the conditions for revolt had long been in existence, and only needed a strong enough impulse from events. This was provided by the student riots in May. Furthermore, certain long-standing tensions within the *Office* had recently been aggravated by internal administrative reforms which strengthened the bureaucratic structure. Among other things, the two TV news services, one for each channel, were co-ordinated into one.[97] The new Director of Television, M. Biasini, was felt by the personnel to be secretive about his plans for the future, while television producers (*réalisateurs*) were worried about the number of co-productions and commercial films on screen.[98] Meanwhile, the government's attempts to introduce brand advertising – which blew up into a wider quarrel over the respective powers of the legislative and the executive branches and the interpretation of Article 34 of the Constitution – brought the problems of *ORTF* once more into the limelight.

Though the controversy over brand advertising was not directly much of a contributory factor in the strike of May and June, some of the incidents surrounding the controversy were symptomatic. Even the conservative *Figaro* was shocked, for example, when the Director General, M. J.-B. Dupont, interviewed on television on 9 April, treated the introduction of advertising as a *fait accompli*, though neither Parliament nor the Administrative Council had yet been consulted on the matter. The following day, *ORTF*'s foreign correspondents were called up on a lunchtime news programme to testify to the general harmlessness of mass-media advertising in the countries they worked in. Once again, the *Office* was endorsing the government view.[99]

About a week later, left-wing deputies filed a motion of censure on the government's information policy. Many of the themes were familiar: the government had made TV and radio into a 'propaganda office'; it had set up regional stations to counteract the opposition views of local papers, and had used regional programmes to put across its own; it had attempted to reduce the freedom of the press in a number of ways, of which the introduction of TV commercials was one; it had excluded the opposition from the media; it had set up the *SLII* as an instrument of censorship. 'Hasty and inadequate' as the motion was[100] – and a pure formality, since the government was highly unlikely not to survive the motion – it at least had the merit of keeping the debate from becoming a purely legal squabble over the interpretation of the Constitution. The government rode the storm and was calmly considering the practical details of the introduction of commercials when the student riots broke out.

It took the extraordinary violence of the student riots, and possibly the hope of a new political set-up after the 'revolution', to shake the *Office* out of its normal state of passivity. (The *SLII* had after all been functioning for five years without serious opposition from within the *Office*.) It was, eventually, an act of censorship which precipitated the crisis.[101] On 10 May, after over a week of student riots, 'Panorama's' report – the first full-scale attempt to deal with the subject – was cut, on the orders of the Ministries of Information and Education. The following day, after threats of strike from a number of TV producers if a complete documentary of the student problem was not quickly shown, the Assistant-Director of Television News broadcast a doctored version of the 'Panorama' report, without the consent of the journalists involved. A 24-hour strike ensued. In the days which followed, and amidst growing chaos in Paris, positions hardened. Police and riot guards (*CRS*) were sent on 16 May to take up positions around the *Maison de la Radio*. The *ORTF* personnel began to formulate their demands: resignation of the Administrative Council, the directors, and the heads of TV news; annulment of the 1964 statute and preparation of a new one.

Meanwhile, a general strike began at *ORTF* at midnight on 20 May. News services kept working for the time being, as part of their duty to the public. However, further incidents exacerbated the tension. On 24 May, de Gaulle broadcast to the nation for the first time since the troubles began. The news services wanted to follow this with interviews and reactions from various politicians. Biasini, the Director of Television, refused to let the recordings go ahead, changed his mind, then on 25 May, refused again, on the grounds of a technical hitch. Ninety-three television news journalists went on strike – to the surprise of the rest of the staff – and news programmes were henceforth produced by a team of 23 blacklegs. While the strikers were men and women of all political colours (including Gaullists), the non-strikers were more unified. The 40 or so employees who kept broadcasting during the strike included 'five former press attachés of ministers, three former writers for the Gaullist party organ *La Nation*, the nephew of a Minister of Information, the wife of a Gaullist deputy, and five journalists personally recommended by the Information Minister Peyrefitte ... '[102]

The strike committees immediately began work on proposals for reform. In a press conference reported on 1 June – and held in a café, since the Director General had refused to allow the *ORTF* building to be used – the inter-union committee explained its demands. A new structure should be voted by Parliament before 1 October, which would guarantee the *Office* independence from political powers of whatever kind, and establish the participation of employees in management. In practice, this would mean: an Administrative Council representing the State, the personnel and the public, without a government majority; the suppression of the tutelage of the Ministry of Information; financial independence, with *a posteriori* control by the public authorities; the designation of the Director General by the Council, without government intervention or pressure.[103] As far as the Council was concerned, it was pointed out that such a reform would merely be putting into practice the intentions proclaimed in the 1964 statute. The strikers, and TV news journalists in particular, were at pains to make clear that their action was apolitical, aimed at obtaining a new statute that would guarantee the honest and impartial news which was the nation's right.[104]

A series of negotiations took place between the strikers and the Ministry of Information. Yves Guéna had replaced Gorse as Minister on 31 May. In the next few days, he met the *ORTF* union delegates but refused to discuss anything other than 'professional demands'. Radio news journalists, who had some time previously 'taken over' radio news and had been putting out a genuinely impartial news service,[105] went on strike after an ultimatum from Guéna on 3 June. In the days that followed, police were sent in to remove strikers from the *Maison de la Radio*. Police and army occupied studios and transmitters elsewhere. The Director

General called in technicians from the army and the private sector, a wildly provocative move.

The early days of June saw a number of changes at top levels within ORTF. In particular, the Director General was replaced. The new man, J.-J. de Bresson, was head of the legal service at the Foreign Office; he had been a member of the ORTF Administrative Council until 1966. An even less encouraging development was the setting up of an anonymous anti-strike committee, the so-called *Comité d'Action Civique*, by the blacklegs. This committee called for sanctions against strikers and denounced certain producers for 'anti-Republican attitudes'.[106] The effect on the strikers was the opposite of that intended. Indeed, the whole conflict had produced a feeling of solidarity and a meeting of minds hitherto unknown in an organization noted for its clans and coteries.[107] Furthermore, the strikers made considerable efforts to enlarge this solidarity, to make the public realize that this was a struggle waged for their benefit. Variety shows, debates, visits to factories in Paris and the provinces brought widespread public support. At the beginning of May, TV reporters covering riots had been reviled by students as little better than government agents. Now a collection made among the police stationed around the ORTF building brought in 1,750 francs in sympathy with the strike. Between 6 and 12 June, and in defiance of a ban on demonstrations during the election campaign, 'Operation Jericho' took place. In an effort to arouse public support, an enormous column of ORTF workers and sympathizers marched daily in silence around the circular *Maison de la Radio*: actors and producers one day, journalists another, administrative staff another. On the seventh and final day, when viewers and listeners were to have marched, the operation was cancelled for fear of violent clashes with police.

France meanwhile was struggling to return to normal. Elections were to take place on 23 and 30 June. After protracted negotiations between ORTF unions and the Ministry of Information, some compromises were reached, mostly in the form of ministerial promises, since a new statute could only be prepared and voted on after the elections. However, the union's final demands, on 17 June, included the creation of an independent 'Wise Men's Council' (*Comité des Sages*), separate from the Administrative Council, to guarantee the impartiality of news; a 'free', that is, non-government commission to prepare a new statute, and the re-establishment of the monopoly of production, giving *ORTF* full powers to produce and organize its own programmes. None of these demands met with any response from the Minister.[108] Within *ORTF*, a split developed between traditional unionists, who felt a strike should be ended when it could obviously gain no more advantages, and the others, who wanted to stay out indefinitely until their demands for more radical reforms were met.[109] 'Statutory' personnel went back to work on 25 June, after the first ballot of the elections, producers and authors on 1 July. Radio journalists voted by a small majority to return on 27 June, but arrived back to find they were sent home and told to await a letter of convocation.[110] Television news journalists stayed out, with union approval, and longer than anyone else, until 13 July, when they too were met on their return with a request to wait for a personal letter: TV and radio news were being 'reorganized'.[111]

In the meantime, the publication of the *Diligent Report*, in the midst of the crisis, had shown that the strikers' grievances had considerable foundation in fact. A popular weekly TV magazine polled its readers late in July: out of nearly 53,000 replies, 87.9 per cent wanted to see reform of the *ORTF* statute, 85 per cent would like to have broadcast news made independent of the government, and 94 per cent wanted more representation of viewers on the Administrative Council.[112] As far as raising public consciousness was concerned, the strike had obviously had some effect.

In the short term, however, the strike was a qualified failure. The government had returned to power greatly strengthened by the election results, and could afford to make its own terms. The public, pleased to have its television programmes more or less restored, and tired of upheavals, was unlikely to pay much further attention to the deeper problems of the *Office*, particularly during the long summer vacation. On 31 July, the Cabinet announced its short-term plans for *ORTF*. The foreign service would be reorganized. The Administrative Council was to be enlarged from 16 to 24 members. The tutelage of the Ministry of Finance was to be made more flexible, with more *a posteriori* controls. The personnel were to be given a larger share in decision-making, in particular by the creation of a Works Committee (*comité d'entreprise*) on the lines of those set up in French industry. At the same time, manpower was to be reduced, especially in the news services; this would create more unified teams. New programme policies would be defined with respect to information and culture. The *SLII* would probably disappear. Finally, brand advertising would begin on 1 October, at the rate of two minutes a day on Channel One.[113]

These reforms did not go as far as the strikers had wanted; they were, none the less, a step in the right direction. In the following days, however, the government's intentions were made clearer. 'Reduction in manpower' meant in reality the sacking, transfer or suspension of over 100 journalists, most of whom had taken part in the strike. Those concerned included some of the most well-known and popular figures: Roger Couderc, Maurice Séveno, Emmanuel de la Taille, Roger Louis. The move was in violation of the constitutional right to strike, and a direct contradiction of earlier assurances by the new Director General and the new Secretary of State for Information that there would be no reprisals.[114]

The reactions of press, unions and public figures were incredulous and hostile. As André Diligent pointed out, the government had recognized that the strikers' demands were justified, by the reforms announced on 31 July. After waving a white flag, it had shot down the enemy [115] By this spiteful and brutal measure – many journalists learned their fate from the carpark attendants, who had been issued with lists of those sacked, which the unions had not[116] – the government poisoned the atmosphere at the very moment it claimed to be making a new beginning.

After the events of May and June 1968, it seemed as if nothing would ever be quite the same again. But though there were important changes, in broadcasting as in other sectors of French life, old habits proved resistant.[117] Hence, a feeling of new beginnings in 1969 gave way to despondency a few years later, until in 1972 the revelation of serious corruption within *ORTF* led to yet another hasty legal reform. At each crisis point, the promoters of commercial television clashed with the defenders of the monopoly: this running debate will be discussed later.

The first of the reforms brought about by the 1968 strike was the enlargement and liberalization of the Administrative Council.[118] Out of 24 members of the new Council, 12 were still representatives of the State, but of these at least five were now to be picked from 'non-political' sectors: the Council of State, the highest courts of justice, the universities and the diplomatic corps. The other State delegates were to be high Civil Servants nominated by the Prime Minister and other ministers concerned. The remaining members were: one delegate of viewers and listeners, chosen from lists drawn up by the 'most representative' associations; two of the press, chosen from lists drawn up by the most representative professional associations of the newspaper industry and journalism; four 'highly qualified' persons; five representatives of the ORTF personnel, again chosen from the appropriate lists, and shared out between 'statutory' personnel (three), professional journalists (one) and production staff (one).

The Council was thus a more representative body; it was also younger. However, as a conciliatory measure, this was timid. The government appointees now numbered 16 out of 24 instead of 12 out of 16; pressures could still be brought to bear on most of the other representatives if necessary. That some improvement in the functioning of the Council did indeed take place was more due to the liberal atmosphere at that particular time than to the actual structures involved. There were no guarantees for the future. For example, in an appendix to the *Paye Report* in June 1970, the Council complained that it was not able to do its job properly. When the Council could in fact be seen directing policy, it appeared to be doing so in ways the government would certainly have approved of, as for example in the case of the famous directive of December 1970, instructing production staff that 'politics' should be confined to information programmes.[119] Furthermore, the uneasy legal relationship between Council and Director General remained unchanged; the former could only 'invite' the latter to take a particular course of action. In short, much depended on personal relations between the Director General and the President of the Council (not to mention personal contacts between these gentlemen and government ministers).[120]

While the change in the Administrative Council touched – in theory, at least – the most important structural element of ORTF, the most controversial area of activities was still information. In December 1968, the *SLII* was replaced by the Interministerial Information Committee (*Comité interministériel pour l'information*), which the Secretary of State for Information promised would have no direct links with ORTF.[121] During the campaign for the referendum in April 1969 (which resulted in the resignation of de Gaulle), some opposition political parties gave up part of their broadcasting time to allow journalists sacked in 1968 to put their case.[122] Then in the presidential campaign that same summer, both the principal candidates promised reform of *ORTF* as part of their programme. Indeed, party political leaders Giscard d'Estaing and Duhamel made it a condition of their support for Pompidou that he guarantee 'objective, living and open' information.[123]

All the presidential candidates had promised to abolish the post of Minister of Information. Thus, after the election, the *ORTF* became the direct responsibility of the new Prime Minister Jacques Chaban-Delmas. In his first speech to the Assembly, in June 1969, Chaban-Delmas promised to see that the *Office* was reformed. In the meantime, he personally would undertake to guarantee its independence from political pressures.[124] Early in the next parliamentary session, on 16 September, the Prime Minister outlined more precisely his blueprint for a 'new society', which would be more prosperous, younger, more generous and more free.[125] For *ORTF*, this would mean autonomy, participation, decentralization, and competition between television channels. To this end, two independent news units, one for each channel, would be created, each with a director having full responsibility for choosing his team of journalists, and complete authority over the means at his disposal. The directors were to be appointed for a specific period, and could only be removed for serious professional misconduct. At the same time, the Prime Minister promised that all political and socio-professional organizations would be given opportunities to express their views on the air.[126]

Despite protests from the conservative wing of the majority party, the liberalization of TV news was put into effect from 1 November.[127] The choice of directors was an interesting one: on Channel One, a comparatively left-wing journalist, and on Channel Two, a staunch but not intolerant Gaullist. Both had links with government, according to critics of the system: Jacqueline Baudrier, on Channel Two, with President Pompidou, and Pierre Desgraupes, on One, with the Prime Minister, Chaban-Delmas.[128] Nor was their independence without limits, particularly with regard to spending on technical equipment.[129] But with all the necessary reservations, it seemed to many observers that TV news indeed became more impartial, more credible and more attractive.[130] There were other signs which seemed hopeful. Some of those journalists sacked in 1968 returned to posts in TV news. Programmes giving opportunities for expression to political parties and socio-professional organizations were planned, though it later transpired that these would not be shown on Channel One, which had the lion's share of the public.[131]

An attempt was also made to deal with the other ORTF bugbear, financial controls. In late 1968 and late 1969, a number of government measures reduced the number of financial operations requiring the prior consent of the State Controller (*contrôleur d'État*), the official representative of the Ministry of Finance at ORTF, and modified the way in which the *Office* presented its budget.[132] Important changes were also made in ORTF's fiscal status as from 1970. Accounting procedures were modernized, to enable production costs, running costs and investment costs to be more clearly distinguished. A number of internal reforms in 1970 would make the *Office*'s administration more dynamic and more appropriate to its special needs.[133] As the Prime Minister had promised, a special commission was set up to look into the possibility of more wide-ranging reforms. The extraordinary improvement of the climate surrounding ORTF at this point can be seen from the fact that in December 1969 the opposition-dominated Senate voted through the *Office*'s budget, for the first time in many years.[134]

The government's special commission, under the chairmanship of Lucien Paye, a liberal Gaullist, diplomat and former Minister of Education, published its report in June 1970.[135] Composed largely of Civil Servants, the commission was caught between two fires: its conclusions were too discreet and unoriginal for those outside, too daring for those inside the government.[136] The report was none the less a genuine and fair attempt to come to terms with ORTF's problems. The large number of persons interviewed included not only those connected with the *Office* itself and the commercial stations, but also politicians, journalists, authors, composers, film producers, an actor and a professor of law.[137] The report certainly did not deserve its immediate fate of burial without benefit of debate.

The main aim of the commission was to look at possible

changes in the *ORTF* statute and structures, which would enable the *Office* better to fulfil its mission as a public service. Paye's *Report* criticized the *Office* on solid and familiar grounds: over-centralization, inflexible administrative procedures, the dual authority of Administrative Council and Director General, and imprecise relations between *Office* and government, as well as a number of failures in specific areas such as education and the foreign service. The remedies proposed were more surprising. The *Report* reaffirmed the monopoly in its existing form, but to combat excessive centralization suggested separating the sections responsible for transmission, programme policy and the technical side of production, and establishing a customer-supplier relationship between the sectors. Furthermore, the whole organization was to be split up into a number of specialized companies affiliated to a mother or 'holding' company, the central core of *ORTF*. A third television channel, for example, was to be completely regional and would form a separate affiliate. This system, in the commission's view, would have the advantages of competition and pluralism, while remaining under the protective umbrella of the State.

As far as structures were concerned, the dualism of authority between Administrative Council and Director General should be resolved by the creation of a new post combining President and Director General in one man, to be appointed by the government for a definite period of at least three or four years. The *Report* also urged changes in the Council, but these did not basically alter the status quo. Relations between government and *Office* should be redefined, carefully and on a contractual basis. *Paye* approved the disappearance of the Minister of Information and the substitution of the Prime Minister as tutelary authority. It also suggested setting up a separate advisory body, a High Council of Broadcasting, as watchdog for the whole field of audiovisual communications.

The *Paye Report* was never debated in Parliament as promised, though in both 1972 and 1974 the government did eventually implement many of its recommendations. Meanwhile, it became clear that the 'new society' was having some trouble coming into being, especially with respect to broadcasting. Gains were certainly made in some areas. The relations between *ORTF* and the government, for example, were clarified to some extent in

October 1971 by the signing of a planning agreement or 'contract': this was in a sense part of a wider movement towards contractual politics in industrial relations in France as a whole, one of the positive results of the events of May 1968.[138] The agreement, based on the recommendations of the Sixth Plan and signed by the Prime Minister and the Finance Minister on the one hand, and the President of the Administrative Council and the Director General of *ORTF* on the other, set out in general terms the *Office*'s objectives and corresponding financial resources for the period 1972–75. This and other specific agreements with ministries (Culture, in March 1971; Education, in January 1972), though criticized on various grounds – in particular, because of the exclusion of Parliament from the equation – were indeed a step towards a more equal partnership and away from the older notion of tutelage or guardianship exercised, however benevolently, by the State.[139]

At the same time, and in spite of the improvement of TV news remarked on earlier, *ORTF* was far from being free from political and moral controls. The President of the Republic had made his position clear at a press conference in July 1970. News, he said, should indeed be impartial, free, independent. But being a journalist at *ORTF* was not the same thing as being a journalist anywhere else. Whether you liked it or not, *ORTF* was the 'voice of France'. [140] The directive to staff, in December that year, inviting them to keep politics out of entertainment programmes was part of the same policy. Again, a number of regular programmes gradually disappeared because they were unwise enough to touch on controversial topics.[141] In 1970, a clip from the film 'Bataille d'Alger' could not be shown on 'Panorama': this led to the resignation of Olivier Todd. A programme on the Resistance, 'Un matin de juin 1940', was dropped after pressure from a Resistants' organization, the *Association des cadets de Saumur*; the film 'Le chagrin et la pitié', which re-examined France's role during the Occupation, was refused a showing on television. Two programmes dealing with industrial unrest, 'Louis et l'aventure' and 'L'Usine', were dropped. A late-night cinema programme, 'Post-Scriptum', got into trouble for a discussion of incest. At Easter 1972 there was a row over an allegedly blasphemous sequence of 'Tous en Scène'.[142] Thus a number of incidents, often petty in themselves, brought the question of freedom of expression to the public's notice and contributed to

[35]

the growing sense of disillusionment after the euphoria of 1969.

There was, too, increasing dissatisfaction among critics and public with the general standard of programmes. Frequent changes of directors of channels, and too many 'reorganizations' in general led to incoherent programme policies and a widespread sense of boredom.[143] Between 1969 and 1972, peak-hour viewing was given over more and more to serials, thrillers, parlour games and boulevard comedies. 'Cultural' programmes tended to be esoteric and were usually shown well after the average Frenchman's bedtime. The policy of competition between channels seems to have encouraged this pandering to 'public taste': directors of channels who did not increase their listening figures were quite likely to be replaced (Maurice Cazeneuve in September 1971 is an example).[144] However, it was by no means certain that the public really wanted this sort of television. In November 1970, one survey showed that 48 per cent of respondents thought that television had got worse during the previous year, others that viewers in fact preferred films, news and documentaries to variety shows and parlour games.[145] By early 1972, nearly half the respondents to a survey were dissatisfied with their TV programmes.[146]

As far as the climate of relations between *ORTF* management and employees was concerned, the 'new society' had mixed results. On the one hand, the creation in 1971 of a works committee (*comité d'entreprise*) and the re-establishment of bipartite committees (*commissions paritaires*) which had existed before 1964 and which were to be consulted on matters such as promotion and dismissal, represented small but real gains for the personnel.[147] But on the other, the pervading lack of trust was such that a number of structural reforms carried out or attempted between 1969 and 1972 were construed by the employees as part of a plot to 'tame' or 'dehumanize' them. The reform of production structures, known as the Riou reforms, which came into operation in January 1971, caused a storm of protest and a second wave of strikes. This reform involved, notably, splitting up the workers in the production process into self-contained units based not on specialized functions but on geographical location. It was presented by the directors as a step towards greater efficiency, economy, and ultimately, better programmes.[148] A significant number of employees, however, saw it as the beginning of a 'dismantling' process which would lead eventually to something very like commercial TV.[149] For others, the reforms were a subtle means to greater control over programmes and producers; in particular, responsibility for choice of programmes was to be given to directors of channels and to a new figure, the 'Director of Co-ordination', while heads of production teams would merely supply what was 'ordered' by the latter.[150] The Director General's own statements confirmed this viewpoint: in the past, programmes were the responsibility of producers and *réalisateurs*, but from now on, programme policy would proceed entirely from director level, 'after discussion with the public authorities'.[151]

The uneasy atmosphere within ORTF and the difficulties encountered in attempting to modernize the running of the *Office* in an authoritarian way can be further illustrated by the long-drawn-out conflict over producers' contracts. The problems raised were complex. However, basically, the directors of ORTF wanted to replace a large body of producers (*réalisateurs*) working sporadically and paid for each production separately, on a temporary basis, by a smaller body of full-time men on two-year contracts and monthly salaries. In return for security of employment, they wanted also to impose an agreement which included clauses enabling the administration to cut all or part of a programme and confiscating the producer's rights over his work. Whatever the particular issues involved, the result was to increase the feeling that the *Office* was turning into an industry, in which producers supplied not creations but products, and in which the mass-produced and ready-packaged – serials, standardized variety shows, anything with a repeatable formula – would eventually oust the original, personal and thoughtful works which had made the reputation of French television.[152]

None of these factors – censorship, the diminishing quality of programmes, internal unrest – were enough to speed up the preparation of the new statute which many people expected as a result of 1968 and again in 1970 after the publication of the *Paye Report*. However, in November 1971, a new scandal broke: certain broadcasters, hand in glove with a State-run advertising and public relations agency, were making money out of introducing brand names into non-commercial programmes. Two special parliamentary commissions of inquiry disclosed alarming evidence of links between the *Office* and financial interests outside.[153] Though ultimately of less significance than the problems of bias and mediocrity, the 'clandestine advertising' scandal caught the headlines and outraged public opinion. Scapegoats were found and for good measure the Director General and the President of the Administrative Council were removed from office. A project for legal reform was hurriedly prepared by the government in May and June 1972. France's leaders had not forgiven *ORTF* its part – as they saw it – in the semi-failure of the referendum on the Common Market in April that year.[154] Furthermore, legislative elections were to take place within the next few months and certainly not later than March 1973. Hence the new statute was unlikely to err on the side of liberalism.

The new legal framework of *ORTF* was the Law of 3 July 1972 together with a decree and two *arrêtés* which followed almost immediately.[155] Though it is the theoretical aspects of this law which mainly interest us here, the 1972 statute should first of all be placed in its immediate political context. In the wake of a number of rather half-hearted measures to ensure that the clandestine advertising scandal would not occur again, the Bill was rapidly prepared and hastily pushed through Parliament at the end of the summer session. Informed public opinion had been conditioned by the *Paye Report* (1970) and more recently by the *Le Tac Report* (1972), the product of the *ad hoc* special commission set up by the National Assembly to look into the scandal and *ORTF*'s problems generally. Both these reports, in different ways, suggested radical decentralization; that is, the splitting up of the *Office* into distinct companies for different activities. Partly as a result, the elaboration of the new statute took place on the one hand among general fears and warnings against commercialization of broadcasting (mainly on the left) and on the other, arguments in favour of the private sector and the end of the monopoly (mainly on the right).

The government, however, had no intention of relinquishing control over the *Office*, particularly with elections looming. On the contrary, the reform of *ORTF* coincided with the replacement of the liberal Prime Minister Jacques Chaban-Delmas by a less independent figure, Pierre Messmer. At the same time, the post of Minister of Information was re-established, in fact if not in name.

It was even suggested that the government's main motive for the new Bill was more to regain control of television news than to remedy financial corruption or malorganization.[156]

Whatever the underlying motives, the government's explicit intentions were set out in the customary *exposé* which prefaced the draft of the new Bill.[157] There were four main objectives. First, the monopoly should be given a precise meaning and one more appropriate to the present state of audiovisual technology. Secondly, a genuine decentralization should take place, leading in the long term to the creation of separate public establishments responsible to the *Office*. Third, the authority and responsibility of the directors were to be reinforced, and last, representation of the public on the Administrative Council was to be improved by means of a new mode of designation of the members concerned.

The 1972 statute was a longer and more explicit text than that passed in 1964. As with the earlier legislation, the Senate rejected the Bill; it disapproved of the text, and wanted the debate postponed until the autumn session. The government, however, was able to use parliamentary procedure to hurry the Bill through, with the result that, with some exceptions, the text finally voted by the Assembly was very similar to the government's first proposed draft.

The new law began by defining the aims and missions of the 'national public service' of French broadcasting. These were: to respond to the needs and aspirations of the population regarding information, culture, education, entertainment and all the values of civilization. The general interest of the community must be the only goal. Furthermore, French broadcasting must help to spread French culture in the world and, with these aims in mind, must take particular care to preserve the quality of the French language (Article 1). This was much more explicit than the 1964 text, which had only stated that the *Office* must fulfil the public's needs with respect to information, culture, education and entertainment.

Article 2 reasserted and defined the State monopoly, which extends to programme policy (*programmation*), transmission and the installation and maintenance of the network. Article 3 allowed for the granting of temporary permission to infringe the monopoly, in special cases determinable by decree, such as programmes for 'particular audiences'; closed-circuit systems in private places; scientific research; national defence and security.

This article was obviously intended to smooth the way for new transmission techniques such as cable television, already being installed in some new towns and housing complexes.

Article 4 repeated the 1964 definition of *ORTF* as a 'State public establishment of industrial and commercial character'. It then went on to innovate in two major respects. First, the *Office* is administered by an Administrative Council chaired by a President-Director General. This new post, a combination of Director General and President of the Council, was defined further in Article 9. Secondly, the *Office* was organized into separate functional units (*régies*) which might later be given even more autonomy in the form of public establishments. This was a hesitant step towards the decentralization recommended by the *Paye* and *Le Tac Reports*. The final clause, which excluded any possibility of control by private interests, was an amendment made by the Cultural Affairs Committee during the Bill's committee stage, and was obviously designed to prevent any channel being given over, later, to the commercial sector.[158]

The following article also represented a change, in theory at least, from the 1964 text. The *Office* was now placed under the tutelary authority not of the Minister of Information but of the Prime Minister or a member of the government delegated by him. The attributions of this authority, however, are identical in the two laws: safeguarding the monopoly, seeing that the *Office* fulfils its duties as a public service, watching over the use made of resources, and, with the Minister of Finance, giving approval to the *ORTF* budget (Article 5).

Articles 6 and 7 dealt with the Administrative Council, the main lines of which remained much the same as before. The Council would have between 12 and 24 members, of which half would represent the State and the other half would be composed of representatives of viewers and listeners, the press and *ORTF* personnel. The category of 'highly qualified persons' disappeared. Viewers' and listeners' representatives (two) would be chosen one by the National Assembly Committee for Cultural, Family and Social Affairs, one by the Senate Cultural Affairs Committee. (This was in fact the major novelty.) The other non-government delegates were to be chosen as before from lists proposed by representative organizations. Each member would serve for three years, although State representatives could be recalled at any time.

The President-Director General had a casting vote (Article 6). Further legislation a few days later completed the framework. The Council would in fact have 14 members, appointed by Cabinet decree. This meant seven representatives of the State, 'chosen for their qualification', that is, not on purely political grounds; two of viewers and listeners; one of the newspaper industry and one of the profession of journalist; three of the *ORTF* personnel, made up of two 'statutory' employees (excluding professional journalists) and one member of those professions concerned with production.[159]

The functions of the Administrative Council were defined in almost exactly the same terms as in 1964. The Council lays down general policy, gives its approval to the budget[160] and follows through its workings in practice. It watches over the quality and moral acceptability of programmes, and the impartiality and exactitude of information broadcast by the *Office*. It ensures that the main currents of thought and opinion are expressed on the air (Article 7). Again, as in 1964, the President-Director General reports to the Council on his management and submits an annual account.[161]

Article 8, on the 'right of reply', was another innovation, though again in some commentators' view it did not go far enough. (None the less, in 1964, the government had rejected a Senate amendment along similar lines.) The article stated that a right of reply would be organized, by decree of the Council of State, to apply to cases where damage to the honour, reputation or interests of a person had been caused by a broadcast. The restriction of this provision to 'physical persons', that is, excluding groups or parties, could be seen as a serious limitation.[162]

Article 9 defined the post and functions of the President-Director General. This post was new for *ORTF*, as also was the three-year renewable mandate. The method of appointment was as before, by Cabinet decree, and the person was to be chosen from among the members of the Administrative Council. The functions of the post were defined as administering the *Office* within the general policy lines laid down by the Administrative Council, preparing and putting into practice the deliberation of the latter, making all major decisions regarding expenditure, and appointing to all posts. Only for appointments at the level of director of a *régie* or 'public establishment' did the law stipulate that he must consult the Council. Theoretically, according to the government, this new post should strengthen the role of the Administrative Council.[163] However, a lot would depend on personalities, and the post was still a government appointment rather than the result of an election within the Council as some people had hoped.

Article 10 dealt with the organization of the separate public establishments under the *Office*'s general control, and was little more than a framework. Article 11 was deeply controversial. After stating, as in 1964, that government messages may be broadcast at any time on condition they are clearly announced as such, and that each parliamentary chamber would have general control over the broadcasting of its debates, it went on to deal with the possibility of strikes. In cases of stoppage, each radio and television channel was to ensure 'the continuity of those elements of service essential to the fulfilment of the *Office*'s missions as defined in Article 1'. The President-Director General was to designate the members of the staff he considered indispensable and who must remain at their posts. This was a considerable extension of the 'minimum service' as previously conceived, and the personnel largely construed it as an attack on the constitutional right to strike, as well as a dangerous precedent for other public services such as education, transport and so on.[164]

Article 12 repeated the terms of the 1964 statute: the *Office* is subject to the financial and economic control of the State as laid down for national public enterprise. The following Article, which dealt with parliamentary control, went further – though not much further – than the earlier legislation. A consultative parliamentary delegation, composed of four deputies, two senators plus the spokesmen (*rapporteurs*) of the Finance Committees and the Cultural Affairs Committees of both Houses, was to meet at least every three months. Its area of competence was more clearly defined than formerly: it was to advise on general aspects of those permissible infringements of the monopoly as set out in Article 3, parts 1, 2, 3; on the creation of public establishments, as in Articles 4 and 10; on general rules concerning relationships between the *Office* and outside bodies regarding production, diffusion and reproduction of programmes, and on any other topic on which the government or the *Office* wished to consult it. This article disappointed some Members of Parliament, Le Tac for example, who would have preferred a permanent committee.[165]

Articles 14 and 15 were concerned with finance. The first restated Parliament's powers to vote or block the collection of the licence fee on the occasion of the annual budget debate. The *ORTF* budget for the past, present and coming years was to be appended to the Finance Act under debate, as well as a report on the state of execution of the planning agreement or contract during the past year and a forecast for the following one. Two new clauses related to brand advertising, which had been introduced since the previous legislation. The amount of revenue from commercials must remain compatible with the *Office*'s missions as defined in Article 1, and with the need for expansion. In the context of the planning agreement then in force, the proportion of revenue from advertising should not exceed 25 per cent of the total receipts of the *Office*. (This last clause was an amendment introduced *en route*) (Article 14). Exoneration or reimbursement of the licence fee would be dealt with in a decree from the Council of State (Article 15).

Finally – and this had not formed part of the government's original draft – Article 16 set up a new body entitled High Audiovisual Council (*Haut Conseil de l' Audio-visuel*), to be composed of members of both Houses and qualified persons from a wide variety of fields, under the chairmanship of the Prime Minister or a minister delegated by him. This body would advise the government on problems arising from the development of new audiovisual technology. Indeed, it could be consulted on any relevant topic, and notably on the ethics of audiovisual communications, on certain categories of infringement of the monopoly, and on the practical application of the right of reply. It would meet at least twice a year, at the request of the Prime Minister.[166]

The Law of 3 July 1972 was essentially a disappointment. Even the debates were grey and academic.[167] There was nothing really new, and no one was satisfied. The statute was instantly attacked on two seemingly contradictory fronts: at one and the same time it represented a further encroachment of government control and an attempt to 'dismantle' the *Office* with a view to giving it over, eventually, to private finance.[168] Certainly, both these intentions could be read into the Bill: the government's power of appointment of the President-Director General and half the Administrative Council, and the limitation of the right to strike for the first, and the creation of *régies* and the let-out clauses in the definition of the monopoly, for the second. Others saw the bill as insufficient and vague, particularly in its failure to produce any new structures which alone could renovate the *Office*. The word *régie*, for example, had no precise legal definition, and in practice there might well be no difference between a *régie* and the present organization of channels.[169] Joël Le Tac, whose report has been referred to earlier, remarked that the new law was a framework surrounding nothing but a big empty hole.[170] The general impression, then, was dull and conformist, with a tinge of the sinister. As Senator André Diligent pointed out, a totalitarian government would not need to change a single line of the new statute.[171]

Thus in the summer of 1972, France had a new government and *ORTF* a new statute. The *Office* also had a new boss. Whereas the new Prime Minister, Pierre Messmer, was a reassuring rather than a stimulating figure, the *Office*'s new President-Director General – whose appointment, it was remarked, caused the greater public interest – was intended as an enlivenment as well as a new broom. In contrast to his predecessors, since 1957 all Civil Servants of one kind or another, Arthur Conte was a politician: a *UDR* deputy, and mayor of a small town in the Pyrenees. His other qualifications for the job included his friendship with President Pompidou, his cultural connections – he had published historical novels and collaborated on several television programmes – and, in general, his expansive Meridional personality.[172] The latter was not only an attraction in itself, but a sort of living symbol of the government's desire to decentralize, 'de-Parisianize' the broadcasting system.

Conte's appointment was received with cynicism, particularly by the opposition. In an election year, Conte, a convert from the Socialist Party in 1962, would be a strong government man. Furthermore, it was rumoured that he had been offered the post as early as 12 May, before the 'resignation' of the previous President and Director General, and before the new statute had even been presented to Parliament. (This was partly true: he had been offered the job on 20 May, after de Bresson's departure, but well before the passage of the new Bill.)[173] Such a move made nonsense of the clause in Article 9 of the new Bill: 'chosen from the members of the Administrative Council'.

Further changes ushered in the new régime. The Administrative Council was almost completely renewed, the only two surviving members being representatives of the *Office* personnel.[174] A number of new appointments were made at high level. However, the various provisions of the 1972 statute were in fact put into practice at widely differing rates. The High Audiovisual Council was not set up until the summer of 1973, while the right of reply provided for in Article 8 was still under discussion in 1974.

One major innovation stemming from the new statute and announced shortly afterwards in late July was the creation of eight *régies* or separate administrative units within *ORTF*: radio; TV Channel One; TV Channel Two; regional radio together with TV Channel Three (the latter was to begin broadcasting in January 1973); transmission; plus three subsections concerned with production and classified by method: video, outside broadcasting (*vidéo-mobile*) and film. These would be set up gradually, and it was hoped the process would be completed by 1 July 1973.[175] At the same time, the directors of these new sections were appointed. Jacqueline Baudrier, the liberal Gaullist formerly running Channel Two news, moved to head Channel One; J-L. Guillaud, the new director of regions and Channel Three, not only came from the Elysée press service, but had been a member of the blackleg Committee for Civic Action which had called for the sacking of *ORTF* strikers in 1968.

From the beginning, there was considerable ambiguity as to the independence of 'la télévision de M. Conte'. The public statements of the new President-Director General engendered anxiety. Conte indeed stressed that his intention was to ensure 'information free from pressures', 'truthful political information'. At the same time, however, both he and Philippe Malaud, the new Minister of Information, had claimed that the government was not good enough at 'selling' its own policies and reforms. Most characteristic, perhaps, and the slogans stuck, was his emphasis on 'making France sing', developing 'the forces of joy and of distraction', simple entertainment for the simple, hard-working French public. This apparently innocuous intention found a more sinister counterpart in the new Secretary of State for Information's thinly-veiled attack on left-wing intellectuals: television must not spread 'catastrophism', he said, referring to 'all these pseudo-intellectual spectacles which claim to transmit what they call messages'.[176]

More significant than these public statements was the announcement of the end of autonomy for the TV news units. The realistic (some said pessimistic) reporting of news by the Channel One news team had long been under fire from the conservative wing of the *UDR* party, and the departure of the politicians' main bugbear, Pierre Desgraupes, head of news on One, was a major victory for the hardliners. In a sense, Desgraupes' departure was inevitable, given the disappearance from power of his chief political support, Prime Minister Chaban-Delmas. But so important was his 'resignation' that some observers asked themselves whether it had not been the primary motive of the whole shake-up, or at least the principal task expected of the new President-Director General by the *UDR* party.[177] At the same time, the *Office* declined to renew the contracts of a number of journalists in the Desgraupes team; others were transferred, or left of their own accord, in protest.[178] All in all, about 200 journalists and cameramen had been arbitrarily moved in the shake-up, according to the unions.[179] Henceforth, TV news was once more to be placed under the control of the directors of channels (or *régies*, in the new order), themselves to be responsible to the President-Director General himself.[180]

To add to the confusion, or perhaps to palliate the impression made by this authoritarian move, Conte shortly announced the creation of a new political programme. This would give all parties with at least 30 seats in Parliament a regular opportunity to address the nation. In practice, 'La parole est aux partis politiques' would give each party concerned 15 minutes every three months. The proposal was received with a certain scepticism by the opposition parties.[181]

After these initial upheavals, one might have expected a period of calm during which the new President would elaborate his policies. On the contrary, it soon became apparent that this régime was no more successful than the old one in coping with the *Office*'s problems. The resistance of the personnel to the reorganization of production structures into *régies* caused a wave of strikes from October to December. By November, there were rumours of M. Conte's resignation.[182] Not all was failure, of course: on 31 December 1972, the prestigious third TV channel was officially inaugurated, and could be pronounced a qualified, if expensive, success. But a year after the new statute had been passed, the balance-sheet in general was a mixed one. The audience was decreasing, in spite of the *Office*'s continuing policy of showing popular programmes in prime time and relegating more demanding material to a later hour. Conte's personal popularity was high, and he had ended the strikes for the time being, but there were rumours of conflict with Philippe Malaud, now Minister for Information, over the extent of the decentralization called for by the 1972 statute. In any case, the situation within the *Office* with respect to the *régies* and the power-relations between directors of various sectors was far from satisfactory.[183]

There had been an uneasy atmosphere at *ORTF* for some time; but in a sense this was almost normal. So when the crisis came, in October 1973, its impact was dramatic. 'Monsieur *ORTF*' was deposed, after only 16 months of his statutory three-year term. Philippe Malaud was replaced as Minister for Information, at his own request, and given the Ministry of the Civil Service as consolation. None the less, though its timing and its amplitude were unexpected, and the short-term causes of the crisis had much to do with personalities, behind the October explosion were in fact the perennial problems of the *Office*: political interference, financial mismanagement, and the eternal question of reorganization.

The immediate impetus of the crisis was the refusal on 12 October of the National Assembly Finance Committee to recommend that the *Office* be permitted to collect the licence fee.[184] A 'hole' of about 40 million francs had appeared in the 1973 *ORTF* budget, and a further deficit of 150 million was being forecast for 1974.[185] Conte's reply to this accusation of mismanagement was a startling counter-attack: he revealed that 'intolerable political pressures' had been attempted very recently by the Minister for Information. The latter, who only in June had been reported as saying that *ORTF* was as free from political interference as the BBC, had on 11 October sent a letter to his old college classmate, the Assistant Director Alain Dangeard. In it, Malaud called for the removal of the director of radio, accused the France-Culture radio network of being a 'permanent Communist pulpit' and threatened that unless heads rolled, there would be no increase in the *Office*'s financial resources in 1974.[186] However ridiculous the charges, the financial pressure was serious. Moreover, Conte's declarations of independence over the previous 16 months were revealed as pathetically fragile while the method of applying pressure was the more sinister for being private, personal and non-institutionalized.

The conflict between Conte and Malaud was a long-standing

one, though both had repeatedly denied rumours of their hostility. The basic subjects of disagreement were not only Conte's degree of independence but also the extent of decentralization required to run the *Office* efficiently. While Conte attempted to set up *régies* within the old hierarchical structure, and went to some pains to consult his staff, Malaud made provocative public statements. In February 1973 he announced that in a few years' time Channel One might be a cultural programme, free from advertising, and Channel Two a popular one entirely financed by commercials. In August he repeated that each channel should be specialized – 'public service', popular entertainment and regions – and have its own financing – licence fee, commercials and regional resources respectively.[187] Conte was caught between Malaud's plans for radical decentralization and the resistance of his own employees to even the most timid attempts at change.

Perhaps the most deplorable aspect of the whole affair was the government's disregard for its own law. The 1972 statute laid down quite specifically that the President-Director General was to be appointed for a full three-year term. Philippe Malaud himself had presented the clause as a guarantee of the *Office*'s new independence. Now, in order to rid itself of its appointee, the government found a loophole: those members of the Administrative Council representing the State could be removed at any time (Article 6); the President-Director General was, perforce, one of the State's representatives on the Council; he could, therefore, be revoked at the government's pleasure.[188] The lack of outrage or even surprise which greeted this manœuvre showed only too well how little the public had come to expect from its leaders, as far as broadcasting was concerned. Meanwhile, the government showed no compunction. Interviewed some months later on Europe 1, Prime Minister Messmer presented the problem as a simple one: if a Minister clashes with a Civil Servant, it is naturally the latter who loses his job.[189]

In his memoirs, published later that year, Conte attempts to throw more light on the affair. Georges Pompidou, already ailing, had become incapable of taking major decisions, and was irritated by anything which presented a political nuisance. The Prime Minister's role had been reduced to a mere shadow, and real power had devolved into the hands of 'anonymous' presidential advisers, men such as Pierre Juillet and Édouard Balladur, who had not been elected but who none the less had more authority than ministers. Conte's attempts (which appear sincere) to give *ORTF* a new dignity and credibility angered these unconditional supporters of the new régime. After a series of subtle pressures from the Elysée men, and a long press campaign directed against the *Office*, Malaud's crude attempts at financial pressure were obviously (according to Conte) part of a larger political manœuvre organized from the presidential palace. The exact reasons are not clear: was this part of a general (and mistaken) divide and rule policy, designed to consolidate the power of the sick President? or, more specifically, did the majority party set out to break *ORTF* in order to introduce commercial television, which it would need if the left came to power?[190]

Whatever its reasons and its legality, Arthur Conte's departure was greeted with satisfaction by the political right, which had found him too independent for its liking. In its choice of a successor, the government, which had perhaps burnt its fingers, returned to the traditional ground of recruitment, the Civil Service. Marceau Long, the new appointee, was a technocrat, with long years of experience and a reputation for carrying through intelligent reforms. Obstinately non-political in the Civil Service tradition, M. Long promised to do his job with independence of mind and respect for the convictions of all Frenchmen. But essentially he presented his task as an administrative one: a law to be put into practice, problems to be solved, consultations and contacts to be made. This was a welcome cooling of the climate.[191]

Tempers continued to run high, nevertheless. Many observers, and the *ORTF* personnel in particular, still feared that the crisis would be used to usher in commercial television in some form or another.[192] Meanwhile, Long's task of balancing the budget for 1973 and 1974 was further complicated by the oil crisis and by a high level of inflation generally. The National Assembly debate on the Budget in October revealed that the figures they had to work with were at best approximate. The 1973 budget could be balanced by an advance of 30 million francs from the *Régie française de publicité*. For the future, the licence fee would go up, and stringent economy measures were to be applied. Among other things, the recruitment of new staff would be cut back, and an expensive new skyscraper would probably be scrapped. In May 1974, a loan of 170 million francs from an American bank was announced, and caused some mutterings. Meanwhile a National Assembly special commission was investigating the *Office*'s financial management and was to publish its report in June.[193]

A dreary Christmas and New Year season on television was exacerbated by austerity measures due to the energy crisis and by general feelings of uncertainty, mistrust and resentment among the *ORTF* staff. In the midst of it all, Long announced his project for the reforms of the *Office*. Under this scheme, the monopoly was to be maintained, and a central body would provide some sort of overall unity. But, as the 1972 statute laid down, the major part of the *Office* was to be split up into five or six separate *établissements publics*: radio, the TV channels, production (possibly) and the foreign service (*DAEC*). Each of these would have a professional *homme de télévision* as director, a president to run the financial side, and an administrative council composed of *ORTF* personnel, outside 'personalities' and representatives of viewers. This plan (which was noticeably similar to that of the *Paye Report* in 1970), was intended as a basis for discussion before being submitted to the government.[194]

The discussions which followed between Long and his staff were punctuated by a wave of strikes in protest against the possible 'dismantling' of the *Office*. But gradually, after consultations with the Administrative Council, the Works Committee, the unions and the permanent parliamentary delegation, the details of the reform were thrashed out.[195] By the beginning of March, the Cabinet had given its approval to the Long project. In its final version the reform involved the creation of a central federating body ('*ORTF*'), which would retain immediate control over financial resources, transmission, computer services and personnel management. It would coordinate six federal establishments: radio, foreign service, TV1, TV2, TV3 with regions, and 'heavy' production. 'Light' production – about two-thirds of the total – would remain under the control of the separate channels. Within TV production, the ill-fated and unpopular division into video, *vidéo-mobile* and film would be replaced by a distinction based on genre (drama, variety shows, etc.) and inspired by the system used at the BBC. Each of the new bodies would have its own administrative council comprising representatives of the State, the personnel, and personalities from outside. The president and director of each would be chosen by the head of the federating body. Decrees setting out these changes in detail were expected by 1 May.[196] Then on 2 April, the death of President Pompidou threw the reform of *ORTF* once more into the melting-pot.

In the election which followed, *ORTF* was not a major issue. None the less, the three main presidential candidates each seemed to offer a different option for the future of broadcasting. François Mitterrand, the left-wing candidate, was hostile to any form of commercial television, including brand advertising on national channels.[197] Jacques Chaban-Delmas had, as Prime Minister, been the chief instigator of the relative liberalization of TV news in 1969. Valéry Giscard d'Estaing was the candidate of the Independent Republicans, the traditional supporters of independent television; his brother had been the author of a Bill proposing commercial TV. One of his campaign advisers was Denis Baudouin, the head of *SOFIRAD*, the government agency concerned with the control of commercial broadcasting on France's borders. However, exactly what were Giscard d'Estaing's own views on the matter, no one quite knew.

After his election, the new President promised France a new liberal era. There was, for example, no Minister for Information in the Giscard government. *ORTF* would be opened up to the opposition and even to minorities.[198] In spite of these assurances of goodwill, however, fears and speculation about the *Office*'s future were not allayed. The publication in June of the *Chinaud Report* on the finance and administration of the *Office* brought fuel to the fire: was *ORTF* really too chaotic to continue? A prolonged strike at this point by technical and administrative staff demanding salary increases seemed to play into the hands of those who advocated the end of the monopoly.[199] Denis Baudouin suggested publicly that Channel One might soon be given semi-independent status.[200]

Amid rumours of the *Office*'s impending insolvency, and growing uproar over commercialization, the government announced its reform project. *ORTF* as such was dead. The monopoly was to remain; this was not really surprising, for its abolition might have meant uniting Parliament against the new President. But a radical decentralization was indeed to take place. On 1 January 1975, the *Office* would split up into six separate establishments, with no central federating organ at all. This reform – indeed, revolution – was rushed through Parliament in a series of extraordinary sittings in late July. Deputies and senators alike complained of the unseemly and unworkmanlike haste of the proceedings, as well as of the Bill's lack of precision which would give *carte blanche* to the government when it came to the details.[201] None the less, the new Bill, with some amendments, was voted through by both Houses before the end of July. It remained to await the decrees and other measures which would fill in the framework, and the appointment of the new presidents and directors upon whom so much would depend.

CHAPTER TWO

Anatomy of Broadcasting

STRUCTURES

ORTF's legal status was defined from 1959 as a 'State public establishment of an industrial and commercial character'. The notion of public, or publicly-owned, establishment (*établissement public*) in French law has never been satisfactorily defined.[1] It was originally applied to public services which were considered as decentralized sectors of the Civil Service. Their employees were classed as Civil Servants, but each institution had its own budget as well as a certain degree of administrative freedom. Later, it was extended to nationalized industries such as gas and electricity, which were not run on the traditional model, whose staff were not Civil Servants, and which were subject to the rules of private and commercial law. At present, each public establishment has its own statute, unique and peculiar to itself (though there are of course similarities of pattern), and its own appropriate administrative structure. However, in each case, the State is the sole shareholder, and retains a degree of control over the management and finances of the enterprise. The denomination 'of an industrial and commercial character' serves mainly to differentiate the institution concerned from an administrative department of the Civil Service.[2]

The head of national broadcasting in France was the President-Director General, or Director General before 1972. Appointed by the Cabinet (*conseil des ministres*), he could until 1972 be replaced at any time. The 1972 statute, which combined into one this post and that of President of the Administrative Council, also stipulated that the new head's term of office was to be three years. Within the *ORTF*, the President-Director General exercised virtually absolute authority. He administered the *Office* along the general lines laid down by the Administrative Council, 'prepared and put into practice' that Council's deliberations, made the major decisions about expenditure, and appointed to almost all posts within the organization. As chairman of the Administrative Council, he held a casting vote.[3]

In theory, there was some confusion about who was responsible for general policy-making: *ORTF* texts ascribe the role equally to the President-Director General and to the Council.[4] In practice, however, the President-Director General had the upper hand, as can perhaps be seen from the fact that it was he who lost his job when things went badly wrong. The *organigramme* or diagram of the official power structure of the organization showed clearly how all lines converged upwards to meet in the President-Director General.[5] The only post which stood outside this hierarchy was that of State Controller, who was employed by and seconded from the Ministry of Finance.

One of the government's explicit intentions in 1972 was to reinforce the authority and independence of the head of broadcasting.[6] In practice, this hastened the breakdown of the system. There were two potential sources of conflict and tension within that system. One was the contradiction between the government's avowed desire to appoint a strong, independent figure and its continuing need to control broadcasting, especially in an election year. This tension found its outlet in the power struggle between Arthur Conte and the Minister of Information, and ended in the dismissal of the former. However, the removal of Philippe Malaud to another ministry showed perhaps that the government did not entirely have the courage of its convictions. What it really wanted was not blatant interference but a broadcasting service which would be loyal without having to be called to heel.

A second contradiction existed within the very terms of the statute. On the one hand, a strongly centralized hierarchy, controlled by a President-Director General with increased authority. On the other, a commitment to decentralization in the form of separate units for separate functions, culminating eventually in the creation of a number of new public establishments under the

Office's general control. Even without the financial crisis of 1973 – which may have been only a pretext – it seems likely that these two built-in oppositions would sooner or later have broken the *Office* apart.

The Administrative Council was set up only in 1964, though it was usual for a 'public establishment' to have such an organ. Its role was defined in 1964 and 1972 as follows: to lay down general policy lines; to approve the budget and watch over its execution in practice; to safeguard the quality and moral acceptability of programmes; to watch over the impartiality and exactitude of news; to ensure that the major currents of thought and opinion were expressed on the air. Its members were appointed by the Cabinet for three years, though the representatives of the State could be recalled at any time. In 1973, it had 14 members: seven representatives of the State, chosen for their qualifications rather than delegated by government ministries; three of the *Office* personnel, chosen from lists drawn up by the appropriate unions (two 'statutory' personnel, excluding professional journalists, and one member of the production staff); two of the press, chosen from lists (one journalist and one from the administrative side); two of listeners and viewers, chosen one each by the Cultural Affairs Committees of each parliamentary chamber.[7]

In theory, the Administrative Council was parallel if not superior to the President-Director General; he was of course one of its members and was obliged to submit an annual report of his administration. In practice, the Council acted as his subordinate. In normal circumstances, it met for several hours once a month, plus one extra morning every two months. It was consulted, but not allowed to make any major decisions. The account of its activities in the *ORTF* handbook for 1973 shows (between the lines) the limits of its powers. On a proposal from the President-Director General, the Council decided to create a new political programme. It set up a sports service and council and a music service and council. It was sent the 1973 programme plans for television and for the France-Culture radio network, for its observations and approval. It received reports on the putting into practice of the planning agreement on educational broadcasting. It was informed of the setting up of new TV production units, and discussed the problems of cable television in France.[8] Described in these terms, the Council's role was evidently a passive one, and the general feeling at *ORTF* appears to have been that this was indeed the case.[9]

Immediately beneath the President-Director General in the hierarchy, a number of assistant directors and delegates were responsible for the various sectors of the *Office*.[10] The Assistant Director General (*Directeur Général Délégué*) had overall control of a number of sections: the general planning service, computer services, the Department of Commercial Affairs (which dealt with the sales of programmes and of rights, and exercised a permanent control over television advertising), the Agency for Economic and Social Information, and the assistant director in charge of 'artistic' employees, that is, actors, musicians, producers and so on. The Delegate for Public Relations was in charge of promoting the *Office*'s activities and of relations with the press and the public.

Apart from the Director of General Control, whose task was to ensure that all rulings pertaining to the *Office* were observed, and in particular to see that the heads of channels or *régies* 'protected the *Office*'s patrimony', the bulk of administrative responsibility fell on the General Secretary for the Administration. General administrative problems, legal problems, those concerning personnel and social matters came within his domain. He drew up dossiers for appointments, contracts to be used for different kinds of employment and so on. Under his authority were placed a wide variety of services, among them the Department of Legal Affairs, the Personnel Department, the Internal Relations Department (which worked in liaison with the Works Committee), in-service training, educational action, documentation, general provisioning and cleaning, and an engineer in charge of co-ordinating the use of technical equipment by the two television news teams.

General financial responsibility was in the hands of the Director of Management and Finance (*Directeur du Contrôle de Gestion et des Finances*), who prepared the budget and followed through its application in practice. He was also in charge of the licence fee collection service. There was also a central accountant appointed by ministerial decree, and a State Controller who as representative of the government was not part of the *Office* hierarchy.[11] The technical side of the *Office*'s activities was controlled by a delegate for equipment, and the Assistant Director General for Technical Action who (in 1973) combined this function with that of Director of Transmission (*régie de diffusion*). The Centre for the Study of Television and Telecommunications at Rennes was also part of the latter's responsibilities.

The Foreign Service (*DAEC*) was a fairly self-contained unit run by the Assistant Director General for External Affairs and Co-operation. Broadcasting stations in French territories overseas – Martinique, Guadeloupe, Polynesia, etc. – were until July 1972 attached to the French regional stations, and then placed in the charge of a separate delegate for overseas stations.[12]

Responsibility for programmes was divided between the three directors of television channels and the Director of Radio. However, in 1972, a new post was created which took a place in the hierarchy above these directors and below the President: the Assistant Director for Harmonization of Programmes. This post carried wide-ranging powers. The Assistant Director was defined as the President's direct representative in matters concerning general programme policy, the drawing-up of annual programme plans and co-ordination between channels. He sat on the Administrative Council's Programme Committee, and kept in touch with cultural bodies outside (the Ministry of Cultural Affairs, the *Comédie Française* and so on). He made concrete proposals for concerted action between channels, and was expected to look for new talents. The channels kept him informed of their projects and programmes in course of production. Certain services were also placed under his control: the Programme Planning Service, the Central Service for Texts and Programme Projects (which examined manuscripts sent in), the Opinion Research Service, the Permanent Secretariat for Language, and the Research Service, which latter retained a considerable degree of independence.

The two programme committees were also attached to the President-Director General rather than to the heads of channels. These committees, one each for radio and television, were composed of between 24 and 26 members, persons from outside the *Office* and appointed by the government. Members included composers, authors, teachers, actors, journalists, Civil Servants and professionals in various fields connected with the social sciences. Their task was to make suggestions and criticisms, study certain aspects of the *Office*'s development and certain specific problems such as violence on television.[13] In practice, their place in the hierarchy was uncertain, their role seems to have been considered insignificant, and indeed, the Administrative Council had set up its own programme committees as a parallel structure.

Two specialized programme areas had their own heads and special advisory committees: music and sport. All other programmes came directly under the responsibility of the directors of television channels and the Director of Radio. In 1972, the three television channels, radio and the transmission sector were redefined as *régies*. (Three other *régies* involved television production methods.) While no precise legal definition can be given for the term (and the details of the organization of the new *régies* was left to the President-Director General), it appeared to be something in-between the previous organization into channels and a 'publicly-owned establishment' which was the status of the *Office* itself. The *régies* were not intended to provide more than a 'deconcentration from within', and a means of increasing the responsibility and independence of the men in charge. The directors of the *régies* were to administer their own staff, equipment and financial resources, and render accounts to the President-Director General.[14] However, it was stressed that *ORTF* personnel remained one body, and that employees were to be able to move easily from one *régie* to another.[15]

Once again, internal contradictions were apparent. While the 1972 legislation had enforced the creation of *régies*, it had also created the post of Director of Harmonization which in theory at least involved a reduction of independence for the heads of television and radio. As it happened the *régies* were expected to come into full operation by July 1973; they did not therefore have much time to show how they functioned in practice.

Television production was also split up into *régies*, and this caused more upheaval and more controversy. Under the overall umbrella of a General Delegation for Television Production, three separate sectors were created. The division was based on the method or tool of production: *vidéo-fixe*, that is, electronic cameras used in a studio; *vidéo-mobile*, that is, electronic cameras used outside a studio (outside broadcasting); and film. The television channels or *régies* 'ordered' programmes from the production *régies*, sending them detailed descriptions of the programme concerned and receiving estimates of the cost before production could begin. (They could also obtain programmes through a special Service for the Purchase of Programmes (*Service des achats et commandes*), which dealt with cinema films, co-productions and private productions.) The division into *régies* angered production staff; they claimed it artificially broke up some successful teams which were based on personal affinities, and that by reducing mobility it would make it more difficult for them to become experienced and well-qualified.[16]

Radio was a self-contained sector which both conceived and produced its programmes. The four national radio networks (France-Inter, France-Culture, France-Musique, Inter-Variétés) each had a delegate counsellor, while an assistant director had control of news programmes. Production was divided up by genre – drama, varieties, etc. – rather than by method. Music, because of its size and importance, constituted a separate section. The Head of Radio was also responsible for the *ORTF* orchestras and for the conservation services used by the whole of the *Office*: the record-library, the drama library, the news documentation service and so on.

At the beginning of 1973, *ORTF* employed 15,406 persons on a permanent basis, and had paid over 30,000 persons fees for some kind of part-time or temporary work during the previous year.[17] Of the permanent staff, about 80 per cent were employed in the administrative and technical sectors.[18] The mass of the permanent staff were governed by the 'statute of *ORTF* personnel', the subject of a special ministerial decree. (A small minority retained the status of Civil Servant which had been that of the whole staff up to 1960.) The statute of personnel was unique and peculiar to *ORTF*; it involved a mixture of public and private law. Its main features were a basic unified legal structure giving the various professions the same rights and duties; a salary scale within each career stream, rewarding experience or additional training; and rules governing promotion with the balance to be struck between inside and outside appointment, and the use of in-service training as a method of selection.[19] The change in 1960 from 'public', Civil Service contracts to private enterprise ones was intended to provide the flexibility required in such an organization. However, it has proved susceptible of misuse, for it makes it easier to promote on political grounds.[20]

'Non-statutory' personnel were employed on a variety of bases. Permanent musicians and choristers had a separate statute. Other creative personnel were paid by fee for each programme, for example, researchers, musicians and conductors, or were given annual contracts, for example, costume- and set-designers and directors of photography. Actors were paid by fee for television appearances, but for radio they had to go before a special auditioning body which issued cards entitling them to radio work.[21] Two categories presented particular problems of organization. Their position – the producer as individual creator and the journalist as individual reporter – in an institution with Civil Service traditions and government control caused numerous tensions which were never properly resolved.

Television 'producers' are of two kinds in France. The 'delegate producer' (*producteur délégué*) is responsible for the intellectual or artistic content of a programme. He may either contribute a detailed plan of the programme or be responsible for gathering together its various constituents, or both. He may also introduce the programme or act as master of ceremonies. 'Delegate producers' are paid by fee for each programme.[22] In television, the post was gradually being phased out from 1970, so that in 1973 the only ones left were in games or variety shows. The real producer had become the production unit.[23] The second kind of 'producer', the *réalisateur*, cannot be eliminated. Like a film director, he co-ordinates the whole production team, preparing the script, casting, choosing equipment and decor and sharing in the preparation of the production budget. He may also have contributed the basic idea in the first place. ORTF had on its books about 1,000 producers of this kind whom it officially recognized as possible employees. This, however, did not guarantee that they would work in any given year, and in fact the number who did work was estimated at about one-third.[24]

The *réalisateurs* have posed a complex problem for a number of years. Until July 1972, they were employed on a short-term contract basis. A system of co-option within the profession meant a virtual monopoly for certain well-established figures, who often earned more than the Director General.[25] In 1972, a new system was proposed whereby about 150 *réalisateurs* would be taken on for two years and paid a monthly salary in exchange for a guaranteed number of days' production. The *Office* presented this as a move towards greater security for its most frequently-employed producers. The latter, however, saw it as an attempt to reduce their freedom by 'institutionalizing' their work.[26] This kind of mutual distrust between the *Office* and its employees seems, unfortunately, to be characteristic.

The problem of the ORTF journalist was likewise a chronic one, which led to bitterness on both sides. The 'Statute of Journalists at ORTF' is a separate legal document differing both from the 'Statute of ORTF Personnel' and the 'Statute of Journalists' for the written press.[27] (President Pompidou's claim that being a journalist at ORTF was not the same as being a journalist elsewhere thus had a sound legal basis.)[28] The reasons given for this divergence are interesting. Not only does the journalist in broadcasting have special working conditions (frequent travel, possibility of posting abroad or to the regions), but he also has special responsibilities. His potential audience – 30 or 40 million, and 12 or 13 million for the evening news on Channel One – enjoins on him 'a habit of prudence, even of reserve'.[29]

The journalists' statute provides for three categories of employees. These are: permanent journalists, on permanent contract (Article 1); 'temporary' journalists, on renewable, fixed-period contracts (Article 2); and even more temporary journalists, who have no contract, and are not covered by the terms of the statute (Article 3). In practice, large numbers of journalists in this last category were as permanent as the other two, in the sense of working as long and as frequently. The system had developed partly to circumvent the insufficient quotas of personnel set by the Ministry of Finance. (The use of this mechanism as a political tool will be discussed in a later chapter.)[30] In January 1973, the *Office* employed about 800 'permanent temporaries' (*pigistes permanents*) under Article 3.[31] Early that year, there were squabbles between the *Office* and its branch of the journalists' union (*SNJ*) over how many of the *pigistes* should be given regular permanent status. Eventually agreement was reached on a figure of 200.[32] By August 1974, 275 journalists were still employed as *pigistes*.[33]

To the audience, it has frequently felt as if ORTF were constantly on strike or on the verge of it.[34] In fact, the personnel are, not surprisingly, extremely disunified. Only major crises or challenges are able to unite the extraordinarily heterogeneous mass of workers of all kinds. The introduction of colour television had such an effect, as did the revolt of May 1968:

In the general assemblies held at the *Maison de l'ORTF*, technicians, 'artists', administrators, from the various Centres met for the first time, and discovered, at the very moment they were trying to destroy them, the thickness of the walls which separated them: methods of payment, training, unions, technical languages, corporatism, distrust, *arrivisme*, defence of territory, ignorance ...[35]

The *Office* personnel were, however, more highly unionized – over 60 per cent – than is normal for French industry as a whole.[36] The 30 or so unions at ORTF were differentiated both by skills and professions and by political allegiance to national union organizations such as *CGT* or *FO*. Within ORTF, the Communist-led *CGT* group of unions was probably the strongest numerically, closely followed by the independent grouping *FSU* (*Fédération syndicale unifiée des personnels de l'ORTF*). There is a co-ordinating inter-union committee, the *Intersyndicale*.

After 1968, and in the context of a general attempt by the French authorities to provide more opportunities for 'participation' in schools, universities and factories, two structures were set up or re-established at ORTF. The *conseils paritaires* or bipartite councils had existed prior to 1964. Composed of equal numbers of representatives of personnel and management, they deal with promotions and sackings, and are (in theory) consulted when necessary. The *Comité d'entreprise* or Works Committee was set up on the lines of similar bodies in private industry. (Every firm with over 50 employees must have such a committee.) It was composed of delegates elected by the eleven metropolitan broadcasting regions and three overseas stations. The committee met every three months, and was largely responsible for social activities and welfare: canteens, libraries, sports, leisure and so on. It could be consulted on all kinds of topics which concerned the personnel: working conditions, training schemes, the budget, personnel relations, etc. Various 'mixed' committees (management-unions) could also be set up on an *ad hoc* basis to look into specific problems as they arose.[37]

The ORTF unions were frequently denounced by critics as 'corporatist' and basically conservative.[38] It is true that they are fanatically opposed to any breach of the monopoly and any consequent introduction of private capital into the structures of ORTF. Thus they were perhaps unnecessarily hostile to certain plans for modernization such as the decentralization proposed by

Marceau Long as President-Director General in early 1974. They have tended to fight against any opening of the *Office* to talent from outside. However, it is untrue that they are only concerned to protect their own interests. In 1968, for example, the unions fought hard for a genuine reform of the *Office* which would guarantee freedom of expression and the freedom to inform. The journalists' union *SNJ* fights for freedom of expression, a better news service and a genuine regionalization policy, as well as for improvements in salaries or working conditions for its members.

The structures of *ORTF* were evidently far from democratic. Power was concentrated in the hands of a few men at the top, together with a small number of well-established producers and 'personalities' who had their own ways of getting things done. The unions had the power to protest, and to paralyse the whole concern by bringing out on strike certain essential technicians, but they had little influence on positive decision-making. The role of the Works Committee was limited to workers' problems and had small say in matters such as general finance, programme policy or reforms. (This may well have been one reason why the strike weapon was used so frequently.) And while a non-democratic institution can form part of a wider democratic structure (political parties are not always democratically run, even in 'democratic' countries), *ORTF*'s numerous internal problems – distrust between staff and management, wrangles over contracts, etc. – hampered the *Office* in its task as medium for a democratic society, and prevented it from evolving to serve that society better.

The reform of broadcasting which began in 1974 after the election to the Presidency of Valéry Giscard d'Estaing, claimed (like its predecessors) to be a 'liberal charter for radio and television'.[39] Presenting the new Bill to Parliament in July, the Prime Minister set out his government's objectives. Independence and pluralism would henceforth ensure a democratic broadcasting system. Secondly, the new organization must look to the education of the public and foster creativity and research in its programmes. It must fulfil its mission as a public service. Finally, the government wanted to see broadcasting efficiently administered. As means to these ends, the Prime Minister enumerated the following: the retention of the monopoly, which must entail duties as well as rights, the encouragement of competition, and the development of a sense of responsibility by the sharing out of revenues according to the double criteria of quality and success.[40] The reform, hastily voted through Parliament in August, was to come into full operation on 6 January 1975.

The intervening period was one of growing confusion and chaos at what had been *ORTF*. The personnel, angry at the prospect of large-scale redundancies as well as inconvenient transfers, launched a series of strikes, punctuated by embittered negotiations. The heads of the new broadcasting companies were hampered in their preparations by delays in the publication of government decrees, and uncertainty as to their budget for the coming year. There were also rumours that political pressures were being exercised over the reappointment of important officials.[41]

The Law of 7 August 1974 gave only the framework of the reform.[42] It needed about 25 decrees (which do not, of course, pass through Parliament) to complete the system; some of these, it is true, were concerned with the problems of the transition from *ORTF* to the new set-up – redistribution of personnel, property, capital, etc. – which were indeed considerable.

The new law defined somewhat more precisely than previously the aims and objectives of French broadcasting.[43] The latter must respond to the needs and aspirations of the nation regarding information, communication, culture, education, entertainment and 'all the values of civilization'; the general interests of the community must be the sole consideration. It must ensure equal access for the 'principal tendencies of thought and the major currents of opinion'; regular broadcasting time (and this was an innovation as far as the law was concerned) should be made available for the different groups. Broadcasting must take an active part in the diffusion of French culture through the world, and has a special responsibility to preserve the quality of the French language.

After this preliminary definition, following articles officially suppressed *ORTF* and replaced it with a number of separate institutions with varying types of organization. There was no central trunk, as the 1970 *Paye Report* and the 1974 reform project of Marceau Long had proposed. Instead, some of the common services, notably, research, archives and in-service training, were grouped into a new Audiovisual Institute.[44] The status of the latter is (like *ORTF*) that of a 'public establishment of an industrial and commercial character'. It is placed under the general control of the Prime Minister or his delegate. It has a President appointed for three years by the Cabinet and chosen from the members of the Administrative Council. The Director General is proposed by the President and appointed by decree. The Administrative Council is a particularly large one: it is composed of ten representatives from government ministries (the Prime Minister, and the ministers responsible for education, culture, foreign affairs, co-operation, youth and sport, professional training, finance, posts and tele-communications, and the universities); two representatives of the personnel, chosen from lists drawn up by the unions; one of the new body responsible for transmission; one each from the new programme and production companies (five in all), chosen by the president concerned; and four persons chosen for their qualifications, two of them to be chosen by the High Audiovisual Council. The Administrative Council members are appointed for three years in the first instance, although the State representatives can be removed at any time. The financial and administrative organization of the Institute, as a 'State public establishment', remains to some degree under State control; there is, for example, as at *ORTF*, a central accountant on the premises.

A second public establishment, on similar lines, was given responsibility for the transmission of programmes and for the extension and maintenance of the networks. Like the Audiovisual Institute, it is placed under the control of the Prime Minister or his delegate. It has a President and a Director General. Its Administrative Council is composed of eight representatives of the State (from a variety of interested ministries), two from Parliament (one from each Chamber, chosen by the appropriate committees), two delegates of the personnel, and one from each programme company.[45]

Responsibility for programmes is divided between four 'national companies' (*sociétés nationales*): radio, and the three television channels. The radio company both draws up its programme plans and produces the programmes. It also has responsibility for the *ORTF* orchestras. The television companies have only 'light' production equipment at their disposal. They are in competition with one another; however, their Presidents must meet regularly to ensure a certain degree of harmony between the programmes. One of the companies – the former Channel Three – includes the regional stations and the overseas territories. It has a statutory mission to give a special place to cinema films and to the organization of programmes allowing direct expression to the differing national currents of thought. Each of the four companies has an Administrative Council of six members: two representatives of the State; one of Parliament; one from the written press; one of the personnel; and one personality from the world of culture, co-opted by the other five, with the government's consent. For the third company, this person must come from the cinema industry. The President of each company is appointed by the Cabinet, for three years, and is chosen from the members of the Administrative Council.[46] It is noticeable that for the first time in French broadcasting, the State representatives are not in the majority on the Council.

For television production, the government created a new company, entirely independent, which would supply the programme companies in competition with other, private firms. Although the State must remain in the majority, shares in this company may be held by other public bodies, by national companies and by companies which have a mixture of public and private capital (*sociétés d'économie mixte*). (This marks out the production company from all the other new bodies, entirely State-owned.) The new company will have greater powers than its direct ancestors, the *ORTF* production *régies*. The latter merely supplied what was ordered, whereas the new company will be able to choose both the subject and the producer of a programme. It will employ about 4,000 people. Reforms in the organization of production structures are planned, notably the disappearance of the much-criticized divisions into production methods (*vidéo-fixe*, *vidéo-mobile*, and film), and the creation instead of new units divided by genre – drama, varieties and so on. A clause expected to safeguard the production company's revenue by fixing a minimum annual quota of orders from the programme companies did not in the end materialize.[47]

A number of Articles of the new statute deal with the relationship between broadcasting and the State. The Prime Minister or his delegate are once more given overall responsibility: for ensuring the respect of the monopoly, and for seeing that the new companies fulfil their duty to the public. In particular, the minister responsible, after consultation with the parliamentary delegation, draws up for each new body a document (*cahier des charges*) defining its objectives in some detail. (This was a major innovation.) The statute gave some indication of the areas involved: information, culture, co-operation (with foreign countries), the access to the screen of political groups, and certain rules governing advertising.[48] The *cahiers des charges* themselves followed some months later. They stipulated, among other things, that children's programmes should be expanded, that the productions of the State-subsidized theatres should be televised (which had never been done before), and that adult education programmes should be further developed. One of the more controversial chapters was the section dealing with relations between broadcasting and the cinema. Television should pay a larger sum into the Cinema Support Fund, and, in return, show a larger number of films, which were what many viewers liked best.[49] The cinema industry complained that it could not possibly supply 500 films a year (Italy, for example, shows about 100, the Netherlands 90), while maintaining any kind of quality. The television screen would be invaded by mediocre American productions.[50] The High Audiovisual Council, consulted on the *cahiers des charges*, also expressed its disapproval.[51]

The *cahiers des charges* also dealt with the details of election broadcasting. At other times, as in previous statutes, the government could broadcast to the nation, but it must make clear the official nature of the communication. Parliamentary debates, as before, were to be televised under the control of each assembly's central bureau. Equal broadcasting time was to be given to the majority and opposition parliamentary groups.[52]

As far as the personnel was concerned, there were important changes. While the staff of the transmission company were to be given a special statute, the employees of the other companies would now enter into collective agreements with the employer, on the lines of those found in the private sector. The statute meanwhile retained the notion of a 'minimum service' to be supplied in times of strike. Each president was to be responsible for choosing those persons or sectors who were to remain at their posts.[53]

At the end of 1974, shortly before the new system was due to begin functioning, the internal workings of the various companies were still not very clear. Among the programme companies,

[67]

a number of variations on the basic pattern had, however, emerged. Radio – *Radio France* – had a President (Jacqueline Baudrier, from TV Channel One) and an administrative and financial director, heads of news and of music, and a head for each radio network. TV Channel One, baptized *TF 1*, had a President (Jean Cazeneuve, Professor of Sociology, from the *ORTF* Administrative Council), a Director General (J.-L. Guillaud, from TV Three) and an administrative and financial director. Channel Two, *Antenne 2*, had a President, but no single director. Instead, Marcel Jullian (from the Plon and Julliard publishing firms) appointed an advisory team: one counsellor, one director to 'harmonize' the artistic and financial sectors, and a programme committee composed of several well-known producers and a former chief editor of the newspaper *France-Soir*.[54] Production was to be organized into small autonomous units, on the lines of the reforms called for by certain producers in 1968.[55] *Antenne 2* has a progressive image: the 'cultural personality' on the Administrative Council is Claude Lévi-Strauss, and Sartre, who has refused to broadcast in France since 1968, has agreed to make a series on contemporary French history.

Channel Three, *FR 3*, the largest of the programme companies, has a President (Claude Contamine, from the foreign service, and Assistant Director General of *ORTF* from 1964 to 1967), heads of programmes, of regional programmes and of programmes for overseas territories. It also has an administrative and financial director, and a head of news (from the Nantes regional news station). *FR 3*'s news will go out at 10 p.m.; it will show films four evenings a week, from 8.30 p.m.

One of the main criticisms of the reform has been the reappearance, in high positions, of men long connected with the ill-fated *Office*. Contamine, Guillaud, de Broglie, Sanviti, Larère, Lemoine, Riou: the list could be continued. Thus, in spite of the renewal of structures, the faces remain the same, and it is to be feared that these men may bring to the new system not only their practical experience but also those very habits of political 'deference' and administrative slackness which led to the breakdown of the old system. The structures, too, may well be, on paper, more liberal – one thinks, for example, of the minority representation of the State on the Administrative Councils of the programme companies. However, this new freedom could be illusory. There are already rumours that the government imposed its own choice of directors on the presidents of the new companies, and that the sacking or recruitment of staff has been the occasion for political manœuvres.[56] Whatever the case – and these are only rumours – it will be interesting to see whether the new structures are indeed more of a guarantee for independence than the old ones.

FINANCE

One reason for the demise of *ORTF* in 1974 was that its financial situation had become almost unmanageable. The government blamed the directors, used the 1973 deficit (not a very large one) as one of its pretexts for dismissing Arthur Conte, and sacked the high officials responsible for the computerized accounting service. Other people blamed the government, which had allowed all this to happen, and which had refused to pay its share. The crisis may have been sudden, but the roots of the problem were long ones.

The total *ORTF* budget in 1973 was estimated at 2,295,020,000 francs, obtained as follows:

	Million frs
Licence fee revenue	1,488.89
Brand advertising	529.28
Commercial and various	172.30
Loan	100.00
Various other	4.55
	2,295.02[57]

Revenue from radio and television licences accounted for nearly 70 per cent of the normal receipts. The main problem here is that sales of television sets cannot expand indefinitely, nor can the licence fee be increased so much as to deter people from buying sets. In France, the rate of expansion of set-ownership began to slow down at an earlier point of development than in other countries. Thus at the very moment when *ORTF* was developing a third TV channel and changing its programmes over to colour, its revenue began to increase more slowly.[58] To remedy this to some extent, it was decided to introduce in 1974 a special licence fee for colour television, which would stand at 50 per cent of the black and white licence. The total colour licence would be 210 francs. It was hoped that sales of colour sets would continue to expand and revenue with it: in January 1973, an estimated 1 million sets were already in use, and sales of a further 600,000 were hoped for that year.[59] Licence fee revenue for 1974 was forecast at 1,703 million, an increase of 14 per cent over 1973.[60]

Another problem was the radio licence. This only concerned those householders without television: that is, in general, the poorer section of the community. Many of these householders, because of their age or low income, were legally exonerated from paying the licence fee. In 1969, the field of exonerations had been considerably extended, and by 1973 it stood at 5.1 per cent of all television and 27 per cent of all radio licences.[61] In these circumstances, it seemed hardly worth the administrative cost of collecting a separate licence fee for radio. On the other hand, however, it could be argued that radio would suffer if it no longer had any independent source of income entirely its own.[62]

Thirdly, there were the problems of collection. Should ORTF continue to collect the licence fee itself, when the cost of collection (in 1973) stood at over 97 million francs and the staff employed (in December 1973) numbered 1,289?[63] While the numbers employed had decreased over the years, costs had continued to go up. The collection service as a whole, though somewhat improved by modernization after 1971, was still not efficient enough. For example, while the number of colour sets in use in January 1973 was put at 1 million, the number of licences taken out was only 702,000.[64] In 1972, a total of over 350 million francs was owing to the *Office* in licence fee revenue, some of this dating back to 1965.[65] In the overseas territories, licence fee evasion reached staggering proportions: about 96 per cent unpaid in the Antilles (the worst example).[66] The *Chinaud Report* in 1974 concluded that the collection service should be removed from ORTF and given to some other Civil Service department, as was already the case in numerous foreign countries.[67]

The second largest source of revenue has been brand advertising.[68] Since 1972, the volume of revenue from commercials has been pegged at 25 per cent of the *Office*'s total resources. In 1973, the estimated income from this source was 529.28 million francs (24 per cent), plus 42.70 million francs from 'collective advertising' (for non-branded goods or nationalized services), and 5.87 million francs from publicity overseas. (In fact, an extra 34 million francs were made on the year's exercise.) In 1974, the revenue expected was 569 million francs (23.5 per cent).[69]

The administration of television advertising was placed in the hands of an affiliated company, the *Régie française de publicité*, in which *ORTF* held 51 per cent of shares. *ORTF* fixed the overall sum to be attained each year, and decided on the tariffs to be applied for each particular slot. *RFP* handled the actual business and saw that the commercials conformed to a strict code of honesty and morality. Financially, the exercise was a successful one; perhaps, as the *Chinaud Report* suggested, this was because *ORTF* did not have the responsibility for administering it.[70]

The heading 'commercial and various' covered a variety of small sources of income: sales of programmes and of copyright, guided tours of the *Maison de l'ORTF* and other public events, moneys paid by government ministries for 'services rendered' and so on.[71] While some of these categories fell outside the *Office*'s control (it could not easily make ministries pay more, for instance), others showed a lamentable lack of commercial acumen on the part of the *Office*: this will be discussed later.

In 1973, the expenditure of *ORTF* could be broken down as follows:

		Million frs.
Investment costs		385·07
TV Channel One		316·47
TV Channel Three	140·32	303·14
Regions	162.82	
TV Channel Two		279·78
Transmission		258·93
Radio		182·56
Foreign service (*DAEC*)		132·37
Licence fee collection		97·41
Copyright and royalties		90·79
Technical and equipment		90·36
Overseas stations		70·26
Administration		57·25
General services		56·21
Television production		49·07
Irrecoverable debts		35·00
Works Committee		25·40
Contingency Fund		24·13
In-service training		20·79
Commission and interest		15·10
Purchase and commissions of programmes		15·09
Social action		8·50
Exceptional expenses		6·01
Research Service		5·80
Education		4·34
		2,529·83
Deduct		
Depreciation (*amortissements techniques*)	226·92	
DAEC's contribution to general expenses	7,89	234·81
		2,295·02[72]

For 1974, the overall budget was forecast at 2,538 million francs, an increase of 10·6 per cent. Expenditure on television programmes was to go up by 8 per cent, and there was to be a special increase in spending on the regions and on the overseas stations (16 per cent each).[73]

Out of its total budget, ORTF lost 13·9 per cent to the government through taxation: 346·5 million francs in 1972. Until 1970, the *Office* had been subject to a variety of small taxes and had also been expected in theory to pay a lump sum into the Treasury (91 million francs in 1969). Then the 1970 Finance Act ruled that the *Office* should be subject to the same taxation system as private enterprise. This meant VAT (Value Added Tax) on all revenue, plus the payment of company tax. Different rates of VAT were imposed on different kinds of receipts: 17·6 per cent on the licence fee, 20 per cent on advertising revenue, 33·3 per cent on sales of records and tapes, 7 per cent on sales of books and productions. VAT paid by ORTF on purchases of goods and services could be reclaimed. The payment to the Treasury was at the same time officially discontinued: in fact, the *Office* had always refused to pay it, and by 1969 owed the Treasury a total of 343 million francs.[74] Of these various provisions, the levying of VAT on the licence fee was the most controversial. The latter had been legally defined in 1960 by the Constitutional Council as a 'parafiscal tax', and not a payment for services rendered. This meant that one tax was now being superimposed upon another. Though this was legal (a special clause in the Finance Act authorized it), it was an unusual and, in view of the *Office*'s financial difficulties, hardly a desirable situation.[75]

As a publicly-owned establishment, the *Office*'s financial management was subject to a number of controls, both internal and external. While the umbilical cord between ORTF and State had been gradually loosening – notably in 1969 as part of the liberalization introduced by Prime Minister Chaban-Delmas – a number of fairly stringent regulations remained. Parliament voted annually for or against the collection of the licence fee.[76] The Ministers for Information and Finance had to give their approval to the ORTF budget. On the *Office*'s premises, the State Controller, the permanent representative of the Finance Ministry, and responsible only to the latter, exercised a largely *a posteriori* control over spending. His preliminary consent was still required, however, for matters concerning investments and salaries. Until 1968, the *Office*'s accounts were submitted for audit to the *Cour des Comptes*; after that date, they went to the Commission for the Verification of Accounts of Public Enterprise. The latter examined the previous year's accounts and sent a report to the *Cour des Comptes* and the Finance Ministry. Certain important areas of expenditure were controlled by *ad hoc* committees which might include members of the *ORTF* management. For example, general salary policy was examined by the Interministerial Salaries Committee, while the purchase or renting of buildings had to be authorized by the Central Committee for Property Operations under the control of the Prime Minister.[77]

Within *ORTF*, a number of departments had responsibility for financial management and controls. The Director of Management and Finance prepared the annual budget, and followed through its workings with the aid of monthly 'statements' (*tableaux de bord*) sent out by the computer services. The Director of General Control, a department created in 1972, grouped together two sections: the *Inspection Générale*, a traditional structure in French public administration, which undertook research into specific areas of management, and the 'internal control' service, set up in 1971, on lines similar to the modern auditing systems recently introduced into private and semi-public enterprise. The latter service examined the functioning of the *Office*'s mechanisms and proposed ways of improving economic viability. The Central Accountant, appointed jointly by the two tutelary ministries (Information and Finance) had overall responsibility for accounting services. Finally, the Finance Committee of the Administrative Council, which brought together four members of the Council, plus the Assistant Director General, the directors of the sections just mentioned, the State Controller and the Central Accountant, was competent to discuss all financial matters pertaining to the *Office*; its role, however, was largely an advisory one.[78]

In view of these numerous safeguards against financial mismanagement, it is perhaps surprising that *ORTF* should have found itself in 1973 with a deficit of 48 million francs and the possibility of a much larger gap – 150 million francs – in 1974. During the course of 1973, it became increasingly clear that revenue from licence fees was not going to reach the target set by the budget for that year. At the end of 1973, there was a shortfall of 12·8 million francs. Meanwhile, expenditure rose well over the forecast level, and in spite of stringent economy measures in the final months of the year, the gap in spending eventually reached 60 million francs. To make matters worse, the analytical accounting service degenerated into chaos, with the result that there existed in fact no reliable evaluation of the financial record for 1973 and no solid forecast for 1974.[79]

The 1973 deficit was not perhaps a very serious one (it was just over 2 per cent of the total budget), and it was tided over by palliative measures, including an advance of 30 million francs from the *Régie française de publicité*.[80] However, for the future, with the Channel Three network still to be completed, costs constantly rising and little hope of increasing revenue, the prospects were alarming. A number of stopgaps were found: further economy measures, the increase of the licence fee and the imposition of a new tax on colour television, and a loan of 170 million francs from an American bank.[81] It became clear, however, that more radical reforms were needed, and the splitting-up of the *Office* in late 1974 was in part a response to this situation.

While the magnitude of the crisis was perhaps due to the general inflation, both the *Office* and the government were also responsible. Within ORTF, there had been mismanagement at a number of levels. According to the *Chinaud Report*, the cost of a finished programme frequently exceeded its provisional budget; indeed the very existence of the 'production norms' (estimates of average cost, man-hours, etc., established as guidelines for different kinds of production) encouraged people to exceed the average. The most notorious example was a Christmas 1973 super-production, 'Sleeping Beauty', which cost $2\frac{3}{4}$ million francs, over 1 million francs more than the 'norm'.[82] In general, too, there was inadequate planning for the use of production units, studios and equipment. One studio, for example, was used exclusively for a weekly variety show and was left empty most of the rest of the time. The cost of this underemployment of men and materials could not be accurately assessed. The *Report* also showed that more and more programmes were being kept indefinitely in stock, others taking longer and longer to finish. Some were described as being 'in course of production' for three or four years in succession.[83]

While the *Office* itself could not of course be held to blame for inflation, it had none the less reacted to the situation with less than adequate speed and flexibility. ORTF had gone through several years of financial euphoria: the revenue from licence fees was in constant expansion until about 1970, and the new revenue from advertising which became available from 1968 cushioned it against the beginnings of saturation. During those years of plenty, it had neglected to set up a rigorous system of financial management, had gone in for costly patronage, allowed itself to be imposed on by government departments, and indulged in a luxurious invest-ment policy. The rise in prices in 1973 had then caught the *Office* unawares. Budgetary forecasts had been based on unreliable data and future price rises had been grossly underestimated. Those responsible seemed to have ignored all the warning signs of the deterioration of the *Office*'s finances. The Administrative Council and its Finance Committee had not acted decisively enough; they had not even been provided with adequate information on which to take action. When the crisis came, the economy measures taken were hardly sufficient. In any case, as the *Report* showed, inflation was not by any means the only culprit, as the directors claimed. A gap of at least 36 million francs out of the total deficit for 1973 could be ascribed to other causes.[84]

Even without inflation, there were areas in which the *Office* had contributed to its own financial imbroglio. For example, in spite of its official denomination as an establishment 'of com-mercial and industrial character', it had always taken surprisingly little interest in selling its products. For 1974, it forecast a revenue of only 32·3 million francs (about 2 per cent of its income) from 'sales of goods and services to clients other than the State'. It made very little money, for instance, from the sale of records, although it maintained a number of permanent orchestras and choirs. The Commercial Service was badly organized. Sales of programmes abroad were the responsibility of the Foreign Service, whose aims were largely cultural and which distributed programmes gratis to underdeveloped countries. In the USA, sales had plummeted from 1 million francs in 1972 to 24,500 francs in 1973, after a disastrous episode involving an incompetent American company. This was a particularly bad example, but the whole system required reorganization and a complete change of attitude on the part of those responsible.[85]

Another debacle for which ORTF could be held largely to

blame was the breakdown of the computerized accounting service, which it had installed in an attempt to revolutionize its financial management. In theory an excellent innovation, in practice the system had been badly introduced and applied. The staff had not been given time to understand and assimilate the new system, which was a highly sophisticated one. (It had been expected to become operational within two or three years, although experts usually advised a running-in period of four or five.) Nor had the system, for a variety of reasons, contributed to improving financial controls. For example, the information it produced was often incomprehensible (because expressed in figures rather than in concrete terms such as days of filming, hours of set-construction, etc., to which the staff were accustomed), overabundant (and therefore ignored), unreliable, and frequently too late to be of any use. As regards the control of expenditure, the bases of calculation were often unrealistic: for example, the cost of the use of equipment was calculated on a base of 365 days in the year, whereas in practice it was frequently impossible to use a particular studio or outside-broadcast van for more than a much smaller number of days. Finally, the system itself had cost over 10 million francs, and its running expenses were particularly high.[86]

The government as guardian of *ORTF* was equally blameworthy. In spite of the continuity of political power in France since 1959, there had been an extraordinary lack of planning for broadcasting. A succession of directors general and other high officials had meant a succession of costly but ineffectual reforms. Where there had been planning, it had frequently been overambitious, more concerned with national prestige than with sound financial possibilities. Channel Three was one notable example; another was the projected skyscraper on the banks of the Seine, which the *Office* abandoned in February 1974 after spending 17 million francs on it.[87]

More specifically, the *Chinaud Report*, the unions and others accused the government of directly contributing to the *Office*'s impossible situation.[88] *ORTF* was the only large public enterprise which was expected to function without State subsidy. It was the government which had imposed on the *Office* the 1971 planning agreement that had led to its unrealistic forecasts of prices and productivity.[89] The government had not reimbursed the *Office* for the repair of the Roc-Trédudon transmitter, blown up by Breton nationalists (115 million francs), nor for the cost of the presidential election campaign (10 million francs). The government and not the *Office* should support the cost of the 800,000 exonerations from the licence fees (100 million francs),[90] since this was part of its social policy. Government ministries consistently got away with paying less than the full price for the 'services rendered' by the *Office*. Since 1971, their contributions had hardly increased at all, in spite of the rise in the cost of living.[91] The Foreign Affairs Ministry was the worst culprit. While the budget for foreign broadcasting had risen by 59·5 per cent between 1969 and 1973, the Ministry's contribution had only gone up by 3·13 per cent.[92] This state of affairs had been denounced for years by successive parliamentary reports on the budget.[93] Taxation policy in particular provided an easy target. The amount the *Office* paid in VAT and other taxes came to more than its deficit.[94] The very principle of imposing VAT on top of a parafiscal tax, the licence fee, was, as we have seen, a subject of controversy.

The transformation of *ORTF* into a number of smaller institutions in 1974–75 was as confused financially as it was on the level of organization. The new statute, once again, provided only a general framework. For the new 'public establishment' responsible for transmission, the Law of 7 August 1974 detailed the various sources of revenue: remuneration from the programme companies in return for the use of the network and other services; a percentage of the licence fee revenue, so calculated as to lead eventually to the complete coverage of the territory and the expansion of overseas broadcasts; loans, subsidies and returns on investments. The budget of the establishment was to be submitted to the government for its approval (Article 5). A number of other Articles dealt with financial matters common to the various other new companies. The provisional budget of each programme company must be submitted for the government's 'observations'. The two Chambers of Parliament would continue to vote annually for or against permission to collect the licence fee. Parliament would also have the right to approve or disapprove the sharing out of the licence fee revenue. The budgets for the past, present and coming years were to be annexed as before to the annual Finance Act, as would also be the state of execution of each company's *cahier des charges*, and the profit and loss sheet of the production company.

The licence fee was henceforth to be collected by the State, and paid into a special account at the Treasury. The criteria for the distribution of this revenue were to be decided on by a decree from the Council of State, after consultation with the parliamentary delegation. The actual job of sharing out the money was to be done by a special committee presided over by a magistrate from the *Cour des Comptes*. The state was to determine and also reimburse exonerations from licence fee payment. Advertising revenue was not to exceed 25 per cent of the total budget for broadcasting; details would be set out in the *cahiers des charges*. The accounts of the transmission establishment and the national companies were to be vetted by the Commission for the Verification of the Accounts of Public Enterprise (Articles 18 to 24).

The basic sources of revenue – licence fee and television commercials – remained the same as before. The government's official recognition of its obligation to reimburse exonerations would, however, save the new system something in the region of 95 million francs.[95] The cost of collection also passed to the government. In this case broadcasting might benefit, but the taxpayer would not: it was estimated that licence fee collection by the government was to cost 40 million francs more than when *ORTF* had been responsible.[96]

The keystone of the new system was the distribution of revenue between the new companies. Two main criteria were to be applied: the quality of programmes (admittedly difficult to assess), and 'success', that is, the volume of the audience. Quality would be assessed by means of a two-tiered organization: on the one hand, by a committee whose members, drawn by lot, would be proposed by a variety of cultural associations, and on the other, by audience research carried out several times a year on a representative sample of the population, and using a questionnaire to be drawn up by the High Audiovisual Council. Quality, thus determined, would then be weighted about three times as heavily as audience volume in the final formula for distribution.[97] The committee responsible would have an audience research team at its disposal. This system could only work properly from 1976 at least, by which time it was hoped that each company could be held responsible for its programmes. For 1975, a transitional system would operate: this consisted more or less in letting the presidents ask for what they needed, and sharing the revenue out accordingly.[98]

The budget for 1975 was in fact something of a mystery. Only two or three weeks before the start of the new régime, the heads of the programme and production companies were still uncertain as to how much they would receive.[99] (That this did not prevent the start of the operation was due to the stocks of programmes inherited from ORTF.) The overall budget was estimated at over 2,600 million francs. Of this, an estimated 2,028 million would come from licence fees and 640 million from commercials.[100] The Audiovisual Institute was to be given a dowry of 95 million francs to begin with, and in later years, would receive a share (10 per cent?) of the programme companies' budget.[101] The production company was to be given a start of perhaps 480 million francs, 260 million from TF 1 and 220 million from Antenne 2: this would form a sort of credit account for those two companies and enable production to get going. However, the production company still felt it would probably have to put up the price of 'tailor-made' productions, in order to ensure sufficient returns. This increase, as much as 35 per cent, would put up the cost of an hour's drama from 850,000 francs in 1974 to 1·2 million in 1975.[102]

The various sets of unofficial figures given in late 1974 for the programme companies' 1975 budgets were particularly confusing. (The uncertainty was partly due to the problems of redeploying the personnel – no one really knew how many staff he would have to take on.) In the budget debate at the National Assembly in November, it was stated that the 640 million francs expected from commercials would go to TF 1 (400 million) and Antenne 2 (240 million); the other two companies carried no advertising. Licence fee revenue would be shared out as follows: TF 1, 208·4 million francs; Antenne 2, 386·3 million; FR 3, 732·37 million; radio, 433·41 million; transmission, 13 million (a total of 1,773 million).[103] Commenting on the debate, Le Monde gave a series of unofficial estimates of what the new presidents had asked for: TF 1, 698 million francs; Antenne 2, 637 million; FR 3, 876 million; radio, 570 million.[104] When it came to the debate in the Senate, the figures had changed: TF 1 needed 809·9 million francs, but had been given 658·4; Antenne 2 needed 739·5 million, was given 643·3; FR 3 needed 876·5 million, was given 770·2; radio needed 569·5 million, was given 477·2.[105]

Whatever the correct figures, it is clear that the programme companies' budgets were to be smaller than they would have liked. Deputy Joël Le Tac, in the National Assembly budget debate, had pointed out that they would indeed have little room for manœuvre. Out of an estimated budget of 720 million francs (yet another figure), Channel One, for example, would have to pay out 220 million for transmission costs and for investments; 80 million to the Audiovisual Institute, 260 million to the production company and 110 million to its news unit. This would leave it with only 50 million to spend on films, co-productions, light production within the company, salaries, upkeep, taxes and so on.[106] In these circumstances, there would be an obvious temptation for the programme companies to spend their money on imported American films (costing 50,000 francs an hour) rather than on French television productions (costing 550,000 francs an hour).[107] The national production company would be the first to suffer.

Once more, French broadcasting was beset by contradictions. The splitting-up of ORTF had been presented, ostensibly at least, as an economy measure. Lighter structures would involve less wastage and would cost less to run.[108] But the bill for the reorganization itself came to 360 million francs, not including the indemnities paid to those made redundant.[109] It was doubtful, too, whether the new system, with its inevitable reduplications, would prove less costly to administer.[110] The most striking of the planned economy measures – the reduction of available jobs by over 2,000 and some drastic cuts in the foreign service, notably in broadcasts to Eastern Europe[111] – caused a public outcry. And finally, the success of the reform depended on new ideas, and a new start for everybody; this seemed impossible in the atmosphere of penny-pinching imposed by the prevalent economic climate.

❦

CHAPTER THREE

Controls and Pressures

'THE VOICE OF FRANCE'

French broadcasting is a public service and is financed largely by the public's money. The French State feels therefore that it should retain some public control over the way that money is spent. This has meant, notably, close statutory links with government ministries. There has been a gradual movement towards granting – in theory at least – greater independence to broadcasting. In 1964, when *RTF* became *ORTF*, the 'authority' of the Ministry of Information legally became 'tutelage' or 'guardianship' (*tutelle*), which should mean a much more distant relationship. A number of changes in the texts relating to financial control also brought a greater degree of autonomy. However, until 1974, *ORTF* continued to be much more closely linked to the government than other State enterprises such as the railways or the electricity industry.[1] Nor were those links always used to non-political ends.

The more controversial of the two tutelary Ministries has been the Ministry of Information (a post which few other Western European countries still possess). The Minister's duties, as defined by Article 5 of the 1972 statute, were to ensure the monopoly was not infringed, to see that the *Office* fulfilled its obligations as a public service, to supervise the use made of its resources and, together with the Minister of Finance, to approve its budget. In that statute, these duties were assigned to the Prime Minister 'or a member of the government delegated by him'. Thus from mid-1969 to mid-1972, when there was no post of Minister of Information, *ORTF* was directly attached to the Prime Minister. For much of their existence, however, French radio and television have been under the wing of a minister or secretary of state for information. Apart from his other duties, this minister also has responsibilities in various sectors of the audiovisual industries: he is chairman of the High Audiovisual Council and is in charge of government policy concerning new developments such as cable television.[2] Until July 1969, he was chairman of the Interministerial Information Committee (*CII*), which replaced the notorious Interministerial Information Liaison Service (*SLII*) and which, it was promised, would have no direct links with *ORTF*.[3] In February 1974, he was given responsibility for a larger, more inclusive information office (*délégation à l'information*) set up by Prime Minister Pierre Messmer. The opposition feared a propaganda machine, but the new office, one of whose tasks was to be the decentralization of *ORTF*, did not have time to show its paces before the change of government.[4]

It is unfortunate, as numerous critics of the French system have pointed out, that responsibility for broadcasting, which brings news and all kinds of information to the general public, should lie in the hands of the man chosen as spokesman for a particular government's policies.[5] The degree of interference practised by ministers evidently depends on the personalities involved: the President, Prime Minister, Minister of Information and Director General of *ORTF* are all possible factors in this equation. While *ORTF* officially claimed that the tutelary role did not extend to the conception or production of programmes,[6] the notion of ensuring that the *Office* fulfilled its obligations as a public service was vague enough to include interference with programme policy in general.[7] Furthermore, although independent committees are asked to submit reports on possible reforms (*Paye*, for example, in 1970), and Parliament may set up bodies of enquiry and modify legislation, it is the minister responsible who prepares the texts of new statutes.

To eliminate the essential ambiguity discussed above, many people have advocated a change in the tutelary ministry. While the *Paye Report* preferred the Prime Minister to retain responsibility for broadcasting, others have suggested changing to the Ministry of Cultural Affairs, on the grounds that information is culture, and conversely, that no genuine cultural policy should neglect to concern itself with broadcasting.[8] This is true, but the change might not eliminate interference.[9] In this, as in other domains, much clearer definitions of relative spheres of power are needed, as well as some drastic modification of well-established habits.

Like all French public enterprise, ORTF was subject to a number of external financial controls.[10] The Minister of Information and the Minister of Economy and Finance exercised joint supervision over the *Office*'s budget, as laid down in the 1972 statute (Article 5). In November of each year, these Ministers were presented with a forecast of the following year's budget for their approval.[11] Moreover, like other nationalized industries, ORTF had to submit its account annually to the Commission for Verifying the Accounts of Public Enterprise, which then sent a report to the Court of Accounts and to both the tutelary Ministries.[12]

A more immediate control was exercised by the permanent presence of the State Controller (*Contrôleur d'État*), the Minister of Finance's representative within the *Office*.[13] In recent years, the powers of the State Controller were gradually lessened, notably in 1969 as part of the general liberalization brought about by the upheavals of 1968. The Controller's general task was to supervise the running of the establishment and more particularly all operations likely to have economic or financial repercussions outside. He had entry in a consultative capacity to all ORTF committees and councils including the Administrative Council. He was sent or could demand any information or documents he thought necessary.

The Controller was to be consulted on any project to be submitted for approval to the Finance Ministry. As the Minister's delegate, he could approve certain modifications made to the budget. Although *a priori* controls had indeed been much reduced by 1972, the Controller still had to give his prior consent to investments involving large sums of money and to certain decisions concerning salaries. He was consulted over other questions which involved personnel.[14] In this latter domain, the 1974 *Chinaud Report* complained that the Controller's supervision was a considerable hindrance to dynamic management.[15]

A second permanent representative on the *Office*'s premises was the Central Accountant (*Agent comptable central*). Appointed jointly by the Minister of Finance and the Minister of Information, the Central Accountant had overall responsibility for the *Office*'s accounting services, for all payments and receipts. Unlike the State Controller, whose position was totally independent of the *Office*, the Central Accountant was placed under the authority of the President-Director General.[16]

The changes made in its financial status in 1968 and 1969 brought ORTF more into line with other 'public establishments of an industrial and commercial character'. It is perhaps worth noting that there has been a general trend towards granting increased financial independence to State-owned enterprise, in the name of more modern and dynamic management.[17] Although financial autonomy is no guarantee of political independence (nor does dependency have to mean interference), it was probably a good thing for ORTF to loosen its links with government ministries as much as possible.

Some contribution to the greater independence of the *Office* – and at the same time, an indication of how close its links with government really are – was the move towards contractual relationships between it and various ministries. The most important of these agreements was the general planning agreement or *contrat de programme*, signed by the Prime Minister and the Director General of ORTF on 29 November 1971. This document, which was based on the proposals of the General Commissariat for the Sixth Plan, set out in broad terms the objectives and obligations of the *Office* and the financial resources available to meet them, for the four-year period 1972-1975. The *Office*'s objectives, briefly, were to extend the coverage and programme hours of the third television channel, to expand regional broadcasting (TV and radio), and to increase activity in the foreign service and services to French territories overseas. To meet these obligations, the *Office* agreed to increase productivity (i.e. to make savings) of 2·6 per cent per annum, while the government agreed to allow up to 78 per cent of expenditure on Channel Three to be financed by a loan. The licence fee would be gradually increased at a rate of about 3–5 per cent annually, while advertising revenue, to be pegged at 25 per cent of the *Office*'s total resources, would also thereby increase regularly.[18]

The main advantage of this system, it was claimed, was that it allowed for longer-term planning than had hitherto been the case.

As far as the negotiation of the contract was concerned, it seems unlikely – given the other factors in the relationship between *ORTF* and government, notably the appointment of the Director General by the latter – that the partners met on equal terms. It is difficult to imagine how *ORTF* could avoid having these terms, however favourable, dictated to it by the government. Another criticism was that the contract would effectively reduce the powers of control held by Parliament. The latter would find it harder to supervise *ORTF*'s spending when the overall financial decisions were taken out of its hands. The annual debate on the budget was thus in danger of becoming a mere formality.[19]

In the context of the same policy, and indeed of the Chaban-Delmas government's general policy on public enterprise, other contracts were signed between *ORTF* and government ministries. In March 1971, the first of these agreements, between the *Office* and the Ministry of Cultural Affairs, set up machinery for co-operation, with provisions for mutual exchange of information and services, as well as some common projects.[20] A year later, with the same Ministry, a specific agreement was reached on the subject of co-operation with the cinema industry, which had long complained of unfair exploitation by *ORTF*. The latter agreed to pay more for films shown on TV, to show fewer films at weekends, to contribute 10 million francs to support cinema production and to have representatives sit on various bodies concerned with the cinema industry.[21]

In the field of education, two conventions were signed. One, in January 1972, with the Ministry of Education, defined general policies for educational broadcasting, for a period of three years in the first instance. The sharing of tasks between *ORTF* and the Ministry of Education's *French Office for Modern Educational Techniques* (*OFRATEME*) was a delicate one. Eight months of negotiations were needed before a specific agreement was reached in May 1973 which gave *ORTF* increased powers of control over the content of schools programmes.[22] A second general convention, between *ORTF* and the Prime Minister early in 1972, concerned the use of audiovisual methods in adult education.[23]

These agreements did not really represent any substantial gain in independence for *ORTF*. Some critics saw them rather as attempts by the State to shuffle off onto the *Office* the cost of its own obligations in the fields of culture, education and foreign policy.[24]

However, whatever the results of these specific contracts (and they cannot be properly assessed here), the general planning agreement signed in 1971 for 1972–75 must be regarded as a failure. It did not succeed in imposing on ORTF the effective long- or even medium-term planning the latter so badly needed. Indeed, its forecasts of prices and productivity, based as they were on a projection of past developments, were essentially unrealistic, and contributed to the *Office*'s confusion when faced with the inflation of 1973–74.[25] Nor, of course, did it reduce political interference.

Before the general planning agreement was due to expire, the 1974 statute made important changes in the relationship between broadcasting and the State. Overall responsibility remained, as in 1972, in the hands of the Prime Minister or a member of the government delegated by him (Article 14). But, the government claimed, its role as guardian would be considerably lessened under the new régime.[26] It would, of course, appoint the heads of the six broadcasting companies. But other than that, its main task would be to draw up the *cahiers des charges* (a sort of list of obligations), which set out the aims and objectives of broadcasting in some detail, and to ensure that these provisions were respected (Articles 14 and 15). These clauses were vague enough to inspire hope in the government ranks and fears and doubts among the cynical.

On financial control, the 1974 law was also rather vague. On some points it was precise enough. The government would continue to examine the companies' provisional budgets before these were annexed to the annual Finance Act and debated in Parliament (Articles 18 and 19). Links between the companies and the Ministry of Finance would, however, differ from the old régime in uncertain degree. Two of the new bodies, the Audio-visual Institute (grouping essential common services such as archives, research and in-service training), and the organization responsible for transmission and the maintenance of the network, were given the legal status of 'public establishment of an industrial and commercial character', which had been that of ORTF. In theory, this should mean that the Finance Minister exercises no prior controls. But the example of the *Office*, where that control had been maintained in contradiction to its legal status, was not a cheering one.[27] The other bodies – those responsible for programmes and for 'heavy' production – while remaining national companies, were given the status of *sociétés anonymes*. This should mean an even greater degree of independence.

Perhaps the most effective and enduring method of government control had been written into the very organizational structures of broadcasting: the government's power to appoint the Director General and other key figures, and, until 1974, its majority representation on the Administrative Council. All reform projects (except the government's) since 1964 have centred on these two vital issues.

The head of broadcasting in France has always been appointed by the government. Before 1972, the Director General could be removed at any time, at the government's pleasure. The 1972 legislation combined into one the posts of Director General and President of the Administrative Council – this would, it was claimed, give the post more authority – and for the first time laid down a stipulated period of office. However, as we have seen, far from completing his three years, Arthur Conte was in fact removed from his post in 1973 after only 16 months. The 1974 statute returned to the principle of separation of powers: a president, still appointed by the government, would serve for three years. He would be free to choose his own directors, except in the single case of the body responsible for transmission and the network.

In 1974, Pierre Schaeffer calculated that the average period in office of a Director General had been one year ten months and six days.[28] The disadvantages of this inbuilt instability at the top are surely obvious. No Director General could risk asserting his independence from the government. He frequently did not have time to put his own personal policies into operation. Furthermore, as the government's men came and went, they were naturally viewed with cynicism and suspicion by the permanent staff at the *Office*. This made it increasingly difficult to carry out any internal reforms.

The government could, of course, have appointed independent personalities and allowed them to get on with the job without interference. Instead, from 1956 to 1974, it put in Civil Servants, usually sympathetic to its views and trained to execute government policy without question. A French parliamentary report in 1972 described the inherent disadvantages of such a choice. The senior Civil Servant is trained to arbitrate rather than to give commands or formulate policy. He tends once at *ORTF* to isolate himself from the rest of the *Office*, surrounding himself with a team of 'technical advisers' from other branches of the Civil Service, trained in the National School of Administration (*ENA*), and often anxious to find their old schoolfriends jobs at the *Office*. The Director and his advisers attack the essentially commercial and industrial problems of the organization with the traditional tools of a conservative administration method.[29]

Again, the French tradition expects a Civil Servant to be totally versatile, to move with ease from one sector of public service to another. Thus the men sent in to run *ORTF* included former ambassadors, prefects, counsellors of state and magistrates. Many of them in addition had been members of ministerial advisory teams, where they could form political loyalties. For example, Jean-Jacques de Bresson, Director General from 1968 to 1972, had in 1964 been head of the advisory team at Peyrefitte's Ministry of Information. For such men, *ORTF* was a stepping-stone in a career; they could not afford disobedience. Nor had they on arrival any experience of the peculiar needs of a broadcasting company. It is to their credit that, government loyalty apart, many of them did their job well.

Examples of faithful obedience to government policies are not hard to find: M. J-B. Dupont's espousal of the government's desire to introduce commercials in 1968; his over-enthusiastic behaviour during the strike that year, notably in calling in the Army to man transmitters; his successor's drastic purge of journalists that same autumn. An interview with M. Marceau Long in November 1973, shortly after his appointment as President-Director General, shows the characteristic discreet obedience of the civil servant. Questioned on his predecessor's dismissal, Long replied that the law making three years the stipulated period of office was too rigid: the President should be sackable in cases such as a change of régime or obvious megalomania. He, Long, could not have refused to take over from Conte, even though the Council of State was in the process of examining the legality of the latter's departure. A high Civil Servant cannot be the judge of the mission offered him, or else the government would be bereft of all authority.[30]

The case of Arthur Conte is an interesting one, in this respect. Put in in an election year, Conte was not a Civil Servant but a *UDR* deputy, and hence even more likely to be responsive to government wishes. In a televised press conference in January 1973, Conte assured the public that 'there is no political control (*tutelle*) over the *Office*. Those are the conditions on which I accepted the post of President'.[31] At the same time, however, TV news had been 'reorganized', and commentators noted a return to pre-1968 levels of censorship.[32] And in his memoirs, Conte describes his secret weekly meetings over breakfast with Prime Minister Messmer during this period.[33] None the less, Conte's eventual departure does seem to have sprung from his attempt to assert his independence from the Minister of Information, a right-wing law-and-order enthusiast. In this context, it is hard to decide whether Conte's consultations with the ORTF personnel (over possible plans for decentralization) were part of a genuine desire to take their views into account, or rather an attempt to enlist their support in the forthcoming trial of strength with the Minister. Whatever the case may be, when the axe fell, the personnel did not react with any great feeling: directors and ministers had already come and gone too frequently.

The splitting up of the ORTF in 1974–75 obviously constituted a radical break with the past. However, the government retained the right to appoint the president of each company, who would be responsible for its overall management. This split could mean a multiplication by seven of the government's powers of control; it could, on the other hand, equally mean division. Future independence would obviously have much to do with the choice of personalities. On 19 September 1974, the new appointments were announced. The body responsible for transmission, a 'public establishment' like ORTF, was given to a civil servant, Jean Autin. Two of the other presidents were experienced in broadcasting as well as being supporters of the majority party: Jacqueline Baudrier, for radio, and Claude Contamine, for the largest television company, Channel Three and the regions. Another two were successful businessmen of the cultural world: for Channel Two, Marcel Jullian, journalist, writer of books and screenplays, TV and radio producer, and head of the Plon and Julliard publishing firms; for 'heavy' production, Jean-Charles Edeline, an entrepreneur in the cinema industry. Channel One was given to Jean Cazeneuve, another majority party supporter, Professor of Sociology at the University of Paris, and a long-standing member of the *Office*'s Administrative Council and Programme Committees. Pierre Emmanuel, a poet and member of the French Academy, was placed in charge of the Audiovisual Institute which was to group services such as archives, research and in-service training.

This reform of broadcasting also ended ten years of government control over the Administrative Council. Created in 1964 to bring *ORTF* into line with other 'public establishments', the Administrative Council was presented by the government as one of the attributes of the *Office*'s new autonomy.[34] But from the start, its structure was far from reassuring. Of its 16 members, eight were to represent the State and eight not: this was in theory the parity principle.[35] The State's members could be removed at any time. Of the remaining members, four were appointed as 'qualified persons': this ensured an effective government majority of 12. Furthermore, the other delegates were not elected but chosen by the government from lists drawn up by the 'most representative' associations. The two delegates of the personnel, for example, were in practice chosen not from the *CGT* union, which has strong Communist sympathies, but from the *CGC* which was one-tenth its size.[36] The 28 million viewers and listeners had only one delegate. In early 1968, the Council's members included Michel Jobert, head of the Prime Minister's advisory team, plus one of the latter's technical advisers, and the head of the advisory team at the Ministry of Information. There were no men from the universities, the theatre, the unions or Parliament.

After the upheaval of May 1968, the Administrative Council was enlarged, made more youthful and rather timidly liberalized.[37] There were now 24 members, and of the 12 State representatives five were to be chosen from non-political sectors such as the Council of State, the diplomatic corps, the university – Civil Servants rather than ministerial employees. There were five representatives of the *Office* personnel, including a producer and a journalist. These were still chosen from lists drawn up by associations or unions. Two delegates of the press, one of viewers and listeners and four 'qualified persons' completed the quota. As in 1964, the government had the power to revoke its own delegates. It now had 16 out of 24 members under its control, as compared to 12 out of 16 earlier. It continued to exercise its prerogatives in the choice of non-government representatives. For example, in

1970 it annulled the appointment of Lamotte, one of the delegates of the personnel, and his replacement was just as unrepresentative, according to the major unions.[38]

Further minor changes took place in 1972 with the new *ORTF* statute. [39] Out of a total of 14 members, seven now represented the State, and of these one was the new President-Director General. The government still appointed all the other members, who were chosen from lists as before. However, the category of 'qualified persons' disappeared. The two delegates of viewers and listeners were henceforth put forward by the Cultural Affairs Committees of each House: this was a new step, and ensured the government at least one supporter from the *UDR*-dominated National Assembly. The government still refused to play fair when it came to the other members. The one representative of professional journalism was chosen not from the largest union (*SNJ*), but from a smaller, more conciliatory one (*FO*). Among the three delegates of the *Office* personnel, the producer came from a small pro-government union affiliated to the *CGC*, rather than from the far more representative Communist *SNRT-CGT*.[40]

In practice, and contrary to the explicit intentions of the statutes before 1974, the Administrative Council has never played any major role in the running of the *Office*. This has been due to its dependence on the government as well as to the difficulties created by the parallel authority of the Director General. It has taken little part in preparing projects for reform, and has often complained that it is not consulted on important issues such as the inquiry into clandestine advertising in 1972.[41] Major policy changes, for example the reorganization of television news in 1969, come directly from the government and are implemented by the Director General. Certain acts of censorship, notably the directive in December 1970 instructing producers to keep politics out of cultural and entertainment programmes, have been announced as issuing from the Council. However, it has been suggested that this could well be a Machiavellian manoeuvre on the part of the directors.[42]

The changes made in the Administrative Council in 1974 were among the most striking of the whole reform.[43] The production company, because of its new legal status, will not have such a council at all. The four programme companies will each have their own council, reduced to six members, appointed for three years. Only two of the members will be representatives of the State, the President and one other; the other four will be made up of one delegate of the personnel, one of the press, one personality from the world of culture, and one Member of Parliament as representative of viewers and listeners. The 'cultural' personality will be co-opted by the other five, with the government's consent. The transmission company, which has the closest links with the State, has a larger council: 14 members, composed of seven State representatives (delegates from appropriate ministries), two Members of Parliament chosen by the competent committee of each House, two representatives of the personnel, chosen from lists as before, and delegates from each of the programme companies. How far these changes mean a reduction in government control in practice remains to be seen.

Another consultative mechanism which the government has in theory been able to control is the Programme Committees. In 1964, two such committees were set up, one each for radio and television.[44] Their twice 24 members – eight representatives of the 'public services', eight professionals competent in family and social affairs, and eight from the arts and sciences – were all appointed by the Minister of Information, who also chose the president and vice-president of each committee. Again, manipulation took place. Two members of each committee had to belong to the central office of a viewers' and listeners' association. In 1971, three persons were picked from a pro-government organization 'Téléspectateurs et Auditeurs de France' and none from the Communist-inspired association 'Télé-Liberté', which had a far larger membership.[45]

Designed to give advice on general programme policy, study projects or manuscripts and keep an eye on programmes in the course of production, the committees in practice had little real power. On general matters, they could only make suggestions. For manuscripts and projects, they were only sent what the Director General or the President of the Administrative Council thought fit. Again, they could preview programmes and express their disapproval, but the final decision on whether or not to broadcast was left entirely in the hands of the Director General.[46]

The real king-pin of government control was in effect the Director General. Until 1974, this post carried with it the power to appoint to almost all posts within the *Office*. This was in itself a guarantee of overall orthodoxy. However, the government itself nominated the most important men on the management side: Alain Dangeard, Assistant Director General in 1970; Xavier Larère, Director of Television Production; Jean-Pierre Angrémy, in charge of 'Harmonization of Programmes' in 1972. It could remove those it considered too independent: a noteworthy example was the sacking of Jacques Thibau, Director of Television, suspected of Communist sympathies, in 1968.[47] Even the heads of television news were in practice government appointees; ORTF journalists still felt this to be true even after the reform of 1974.[48]

The pyramidal, heavily-centralized power structures of the *Office* before 1974 gave these government appointees considerable powers of control.[49] As far as imposing orthodoxy was concerned, their task was made easier by the conditions of employment within ORTF. While the large majority of the personnel are 'statutory' appointments – that is, they are salaried, and have a certain security of tenure – two of the most important categories – producers and journalists – include a large proportion of 'non-statutory' persons paid by fee or on short-term contracts of varying duration. There are good reasons for this situation. Producers and journalists often prefer freedom and mobility to security. Creative jobs cannot be made as secure as technical or administrative ones. And the quota system of recruitment imposed by the Ministry of Finance could be circumvented only by taking on 'temporary' or 'part-time' staff who might then work as long and as hard as the permanent employees. None the less, in practice, the *Office* also used dismissal or the threat of it to keep its journalists and producers under control. Those who conformed were rewarded with a new contract or promotion. Others were dismissed for political reasons, often on the pretext of re-organization or cutting back. The most notable large-scale examples occurred in 1968 and in 1972, when numbers of journalists were removed, ostensibly on these grounds.

In the face of these enormous possibilities for government control, and in the absence of any effective citizen involvement, the supervision of broadcasting by Parliament provides a useful counterweight, and has contributed in recent years to bringing the important issues of French broadcasting to the public's notice. Parliament's powers of surveillance are organized in a number of ways, some of which are considerably more influential than others.

The primary financial check is provided for with the annual parliamentary debate on the state of the nation's finances. Both the 1964 and 1972 statutes laid down that the Finance Committees of both Houses should submit reports on the *ORTF* budget, which was to be presented in some detail as an appendix to the general Finance Act of the following year. In 1972, the law also stipulated that the report must include a statement on the fulfilment of the planning agreement for the previous year and forecasts of its execution in the year to come. On the basis of these reports, both Houses can vote for or against the collection of the following year's licence fee. The 1974 statute also gave Parliament the additional right to approve the distribution of the licence fee revenue between the different broadcasting companies.

Thus Parliament has no direct influence over the *Office*'s budget nor over the amount of the licence fee, but has the right to detailed information on these matters and can voice its disapproval if necessary by refusing to vote for licence fee collection. This has meant a considerable gain in independence for *ORTF*, and a reduction in Parliament's powers, as compared to the period before 1959 when the *RTF* budget was an integral part of the general administrative budget of the State and thereby subject to much closer scrutiny. Indeed, what legal powers Parliament has in this respect are often derisory in practice. In 1971 and 1972, it complained that the manner in which the *ORTF* budget was presented made it difficult to interpret correctly and indeed that certain sections were incomplete.[50] In October 1973, the National Assembly came near to refusing to accept the *ORTF* budget, and the *Chinaud Report* in the following June confirmed that the figures presented to Parliament were becoming further and further removed from reality.[51]

The annual budget debates each autumn tend to enlarge their scope into more general criticism of *ORTF*'s performance or of the government's interference in the previous year. The Minister for Information or the Prime Minister is obliged to answer questions from deputies or senators on matters as various as decentralization, advertising, regional programmes or the organization of TV news. Refusal to vote the licence fee can be a reflection of general dissatisfaction rather than a judgement on

ORTF's financial management, though the latter was indeed the case in 1973. By 1969, it had become unusual for the Senate – where the opposition is in the majority – *not* to refuse permission to collect.[52]

Parliament's powers in this area are largely ceremonial, then, a right of remonstrance rather than a real control. Quite apart from the Fifth Republic's general tendency to weaken Parliament and strengthen government, the deputies themselves have also been to blame. For example, in the National Assembly budget debate in November 1971 (admittedly a year of relative calm at *ORTF*, at least up to that point), out of 487 deputies only eight were present when the debate opened and only 18 at its end. This is an all-too-frequent occurrence; the average attendance has been put at about 30.[53]

Debates on broadcasting can of course be called at any time. When legislation is not involved, however, these too have mainly the (salutary) effect of calling the government to task for its actions, without any coercive power. Furthermore, since the majority party controls the parliamentary timetable, the opposition's chance to complain about abuses can be strictly curtailed. It should be remembered, however, that governments can on occasion be more liberal than their parliamentary party. In 1969, for example, the Prime Minister had to defy the *UDR* deputies, many of whom were opposed to the liberalization of broadcasting he wanted to introduce.[54]

A second statutory control mechanism is the consultative parliamentary delegation (*délégation parlementaire consultative*). First established in 1964, this body now consists of five deputies and three senators plus six spokesmen from both Houses' Finance and Cultural Affairs Committees.[55] It meets at least every three months[56] (though before 1968 this rule was not strictly adhered to), and submits an annual report to Parliament. In 1974, this delegation was not only made larger than previously, but also given wider and more precise functions. It must be sent the special reports of the Commission for Verifying the Accounts of Public Enterprise. It must be consulted by the government on cases of infringement of the monopoly and on any agreements signed by the new broadcasting companies concerning the production, reproduction and transmission of programmes. It may also be consulted, or may proffer its opinion, in any area covered by the new statute.

[95]

The parliamentary delegation was indeed consulted during the elaboration of Marceau Long's reform project in February 1974. By virtue of the 1974 statute, it was given right of consultation in the putting into practice of the new broadcasting régime. Thus it must be consulted by the Prime Minister when drawing up the *cahiers des charges*, and by the Council of State when defining the criteria to be used in the distribution between the companies of the licence fee revenue.[57]

In 1973, the delegation included some able men with considerable knowledge of the *Office*'s problems, notably Senator André Diligent and Deputy Joël Le Tac, both authors of important parliamentary reports in recent years. In June 1973, its membership became more eclectic (i.e. less governmental) than formerly, with the appointment of two left-wing deputies. And the 1974 statute expressly stipulates that its composition must ensure 'a balanced representation of political groups'. However, in spite of its obvious progress, the advisory nature of the parliamentary delegation and its rather infrequent meetings give it little real say in the running of the *Office*.[58] There is also some overlap of tasks between this body and the new High Audiovisual Council.

A more successful parliamentary instrument for control and reform has been the special *ad hoc* commission: the commission of inquiry (*commission d'enquête*), which investigates 'established facts' (*faits determinés*), that is, particular scandals, and the commission of control (*commission de contrôle*) which looks into the administrative, financial or technical aspects of public services or nationalized industries. These can be created by either Assembly, and their members are elected by the House concerned.[59] In recent years, such commissions have forced into the public gaze matters which both ORTF and the government had attempted to sweep under the carpet, informing the public and stimulating debate. However, these commissions have the disadvantage of being the products of crises, and they have no coercive power. The Senate commission of control which reported in June 1968 (the *Diligent Report*) was proved right by the events of that year, but it seems unlikely that without the violent upheaval at ORTF and elsewhere, serious attention would have been paid to the suggested reforms.

The Fifth Republic reduced the powers of parliamentary special commissions, limiting their duration to four months and excluding from their scope any question which is *sub judice*.[60] It has also resisted attempts since 1958 to make the system more effective.[61] A recent study of the eight parliamentary commissions of inquiry set up for a variety of reasons between 1958 and 1972, and the 42 proposed in Parliament without success, shows the extraordinary power of the government to limit the inquiry procedure.[62] For a commission of inquiry, not only must facts be 'established' and not *sub judice*, but they must not form part of the 'reserved domain' of the executive branch. Other possibilities of pressure exist: from government control of the parliamentary timetable (which in 1967 prevented an inquiry into regional television programmes); from the limited time allotted to the work (though this can be remedied by turning the inquiry into an information mission or *mission d'information*); and from the various forms of official secrecy which can be invoked – judicial, national security, and administrative – the last-named used by ministers in 1968 to justify refusal to co-operate with the Diligent Commission.[63] Indeed, the commission's powers are effectively limited to those the subjects of the inquiry allow them; no one is obliged to appear, and ministers can refuse to let their Civil Servants testify. The final report of a commission may exclude the observations of the opposition members, and the Assembly may refuse to allow publication altogether. Finally, the commission's report has only the force of suggestion or proposal; the government and the broadcasting company can thus choose to ignore its conclusions.

In the face of these obstacles, the work of the four special inquiries into *ORTF* in the last few years – the *Diligent Report* in mid-1968, the two inquiries (one a mission of information) into clandestine advertising and other problems in 1971–72, and the *Chinaud Report* in June 1974 on finance and management – has been remarkable. Clear, impartial, stuffed with facts and constructive criticism, the 1968 report was, as we have seen, swallowed up in the strikes and riots of that year, and may not have had much to do with the reforms that followed. The 1972 reports, on the other hand, performed a vital informative function, and prevented government and *ORTF* alike from minimizing the affair. However, they too had little effect on the preparation of the new statute. The credit for Parliament's relative success in this domain must in the end be given to a group of dedicated and hard-working men

(André Diligent in particular) rather than to the mechanisms involved, which are evidently inadequate.

Finally, Parliament can, of course, attempt to change *ORTF* by means of legislation. Recently, however, legislative measures concerning broadcasting have tended to show once more the government's strength and Parliament's weakness. (This is a general pattern in the Fifth Republic.)[64] In 1968, for example, the government decided to introduce brand advertising on television. The Director General of *ORTF* appeared on television to justify the decision, which he treated as a *fait accompli*, even though the matter was still under debate in Parliament.[65] The latter in any case turned the debate into a wider motion of confidence, while a ruling of the Constitutional Council on whether or not the matter fell within Parliament's jurisdiction, was vague and ambiguous. The government was therefore able to act by decree. In this case, everyone was to blame:

> Through Parliament's neglect of its duty, the bored resignation or cynicism of public opinion, and the increasingly offhand behaviour of governments, the French people have been deprived of a free radio and television service.[66]

Another instance of Parliament's failure to make reforms in the face of apparent government determination to prevent it has been the question of a right of reply for broadcasting. Several projected Bills to install such a right have been killed in Parliament by various government procedures.[67] The 1972 statute did include a clause granting a right of reply, restricted to 'physical persons', as opposed to the comparable right in the written press, which includes both persons and groups. Over a year after the passing of the 1972 statute, the relevant decrees setting out the practical details of the promised right had still not appeared. It was later announced that the High Audiovisual Council was working on the problem, so taking it out of the hands of Parliament, at least for the time being.[68]

As far as the two most recent statutes are concerned, the 1972 Law showed once more the government's supremacy over Parliament: indeed, this law was frequently referred to in the French press as the 'Malaud reform' after the Minister for Information who prepared the Bill. The Senate refused to pass the measure, largely on the grounds that it was being pushed through far too hastily. This refusal is of course a gesture, since the government can force Bills through in the National Assembly whatever their fate in the Senate. The National Assembly made only a few amendments. It complained that the real changes would depend on the accompanying decrees – the composition of the Administrative Council, for example, and the personality of the Director General – and that these were in the government's hands alone.[69]

At the debates on the 1974 statute, senators and deputies again complained – with justification – of the ludicrously short time in which they had to examine the new measures. Once more, the law was a framework, and the important decrees and appointments were out of their hands. But at the same time, Parliament benefited from a change in the atmosphere (if not the real power structures) of the relations between it and the government. The new President in any case could not afford to unite a majority against him. Thus Parliament did in fact manage to introduce several amendments to the government project: a ceiling on advertising revenue, for example, the creation of regional committees, and provision for the harmonization of programmes between the separate TV companies. On certain points, the government imposed its will: the Prime Minister insisted that representatives sent by Parliament to the Administrative Councils of the new companies be reduced from four to two (for the transmission company) and from two to one (for the others). Again, the regional committees were not given any financial resources of their own, thus considerably reducing their real powers. But overall, Parliament had had more say in the new reform than was usual under previous governments.

A number of independent bodies also have some rights of control or supervision over broadcasting. One of the amendments Parliament succeeded in passing in 1972 was the inclusion in the statute of a clause (Article 16) creating an independent advisory council to be known as the High Audiovisual Council (*Haut Conseil de l'Audio-visuel*). This body is composed of six Members of Parliament (four deputies and two senators) chosen by their Assemblies, and 34 'highly qualified persons' in the fields of general culture, the arts, science, technology, the law, professional and family associations, and the unions. These persons are chosen by the government and serve for a period of three years, after which their appointments may be renewed.[70]

Convoked by the Prime Minister, the High Council meets at least twice a year, under his chairmanship or that of his delegate, normally the Minister of Information when that post exists. As its name suggests, the High Council's job is to advise the government on the direction and development of the whole field of audiovisual technology, and on the problems which the latter may pose to the authorities. On specific problems, the text of the statute is vague, presumably in the interests of flexibility. However, it does specify three major areas of consultation: the ethical problems of audiovisual communications, certain kinds of breach of the monopoly, and the right of reply.[71] The High Council was given no direct supervisory control over the workings of ORTF.

Established by law in July 1972, the High Council remained in limbo until almost a year later. The members chosen by Parliament in June 1973 showed a reasonable spread of political allegiance with a general leaning towards the centre. Three of the four National Assembly members were majority party supporters: one UDR, one Centrist Union and one Independent allied to the Independent Republicans. The fourth was a Reformer, that is, in moderate opposition. (The Reformers were not part of the majority under Pompidou, but joined it under Giscard d'Estaing after his election in May 1974.) Their substitutes were two UDR men, one Communist and one Socialist. The senators were one Socialist and one Independent Republican, with a Communist and an Independent allied to the Independent Republicans as substitutes.[72] This particular concoction is of course dependent on the fates of members in general elections.

The 34 members appointed by the government show a formidable array of talents and qualifications. Some had already had experience of ORTF, either as directors: Jean d'Arcy, ex-Director of Television (1952–1959) and now President-Director General of *Multivision*, a cable TV company; Claude Contamine, ex-Director of Television (1964–1967), then Director of the Foreign Service (*DAEC*) and later head of Channel Three; or as creators: François Billetdoux, writer for stage and radio, and at that time in charge of the reform of the radio network *France-Culture*; Lazare Iglésis, producer; Pierre Schaeffer, writer, musician and Director of the Research Service at ORTF; or as union leaders: Pierre Simonetti, member of the Administrative Council and perhaps the most powerful unionist within the *Office*. Others had connections with related organizations: Denis Baudouin, Director of *SOFIRAD*; Jean Raynaud, Director of *OFRATEME*; Jean-Claude Servan-Schreiber, Director of the *Régie française de publicité*. More than a few have backgrounds in government and the Civil Service; others have had distinguished careers in the press – Hubert Beuve-Méry, co-founder of *Le Monde*, for example – or in the cinema industry.[73] The average age of the High Council in 1973 was 55.[74]

The value of the High Council as an effective influence on broadcasting or on government policy cannot yet be adequately assessed. At present, it has sub-committees working on a number of questions: the preparation of a legal text for a right of reply, cable television, and the social implications of audiovisual communications together with the ethical problems they involve. It may also be set to work on the complex problem of copyright.[75] On the debit side, one can note that it meets only twice a year, at the Prime Minister's behest, that its members are largely appointed by the government, and that most of them are safe, if worthy figures. However, these factors may not necessarily prevent its working as a creative and independent body.

The reform of 1974 introduced two new bodies with differing degrees of control over broadcasting. The distribution of licence fee revenue between the programme companies was now placed in the hands of a special independent committee chaired by a high-ranking magistrate. In theory, this body's decisions could have considerable influence on the future quality of broadcasting. Secondly, regional audiovisual advisory committees were set up in the regional broadcasting centres. It would obviously take time to measure the practical powers of these committees, which it was hoped would be truly representative of the regions concerned.[76]

'MONOPOLY'?

For those who rebuilt France after the war, State control was not a licence for government interference but rather a guarantee of freedom from the harmful grip of profiteers. Indeed, in the on-going public debate over French broadcasting, 'monopoly' is usually proffered as the opposite to 'commercial'; while 'commercial' itself is ambiguous, denoting as it does, to some, free competition and the free expression of opinion, and to others, the denial of any kind of public service, the exclusive concentration on profit to the detriment of political life, education and culture. Certainly, as a State monopoly within a free enterprise system, ORTF has been unable to keep itself entirely free of contacts with commercialism. Its jealously guarded monopoly is broken in practice by the privately-run radio and television stations operating on France's borders, and (legally) by the numerous private companies which are called on more and more frequently to supply for the screen. Brand advertising in 1968 introduced the commercial ethos into the very heart of the public broadcasting system, and the clandestine advertising scandal in 1972 revealed an insidious and related form of corruption. Meanwhile, the lobby for a commercial television channel in France has renewed its efforts at the *Office*'s every crisis point. There are now fears, too, that the new cable television and video-cassette industry will be opened up to private profit.

Commercial radio was banished from France in 1945, leaving RTF and later ORTF with the legal State monopoly of broadcasting. In practice, however, the commercial stations merely set up shop again just outside the national boundaries. This situation is tolerated and even encouraged by the French government which has acquired shares in many of these stations, thus helping to finance ORTF's rivals at the same time as gathering revenue for the French Treasury. The 'peripheral' stations, as they are called, mainly French-owned and backed by French advertising, have expanded their operations every year, and have mostly made ever-increasing profits. Their presence has had a number of effects on national broadcasting inside France.[77]

The oldest of the radio stations is Radio-Luxembourg, which was set up in 1929 and extended its activities to television in 1955. Financed, like all the 'peripheral' stations, entirely by advertising, RTL (Radio Télévision Luxembourg) has studios in Paris and Lyons and transmitters in the Duchy of Luxembourg. A commercial contract between RTL and the French postal authorities (PTT) allows for a direct cable link from studios to transmitter. Radio-Luxembourg's programmes reach most of France, Belgium and Switzerland as well as the Duchy itself. Its audience is estimated at $7\frac{1}{2}$ million.[78]

Radio-Monte Carlo was created in 1942 by Nazi Germany to broadcast to North Africa. Taken over by France at the Liberation, it is at present owned jointly by French and Monacan interests. It is the only commercial station with transmitters actually on French soil. Until 1974, Radio-Monte Carlo's broadcasts covered the whole of southern France up to the Loire, as well as parts of Italy.[79] In 1973, it was given permission – among protests from ORTF – to erect two new transmitters at Roumoules, inside French territory. This blatant breach of the monopoly could extend the station's range to Mâcon, Dijon, Bordeaux and even Paris, doubling its audience (at present about 2 million) within four years.[80]

Europe 1, the radio station set up in 1955 by an international group 'Europe 1 – Images et Son', has studios and transmitters in the Sarre, with the same cable-link arrangements as Radio-Luxembourg. Its rapid and lasting success was due to genuine innovation in radio techniques, especially in journalism. In 1973 it had an audience of about $7\frac{1}{2}$ million, about 20 per cent of the total French radio audience.[81]

These three giants together have a listening figure (in 1972) of about 51 per cent of the national audience in France,[82] and are in constant competition for a larger share, both with each other and with ORTF's radio networks. A smaller and more regional station is Sud-Radio, based in Andorra, whose programmes reach about ten French departments, including Toulouse. Sud-Radio (the name dates from 1966) was set up in 1951 after a certain amount of conflict between France and Andorra over Radio-Andorre, the other private, Spanish-controlled station on the latter's territory.[83] From September 1958, the Fifth Republic encouraged the development of the station as a political counter-weight to the regional newspaper, La Depêche du Midi.[84] Sud-Radio alone is allowed to broadcast news and current affairs programmes in French.[85] Its audience is estimated at 1 million, in a region stretching between Sète and Bordeaux. Since 1971, it also has a small daughter station, Radio de les Valls, which broadcasts a few hours daily in Catalan.[86] Some of its programmes are re-transmissions from Radio-Luxembourg whose own transmitters do not reach that area.[87]

All these radio stations are tolerated officially, if discreetly, by the French authorities. Pirate stations do, however, occasionally spring up. 'Atlantic 2000', for example, began broadcasting from Spain into south-west France in 1972. The French government rapidly began negotiations to link the new station with its agency *SOFIRAD*.[88]

'Peripheral' television is at present much less of a threat to the monopoly, for obvious technical reasons. However, in 1972, Télé-Luxembourg had an estimated 1 million viewers, in ten French departments. Télé-Monte Carlo, a separate organization from Radio-Monte Carlo, is an affiliate of the Europe 1 group. It covers most of the Côte d'Azur and part of Marseilles, and has about 300,000 viewers in France.[89] Furthermore, in politically-sensitive Alsace, many viewers prefer to watch German television rather than *ORTF*, which has traditionally been less well adapted to regional needs.[90] The choice of Nord, Alsace and Lorraine as three of the first four French regions to receive *ORTF*'s third, regional channel was probably influenced by the need to compete with German television and Télé-Luxembourg in these areas.

Since no monopoly can be practically enforced – except by jamming, as France did in 1950 to Radio-Andorre[91] – and since the commercial stations are in any case extremely popular, the French State has decided to control them from the inside, as far as possible. A government agency, *SOFIRAD* (*Société financière de radio-diffusion* – Financial Broadcasting Company), administers the French State's shareholdings in radio and television stations outside France. In 1972, *SOFIRAD* made a net profit of over 6 million francs.[92] Ten out of its twelve directors are senior French Civil Servants, the other two are directors of newspapers. The President of *SOFIRAD* is at the same time Vice-President of Radio-Monte Carlo, President of Sud-Radio and a director of Europe 1.[93] In 1973, the head of *SOFIRAD* was Denis Baudouin, a former presidential adviser on information.[94]

SOFIRAD has various holdings in private radio and television stations: Sud-Radio is 99 per cent *SOFIRAD*-owned; 83 per cent of Radio-Monte Carlo's capital is held by *SOFIRAD* and the rest by Monaco; *SOFIRAD* has 13 of the 18 members of the Administrative Council. However, the Monacan members have the power to block decisions, either by action within the Council or in the general assembly of shareholders.[95] In Europe 1, its principal source of income, *SOFIRAD* holds 35 per cent of the capital and has about 47 per cent of the vote on the board of directors.[96] Télé-Monte Carlo is run by a Monacan company, the *Société spéciale d'entreprise*, itself an affiliate of Europe 1. *SOFIRAD* holds

11 per cent of its shares.[97] The only other major station, *RTL*, which is run by the *Compagnie luxembourgeoise de télédiffusion* and controlled to some extent by the Luxembourg government, has so far resisted *SOFIRAD*'s attempts to acquire shares. However, the advertising agency *Agence Havas* (56 per cent French government-owned) holds 15 per cent of *CLT*'s shares and has the station's exclusive advertising rights, via an affiliate, *Information et Publicité*. Until recently, French financial interests were in the majority, but a new grouping of shareholders in January 1974 has given the edge to a Belgian group.[98] *RTL* has links with the powerful French publishing firm Hachette, and its manager (in 1974), Jean Prouvost, is the owner of *Paris-Match* and *Le Figaro*, two lively (and conservative) French publications.[99]

Theoretically then, the French government has considerable opportunities for control of the commercial stations. It can interfere by means of its financial holdings and its representatives on boards of directors and administrative councils. It can also, if necessary, bargain on the basis of its permission to use French territory for cable links or transmitters, as well as on its help in setting up foreign stations. The more drastic measures are very rarely needed: the cables were however cut in 1958, and two famous journalists at least have been forced to leave their stations because of French government pressure in administrative councils.[100] On the whole, as one might expect, government interference has been much less apparent than at *ORTF*. But the appointment in 1973 of Denis Baudouin as head of *SOFIRAD* to replace Pierre Lefranc, a Gaullist unsympathetic to President Pompidou, was probably a political move. The sacking of Maurice Siégel, Director General of Europe 1, in October 1974, was one of Baudouin's tasks. The latter claimed that Siégel had been at his post 20 years; new blood was needed. At the same time, however, he objected publicly to the 'bantering tone' (*persiflage*) of the station's journalists. The move was generally seen as an example of blatant political interference by a government which claimed to be liberal.[101]

The commercial stations are a small but valuable source of income to the French State – over $3\frac{1}{2}$ million francs in 1972[102] – and their advertising can be seen as a useful stimulus to the traditionally underdeveloped French publicity market. The government has even on occasions used the stations to further its own policies. Télé-Monte Carlo's expansion towards Italy in 1971 was encouraged (though it meant two new transmitters on French soil) because the Italians, who had not yet decided on a colour system, might thereby be given a good chance to sample the French process SECAM.[103] Radio-Monte Carlo, the most 'governmental' of the commercial stations,[104] was given French approval to set up a relay transmitter in Cyprus – 'Radio-Chypre' – which would extend its coverage to Lebanon, Syria and the Persian Gulf. Though the French foreign broadcasting service felt its toes had been trodden on, a French parliamentary committee welcomed the new venture, which it felt would be less 'rigid' than an *ORTF* one.[105] In both these cases, the French State appears to have used commercial stations for purposes which it would have been inappropriate or impossible for the *Office* to fulfil.

The commercial television stations have contributed little besides old films and popular American-style entertainment to the public's choice of viewing. Their main advantage may have been to stimulate the development of the *ORTF*'s regional channel in certain areas. However, during the presidential elections of 1974, Télé-Monte Carlo, in connection with the radio stations, Europe 1 and Radio-Monte Carlo, televised debates between the major candidates. This led to the organization of a similar duel on national television just before the second ballot – a striking innovation for campaigns on *ORTF*.

The radio stations, on the contrary, have had several salutary effects on national broadcasting. Their treatment of news and current affairs has been generally recognized to be freer and more impartial than that of the *ORTF* radio news services, and the latter, partly because of this competition, were in turn allowed more freedom than television news in France. Their political programmes have been more open to a wide spectrum of personalities and opinions. (In 1965, Europe 1 and *RTL* successfully resisted an attempt by the Ministry of Information to limit presidential candidates' election broadcasts to *ORTF*.)[106] This superiority is tacitly recognized by the French authorities: in December 1973, for example, it was on Europe 1 that the Prime Minister made an important speech replying to criticisms from the French press, and, among other things, explaining why he had sacked the Director General of the *Office*.[107] Their style, too, has had an enlivening effect on national radio programmes, though in its extreme form it has also contributed to the innocuous *FIP* channels (muzak, and 'news', i.e. traffic and weather) which have been set up in recent years by *ORTF* as an apology for genuine local radio.

The tacit coexistence of *ORTF* and commercial radio has long been accepted. Journalists and personalities move between the two, or even (since 1968) appear on both on the same day.[108] Even the left-wing opposition's 1972 election manifesto promised merely that the commercial stations would be taxed more heavily, to allow the *ORTF* to operate without resort to advertising, thus enabling the French public to go on having the best – or the worst – of both systems.[109]

While the monopoly of transmission and reception has long been a legal fiction in France, a monopoly of production has never really existed, if only because of the televising of cinema films. However, since 1964, when there was a change in the ruling regarding outside production, *ORTF* has had increasing recourse to the private sector.[110] Links with the outside fall into a number of categories. Programmes may be bought or hired ready-made as in the case of films and many serials; co-produced; or made to order by private companies at *ORTF*'s request. Personnel or equipment may be hired from private firms for a particular production. Certain technical operations such as montage may be farmed out. Finally, of course, *ORTF* has had to buy its production equipment, and some of its dealings in this area have caused controversy.

In 1973, the percentage of hours of outside production for the three television channels together was put at 22·3 per cent, compared with 19·1 per cent in 1972.[111] The main reason for the rise in outside production was the entry into service of Channel Three which gives a relatively large place (40 per cent) to the private sector.[112] Over 9 per cent of the 22·3 per cent was accounted for by full-length films. Thus, out of the 1,500 hours of programmes produced outside the *Office*, over 600 were taken up by films. Co-productions accounted for a further 210 hours of fiction and 60 hours of documentaries and variety shows. [113]

The policy of opening up television to outside production was begun by Albert Ollivier before 1964, in the hope of bringing some fresh air into *RTF*'s bureaucratic world.[114] Indeed, it would be foolish to think of co-productions and purchased programmes as merely commercial ventures. Many of the latter are bought from other national television companies: 'Elizabeth R' from the BBC, the 'Revolt of the Haiduks' from Romanian television. Co-productions, too, often involve other non-commercial broadcasting systems: the 'Aeneid' with *RAI* (Italy), 'Un grand amour de Balzac' with Polish television. Or they may bring together well-known French producers and private or semi-private production companies: 'Vidocq', by Marcel Bluwal, produced (in the financial sense) by *Technisonor*; 'The Battle of Stalingrad' by H. de Turenne and Daniel Costelle, produced at *Pathé*.[115]

Many of the outside productions have been of high quality; others, of course, have been stereotyped American gangster series which can be sold cheaply to Europe after they have paid for themselves on the home market. And it is true that recourse to the private sector has caused *ORTF* some problems. In 1970, the *Paye Report*, which was strongly in favour of competition, criticized the unhealthy relations between *ORTF* and a number of private companies which appeared to have sprung up merely to feed the *Office*'s needs.[116] Some of these parasite companies had been set up by men who worked regularly for *ORTF* on a contractual basis and who could use their contacts to get their productions screened. No legal obstacle prevented such people (among them some of the best-known TV personalities and producers) from holding interests in private companies engaged in television production. Nor was there any reason why the *Office* should have suffered. However, the *Le Tac Report* in 1972 implicated several of these companies in certain aspects of the clandestine advertising scandal and suggested that it was, to say the least, undesirable for a person to use his position at *ORTF* to make money outside.[117]

Another problem is financial. The large-scale use of private companies means that *ORTF*'s own expensive equipment may not be used to the full. The *Office* was itself to blame, to a large extent: its inaccurate accounting system and methods of planning for the use of equipment and buildings artificially inflated its own costs and made the private production companies' offers look more attractive.[118] Furthermore, it can be argued that in some cases public money is being used to finance the private firms. Thus for certain kinds of co-production, *ORTF* provided 70 per cent of the funds. The other producer could reimburse his 30 per cent by selling the production to a foreign network.[119] It was also suspected that the private producer did not always put in his full share.

For some observers, *Paye* for example, the use of private firms provided healthy competition for *ORTF*. But it could be argued too that this competition was essentially unfair. The *Office* was both asked to compete with the private sector and at the same time to provide a public service which could not be measured in commercial terms. For example, its costs could never be brought as low as those of small private companies, if only because of its heavy responsibilities in education and the foreign service.

ORTF producers too have had varying reactions to the existence of private companies – quite apart from those who were making money out of them. While some felt freer working for a smaller unit away from the constraints of the *Office* bureaucracy, others claimed that they were more restricted by the necessity to produce something commercially viable.[120] Yet others see the whole system as another aspect of the political muzzle; *ORTF* producers kept in check, that is, by the threat of losing their work to private contractors.[121]

The system set up in late 1974 changes the whole relationship between the public and private sectors. After an initial period of three years during which its competitive capability will be aided by a subsidy from the licence fee revenue, the national production company will be placed in direct competition with the private production firms. The three national TV programme companies will be able to order productions from whatever source they choose. It will be interesting to see whether fears of 'commercialization' – standardization of programme length and format, appeal to the widest possible audience – will turn out to be justified under these circumstances.

Links between public broadcasting and the French electronics industry are, of course, inevitable. But as a public enterprise and State monopoly, the *Office*'s connections have sometimes entailed ambiguities. (One thinks of the National Health Service in England and the problems of its links with private profit-making drug companies.) The choice of an 819-line definition for television after the war and of the SECAM colour system in the 1960s were both cases where not only national prestige but a mainly private industry gained at the expense of the *Office*'s development. The case of the *Office*'s special relation with the major electronics firm

Thomson-C.S.F. was examined by the *Chinaud Report* in 1974.[122] Thomson-C.S.F., it claimed, was in a position of virtual monopoly with respect to the supply of large-scale equipment for *ORTF*. It had, for example, constructed all 75 main transmitters for Channel Three. A special agreement renewed for three years in 1973 provided for permanent co-operation between the *Office* and the firm. In particular, the *Report* noted, *ORTF* was to give financial aid to Thomson's research, and to help in promoting sales of Thomson equipment abroad, by means of its numerous international contacts.

In defence of the arrangement, it was argued that on the contrary, here was a model of relations between industry and public bodies. For small-scale equipment, there was in any case no monopoly. For transmitters, it would make no sense to have more than one supplier: costs would rocket if the numbers constructed were any smaller. The 'special agreement' concerned only SECAM, the colour TV system. *ORTF*'s annual contribution to the research budget was only 2 million francs compared to Thomson's 20 million, and the latter paid *ORTF* a percentage on its sales of SECAM materials abroad. The choice of SECAM had been a national one, and perhaps it was the government rather than the *Office* which should give financial aid to the development of the system.[123]

Few national broadcasting systems have rejected the additional revenue brought by television commercials. In France, the notion of *ORTF* as a 'public service' could once more serve both sides of an argument. For those who believe in the dangers which publicity on a massive scale presents for the mental and moral health of the nation, a public broadcasting system should protect the public by rejecting advertisements and indeed the whole commercial ethic: it should, for example, choose its programmes for their intrinsic value rather than their value for money. As Pierre Schaeffer put it in 1967, would *ORTF*'s statutory mission now have to be amended to read 'inform, educate, entertain ... and sell'?[124] For others, advertising is a necessary and acceptable part of a free economy, and a public service should have no shame in providing an added stimulus for the country's industry and agriculture. This debate – not of course the only point of discussion – can be paralleled by another, on the results of accepting advertising revenue. Thus, for some, the clandestine advertising scandal of

1971 would not have happened had *ORTF* steadfastly turned its back from the start on mercantile matters. For others, the whole problem was that there were not enough TV commercials, so that advertisers had money to spare and pushed it into the pockets of certain not-too-reluctant *ORTF* producers.

In a sense, commercials in France date back to 1951, when the government passed a Bill allowing broadcast campaigns in favour of certain kinds of unbranded products, mostly agricultural to begin with.[125] In 1959, this 'Eat more lettuce' type of commercial, officially entitled *publicité compensée*, was extended to television, quietly and without any official ruling or change in the law. Under the control of various ministries, sponsored programmes were used as well as short commercials. For example, the programme 'La Roue tourne' was made by *RTF* but paid for by the *Commissariat général au Tourisme*, the *Groupement des Assurances Accidents* and the nationalized car producer Renault.[126] As time went on, more manufactured goods were advertised as opposed to agricultural produce. In cases where only a very few large private firms had cornered a market – as in the case of glassware and chicory – it could easily be charged that brand advertising was already installed and that these firms should at least pay the market price for their publicity rather than be given it at the government's expense.[127]

In 1963 and 1964, the volume of 'compensated' advertising increased significantly, from 9,439,810 NF's worth in 1962 to 19,820,780 NF's worth in 1964.[128] It was probably no coincidence that in 1964 the government announced that the possibility of brand advertising on national television was being seriously considered. Originally planned to begin in 1966, the project was shelved as economically inopportune, the opposition claiming that this was because of the forthcoming elections.[129]

When the question was raised again in the autumn of 1967, the government and the advertising agencies seemed to be the only champions of TV commercials. The press, which feared it stood to lose a damaging proportion of its revenue, was extremely hostile. The public was unenthusiastic – only 18 per cent in favour, according to a survey in late 1967 – though few went as far as a Lyons industrialist, who threw a TV set from the top of the Eiffel Tower in protest.[130] Both the Senate and the National Assembly refused to vote the collection of the licence fee as a protest against brand advertising.[131] A majority of the legal experts referred to on the problem stated that advertising was contrary to *ORTF*'s statutory mission of providing information, culture, education and entertainment.[132]

Public debate turned on three main issues, none of which was directly concerned with the general effect on *ORTF* or the public of television commercials as such. One was the question whether the introduction of publicity should be done by regulation or by a change in the law, an issue which was part of the ongoing struggle between government and Parliament in the Fifth Republic.[133] The second was the possible effect on the press, which could not afford to lose its advertisers. The third was the government's misuse of broadcasting over the previous years, which allowed the opposition to claim that the present project was a deliberate attempt to muzzle the written press as well.[134] All three issues were important ones, but prevented any reasoned consideration of the problems involved for *ORTF* itself. Meanwhile the government claimed that *ORTF* needed the money, which it would use to finance all kinds of expansive – and expensive – projects, and the economy needed the stimulus, especially at this time when France had to compete within the newly opened frontiers of the Common Market. In any case, 'peripheral' television and satellite stations would soon be saturating the nation with commercials for other countries' products.[135]

Much of the argument on both sides was based on supposition, since foreign models could not necessarily be applied to the French situation and much would depend on France's economic performance in the years to come. The argument that *ORTF* needed extra revenue because sales of television sets had reached a plateau and licence fee revenue would not therefore keep pace with the *Office*'s expansion was sound enough, but opponents claimed that a loan would be more suitable in the circumstances. Others pointed out that relieving *ORTF* of taxes and other moneys due to the Treasury, and forcing government departments to pay the full cost for 'services rendered' (notably in education and the foreign service) would in itself go a long way towards providing the extra money. The *Diligent Report* (1968) even claimed that the government had artificially produced a paper deficit in the *ORTF* budget in order to justify the introduction of brand advertising.[136]

Whatever the overall economic consequences might be, both sides were agreed that the practical details of the project were of the highest significance. Advertisements would have to be introduced very gradually, to avoid any sudden catastrophic effect on the publicity market generally. The quality and content of commercials must be carefully controlled, and no programmes must be sponsored. The agency responsible for selling and sharing out broadcasting time must be under State supervision, but at the same time must attempt to combine the advantages of both State monopoly and a capitalist mechanism: quality and the public interest on the one hand, and flexibility, efficiency and competitive spirit on the other.[137]

In the event, the government (helped by the confusion of 1968) won its battle against Parliament, and brand advertising began as planned on 1 October 1968. A new agency was set up shortly afterwards in 1969 with sole competence to handle ORTF advertising. The *Régie française de publicité* (RFP) is run by Jean-Claude Servan-Schreiber, a former UDR deputy. Its shareholders were as follows: ORTF, 51 per cent; SOFIRAD, 13·5 per cent; *Fédération nationale de la presse française*, 7 per cent; *Confédération de la presse française*, 7 per cent; *Union des Annonceurs*, 8 per cent; *Confédération de la publicité française*, 8 per cent; *Institut national de la consommation*, 3 per cent.[138] The Administrative Council is composed of seven 'State' representatives (three for ORTF, one each for the Court of Accounts, the Council of State and the *Cour de Cassation*, and one for SOFIRAD), and five others, one for each of the private shareholding associations mentioned above. RFP takes a commission of 0·5 per cent on its receipts, as opposed to between 6 and 10 per cent normally taken by private agencies. Both ORTF and the Ministry of Finance can intervene in questions of tariffs, while a committee including representatives of RFP, ORTF, advertisers, consumers and ministries is responsible for seeing that quality is maintained and the rules observed.[139]

Commercials were introduced very gradually beginning with 2 minutes a day on Channel One only, just before the 8 o'clock evening news. On 1 January 1969 this was increased to 4 minutes daily, while 'compensated' advertising (or 'collective', as it is now called) was to be introduced onto Channel Two in November that year. From 8 minutes daily in 1970, commercials went up to an average of 12 or 13 minutes in 1971. Channel Two was also being used by now, and 'spots' were timed at 9.30 p.m. as well as between 7 and 8.30 p.m. To compensate for off-peak periods such as the summer holiday months, other periods could have as much as 17 minutes a day.[140] In January 1973, the average daily commercial time was to be 11 minutes on Channel One (as opposed to 10 minutes 15 seconds in 1972) and 7½ on Channel Two (5 in 1972).[141] In April that year, commercials were restricted to periods immediately before or after news bulletins (midday included), thus ensuring a high audience and a minimum disturbance of the evening's viewing.[142] There are no commercials after 8.45 p.m.,[143] and none on Channel Three or on regional programmes. On radio only collective advertising is allowed, and is restricted to one channel, France-Inter.[144] There are no sponsored programmes.

The clustering of commercials around news bulletins means high tariffs as well as high audiences. Costs ranged in 1973 from 11,000 NF for a 15-second message between 7.15 and 7.30 p.m. on Channel Two to 144,000 NF for a 1-minute spot between 8.15 and 8.30 p.m. on Channel One.[145] In summer, there is a discount of 40 per cent. The cost of collective advertising is normally 50 per cent of the cost of a brand commercial.[146] Fears that high tariffs would work against small and medium-sized French businesses and in favour of large international companies have not been entirely unfounded. In 1971, nearly a quarter of ORTF's advertising revenue came from Unilever, Colgate Palmolive and Procter and Gamble.[147] In November 1972, limits on advertising by large firms were announced.[148]

To avoid excessive 'commercialization', as well as harm to the written press, the 1971 planning agreement stipulated that not more than 25 per cent of ORTF's total budget should come from advertising. In 1972, Parliament forced the government to write a similar clause into the statute. The ceiling of 25 per cent has not yet been reached. In 1974, advertising was expected to contribute 23·3 per cent of the budget.[149] ORTF's share in the overall French publicity market stands at present at about 18 or 19 per cent: in the USA, radio and television commercials take a similar slice of the advertising market, while in Britain their share is somewhat higher.[150]

The 'moral' controls over advertising in France are particularly strict. Commercials should be of artistic, documentary or educational interest, contribute to the consumer's information, and form part of an effort towards better quality and lower prices for goods and services. They must be free from vulgarity and bad taste, use good French, and be of excellent technical quality. In general, commercials should be truthful and decent; they should not abuse the customer's trust nor his lack of experience or knowledge. No claims should be made which cannot be substantiated; no superlatives may be lightly used, nor comparisons made with other brands or services.

Alcohol and tobacco and legal advice may not be advertised. Certain other products are subject to restrictions: commercials for medicines must be approved by the Ministry of Social Affairs, loans and investments by the Ministry of Finance, correspondence courses by the Ministry of Education. In car advertisements, which were not allowed until 1971, speed must not be presented as an end in itself, but only as an additional contribution to safety. Children are especially protected. If they appear in commercials, they must behave properly and show they are well brought up. Moreover, no commercials may cause harm to children nor take advantage of their credulity. More detailed rules specify, for example, that children must not be made to feel that their health or their future will suffer, or that they will be the object of ridicule, if they do not possess the product in question.[151]

By means of these stringent safeguards – so stringent that the advertising industry has complained[152] – *RFP* and *ORTF* have avoided some of the worst features of television advertising. Programmes are not sponsored and are clearly separate from commercials. They are not broken into by advertisements – though critics claim that this has been achieved largely by putting on very short programmes around news time. There are long stretches of viewing without any interruption at all. So far, the public has shown no conspicuous signs of dissatisfaction. A survey in June 1972 disclosed that a small majority of viewers felt that too much time was given to commercials. In sociological terms, these people tended to be professional or managerial, and politically left of centre. However, more than seven out of ten felt that the adverts themselves were tolerable and well-presented. A certain phenomenon of habituation seems to take place, not always to the benefit of the advertisers. Thus in June 1972 more people found commercials irritating and overdone (*exagérés*) and less found them original or convincing, than in April 1969.[153]

There are still many serious critics of television advertising in France. The argument that commercials are economically unnecessary, since three-quarters of the revenue from them goes to pay the *Office*'s VAT and other taxes is still a valid one.[154] From the point of view of programmes, news and current affairs need not suffer. The experience of television news in the USA, and of ITN in Britain, as well as that of radio news on the commercial stations, shows that a privately-run system does not have to lead to biased or trivialized information programmes. More dangerous is the possible effect on the content of peak-hour viewing: because advertisers need and will eventually only pay for the maximum audience, these programmes will be forced to cater only for the mass public in its worst sense. Some people feel that this has already happened in France, though with the extension of the third channel, which carries no advertising, the effect should be considerably lessened. Several politicians have at various times promised to remove commercials from the national screen. In 1969, Alain Poher, a candidate for the presidency, made the promise, and in 1972, the opposition manifesto included the same proposal.[155] But with advertisements bringing in over 20 per cent of broadcasting revenue, even if the tax situation were regularized it is difficult to see how this could be done without government subsidy. In view of the *Office*'s history, that would not be a reassuring prospect.

Television advertising is affected in a number of ways by the change in the law in 1974. Channels One and Two, whose combined budget was about 500 million francs, will now be financed almost entirely from the revenue from commercials (a total of nearly 578 million francs before tax in 1973).[156] The channels will henceforth be allowed to fix their own tariffs[157] – a limitation of the role of the *RFP*, which will continue to exercise general surveillance. The amount of broadcasting time to be allotted to commercials will be set out in the *cahiers des charges* which are drawn up by the government and the broadcasting companies. There will be no commercials on Channel Three or on national radio, though these will benefit from the receipts to some extent.[158] The proportion of advertising revenue as a percentage of the total budget is fixed at 25 per cent.[159] Critics claim that with the expansion of broadcasting and its splitting-up into several companies, there will inevitably be more commercials,[160] and that with each channel fixing its own tariffs the way lies open for cut-throat competition on the American model.

Those who feel that advertising contributes to the mercantile climate in which games, sports programmes and variety shows foster and glamorize a highly commercial ethos are unlikely to be pleased by the new legislation. They can point to the 'clandestine advertising' scandal of 1971–72 as evidence of the pernicious effects of introducing commercials onto national television.[161]

This scandal, which was eventually to lead to the new statute of 1972, was first revealed to the public by Senator André Diligent during the budget debate of November 1971. His forceful accusations of 'methodical and systematic corruption' within *ORTF* were followed by the publication in the national press of a note from the Havas public relations agency concerning the introduction of a brand name into a programme. The directors of the *Office*, who had had such cases brought to their notice from 1969 at least, quickly set up an inquiry. They hoped to get the matter rapidly over with. But it was too late. Public opinion was aroused and both Houses set up special commissions to investigate further.[162]

The dossiers eventually made public in 1972 by the two commissions contained a staggering record of corruption. Brand names had been consistently introduced into programmes. A golf tournament, renamed after a brand of perfume, was given nearly 2½ hours' television time, though the sport is hardly popular in France. A new racing magazine was plugged on regional sports programmes all over the country. Television games were controlled by a powerful clique of producers who were making money out of them. Other *ORTF* men had unhealthily close contacts with commercial ventures – private production companies, advertising agencies and so on. Perhaps the revelation which most shocked the public concerned the *Office*'s charity campaigns. Private agencies such as Havas, called in to organize the campaigns, were taking a fat commission on the proceeds. Worse, some of the *ORTF* personnel involved were accepting payment from these agencies for work which could equally be considered part of their normal work for the *Office*.[163]

The reactions of government and *Office* were perhaps to be expected. Both tried as long as possible to pooh-pooh the affair. The Director General sacked 18 persons in March 1972, but these did not include anyone of importance, and *Le Figaro* called it window-dressing.[164] The Prime Minister declared in the National Assembly that the Director General and President of the *Office* were blameless – then sacked them three days later.[165] It was rumoured that the *Office*'s list of licence-holders (names and addresses) had been stolen from the Rennes Centre and offered for sale to a mail-order firm. The Administrative Council denied the very existence of the affair. But in November 1973 the head of sports programmes was accused in court of that very crime.[166]

The public disclosure of the clandestine advertising affair led to the setting up in October 1972 of a permanent control mechanism and in general to an effort to keep *ORTF* staff aware of the problems and dangers involved. The temptations still exist, of course. Indeed, some critics blame the authorities for not allowing certain types of product or service access to television advertising. Thus Air-France is still frequently mentioned, even though the Minister of Transport refuses to allow airlines to advertise, in an attempt to protect the French company from international competition. Renault refuses to advertise, after the breaking off of its special relationship with *ORTF*, which was severely criticized in 1970. None the less, *ORTF* continued to devote several minutes of its news bulletins to Renault's latest models when they appeared. These then are cases where *ORTF* provided 'advertising' and received nothing in return.[167]

If advertising has raised problems, what about a commercial channel in France? At almost every crisis or point of change in *ORTF*'s history, the voice of the commercial TV lobby has been heard, in the press and in Parliament, crying out for an end to the State monopoly of broadcasting. This has meant over the years a considerable number of Bills presented to Parliament, all of which governments have so far rejected. The wording of the 1972 statute excluded private capital from large-scale holdings in *ORTF*, and the 1974 statute confirmed this, though as we shall see, other changes were made which did not reassure the defenders of the monopoly. The introduction of commercial television still requires a change in the law, and in general up to now there has not been a parliamentary majority in favour of such a change.

Apart from the businessmen who hope to make a profit from it, the promoters of commercial television have traditionally been the Independent Republican party in Parliament, and outside it a number of liberals, who would welcome the change without necessarily campaigning for it: economists such as Henri Mercillon, journalists such as Bernard Voyenne, television men such as Pierre Desgraupes, ex-head of Channel One news.[168] The public has also been generally in favour,[169] though its opinion is very likely ill-informed, and is probably largely a reflection of its dissatisfaction with *ORTF*'s performance. The opponents of a private channel have included such apparently diverse characters as General de Gaulle and the Communist and Socialist parties. The *ORTF* unions have also been solidly opposed to any attack on the public system.

The arguments for and against a commercial television channel have been various, some based on general economic reasons, others on the improvement (or otherwise) of *ORTF* and of broadcasting generally. It was claimed for example that a commercial channel would expand the publicity market and hence the French economy generally, that it would rescue the ailing cinema industry by employing its producers and other staff, and that it would help the electronics industry by boosting the sales of TV sets. (As France reaches its point of saturation of TV receivers, this last argument loses much of its point.) The good effects on broadcasting were to be considerable: better and freer news, because of competition (and here one could indeed point to the experience of radio); more money available to *ORTF*, because of the increased sales of TV sets, and so better programmes on all channels; greater efficiency all round, because of the effects of competition on *ORTF*'s administration and financial management; an increase in artistic freedom, a greater pool of talent and more opportunities and mobility for everyone. It was also argued that since *ORTF* already carries commercials, there was no reason why a totally commercial channel should not exist alongside it, and that in any case the advent of satellite television would soon make the monopoly an anachronism.[170] Perhaps the strongest argument has been based on the model of the written press, which has certainly provided a freer and more varied news service (in particular) under a commercial régime than has *ORTF* under its 'public service' structure.[171]

Against commercial TV, it has been argued that standards would be lowered on all channels, by the extension of the race for the ratings, and that the 'freedom' claimed for the private system is illusory, since government control would merely be replaced by the *diktat* of big business.[172] Only heavily populated areas would be thought worth covering by a commercial channel, although everyone would have to pay for the adverts. Furthermore, in the United States, it is argued, commercial television now appears to be a failure, and 'public' broadcasting is springing up everywhere to remedy the situation. (This really only proves the need for a public service, and not that commercial television alongside public television could not provide a useful complement.) However, the arguments which seem most likely to carry weight are the economic ones: in the context of the present slow growth rate of France's advertising market, neither the press nor *ORTF* could sustain the loss in revenue which would inevitably result from a nationwide commercial channel. The *ORTF* licence fee would probably have to go up by 50 per cent.[173]

Projects for commercial channels have tried in various ways to meet some of these objections. The 'projet Vivien', a Bill drawn up in July 1968 by M. R.-A. Vivien and other *UDR* members, based its arguments primarily on France's economic interests, and suggested moreover that the press could share in the profits. The goals of broadcasting – to inform, cultivate, educate and entertain – would be extended to the private channel. Control of programme quality would be placed in the hands of an independent council on the lines of the Independent Television Authority in Britain. Advertisements would be limited to 10 per cent of programme time; no programmes would be sponsored. *ORTF* would 'hire out' its transmission installations to the independent companies concerned, who would have contracts for 10 years at a time. News, which would take the form of 'short flashes', could be supplied by a separate news agency created in agreement with *ORTF* and *Agence France Presse*.[174]

A project which made considerably more impact was 'Canal 10' ('Channel Ten') or *NTV* (*Nouvelle Télévision*), put forward in 1970 by Jean Frydman, head of Télé-Monte Carlo. Canal 10 would have covered 70 per cent of French territory. It was to install its own transmitters in *ORTF* buildings, under *ORTF*'s general management, and pay the *Office* in exchange a sort of commission on its revenue. Advertising would have been restricted to six minutes an hour, with no breaks in programmes. The regional press was to be invited to participate in programme production, and regional advertisers encouraged to use the new medium. No one private financial group was to be allowed to gain control of the company. The promoters' plans for programmes were described as vague and seemed to augur ill for quality and homogeneity. However, a supervisory committee, half of whose members were to be nominated by the State, was to have overseen the operation and protected the public.[175] The director of programmes was to have been Jean d'Arcy, director of RTF from 1952 to 1959.[176]

One of the few projects to be based more on principles than on personal or national economic interests was put forward by an economist, Henri Mercillon, in 1972. Inspired partly by systems in Germany and Holland and by the *Pilkington Report* in Britain, this project would give control of a private channel to the press and to the public. A possible administrative council might be composed of six State representatives, six of the press, and ten of the audience, with two others. The press should also have financial interests, though no one group should be allowed undue influence. A national company would administer equipment and a common national programme (about 50–60 per cent of the total). The rest would be provided by regional companies responsible for production and programming, who would hold renewable subcontracts from the national organization. These would be run by separate councils and be financed by local and regional advertising. No control of programmes by advertisers would be possible. According to Mercillon, this system would give the 'consumer' back his rights, while the press would gain from its new mobility of capital and talent.[177]

For technical reasons, France has room for only four national networks of the traditional Hertzian kind. Three of these are already occupied by ORTF and a fourth may not in fact prove practicable, for air-space is already crowded and many television sets now in use are not sufficiently sensitive to different wavelengths.[178] Though projects for commercial television channels continue to be put forward, for example by the Giscardian *Perspectives et réalités* club in 1973,[179] the Pompidou Government's continued opposition and the development of new audiovisual technology to some extent dampened enthusiasm.[180] Promoters are probably waiting to see whether they can get their foot in the door of the video-cassette or cable television industry rather than embark on the extremely expensive task of creating a national network. As for hiving off one of the existing national channels onto the private sector, the Minister of Information who proposed such a solution in August 1973 caused uproar at *ORTF* and did not appear to have the support of the rest of the government.

Fears and speculation that *ORTF* would indeed go commercial in part or in whole were revived in the summer of 1974 when Valéry Giscard d'Estaing was elected President. The new President's party, the Independent Republicans, had traditionally been the strongest supporters of commercial television in Parliament. Indeed, his brother Olivier Giscard d'Estaing had proposed a Bill along those lines in 1972.[181] With the *Office* obviously in financial difficulties, independent television seemed more likely than ever before. Two different projects were already in the offing. By virtue of international agreements, the Europe 1 group already had 'Channel 39' at its disposal. With a new transmitter in the Sarre – and negotiations were under way between Paris and Bonn – this network could serve an area as large as that of Télé-Luxembourg. It was suspected that the new Radio-Monte Carlo transmitter in the Alps might also be a link in the new project.[182] Another possibility was that one of the *ORTF*'s own channels could be given over wholly or partly to the private sector, remaining under government control via *SOFIRAD*. This was suggested in June 1974 by the head of that agency, Denis Baudouin.[183]

Any Bill to introduce commercial television could still have united the left and most of the Gaullist party against the government, not to mention provoking the hostility of the press and maybe a general strike at *ORTF*.[184] In the event, the 1974 statute was a compromise. On paper, the monopoly remained, but the government's talk of a 'new chance' for the public service had a sinister ring. Clearly the new system had more in common with the private sector than before: the legal status of the new bodies, for example. While the transmission company retained the title of 'public establishment', the programme companies were placed under the legal system governing private commercial companies (*sociétés anonymes*). The State remained the only shareholder. The production company – and this was the major innovation in this respect – was now opened up to private capital in the form of 'mixed economy' companies (*sociétés d'économie mixte*), so-called because their shares are owned by both the State and private interests. The State and other public enterprises were to remain in the majority and the State retained the right to veto any financial transactions concerning the company's distribution of shares. For all the new bodies, except the transmission company and the Audiovisual Institute, salaries and working conditions were to be governed by collective agreements rather than by the sort of statute applicable in the Civil Service or in nationalized industry. After analysing the new bill, a group of legal experts concluded:

> ...even if it is not its avowed aim, the result of this project is to prepare the way for going private, by setting up the appropriate mechanisms, and, in the short term, to reinforce the powers of the government to control radio and television.[185]

There were other features which contributed to the general anxiety. The basic principles of the new system – competition between channels, the client-supplier relationship between the companies – were patently those of commercial television. The new formula for Channel Three, 'cinema and free speech', was seen as an imitation of the commercial radio and television stations on the borders.[186] Finally, at the head of the production company, the closest in format to a private firm, the government placed M. Jean-Charles Edeline, under whose management the *Union générale cinématographique* (General Cinematographic Union), a national body, had been given to the private sector. Both M. Edeline and the Prime Minister, however, quickly denied that any such fate was in store for the production company.[187]

Whether or not traditional television in France is allowed to go commercial, private interests have already managed to plant a stake in the new technology. A number of private companies were formed with the intention of promoting and exploiting cable television. Among them were *Multividéo* (now called *Vidéocités*), headed by Jean d'Arcy, ex-director of RTF, and composed of seven financial and industrial groups: *Financière de Suez, Soditel, Information et Publicité, Publicis, Sodete* (*Société pour le développement de la télévision*) and two American groups *Teleprompter* and *International Communication Systems*. Another was *Télétudes*, whose members included Hachette, *Sodete*, banks such as the Bank of Paris and the Netherlands, plus the nationalized banks, *Crédit Lyonnais* and the *Société Générale*. The networks themselves are not expected to be dominated by the commercial sector but the latter will not be excluded.[188] For example, at Nice, the shareholders in the cable system are expected to be the town council, the local newspaper *Nice-Matin*, and the *Société française de télédistribution* (which is an affiliate of *ORTF* and the Ministry of Posts).[189]

Perhaps the most controversial case involving the imbrication of public and private capital in this domain has been the *Société française de vidéogrammes* set up in October 1971 to 'study, publish and distribute' sound and vision recordings, in the form of cassettes and 'videodiscs'. This company, at its beginnings, had a capital of 1·6 million francs, the shares being held equally by *ORTF* and the giant French publishing firm Hachette. This agreement was greeted with widespread criticism in France. Why should a private publishing house make money out of *ORTF*'s television programmes, already paid for by the public with its licence fee contributions?[190] Would educational establishments (one of the main markets) be forced to pay commercial prices? Would any control be exercised by Hachette over the 'cultural tendencies' of the various projects?[191] Other matters for concern were Hachette's financial interests in *RTL* (*Radio-Luxembourg*), and its links with government: Simon Nora had moved from the Prime Minister's office to a directorship at Hachette six months before this agreement was reached. (He later joined the Administrative Council at *RTL* as well.)[192]

ORTF defended its choice of partner. It could not itself set up an adequate network for distributing its programmes in cassette form: Hachette already had 40,000 sales outlets as well as numerous contacts abroad. In any case, the new company was not a monopoly; Hachette had not been given exclusive rights over *ORTF*'s productions.[193] Furthermore, it was not intended that Hachette and *ORTF* should remain the only shareholders. Indeed, by October 1973, the Paris and regional press had acquired shares (12 per cent) and so had *Vidéo-Cinéma*, an offshoot of the *Union générale cinématographique* (10 per cent). Hachette had agreed to reduce its holdings to below 34 per cent so that it would be unable to act as a blocking minority.[194]

The enmeshment of public and private enterprise in French broadcasting is understandable in the context of France's mixed economy, in which successful state-owned industries and powerful government departments coexist with large and often monopolistic private companies. Given this system, it would be naïve to hope for any clear separation of the public and the commercial. Broadcasting cannot be taken entirely out of the marketplace, any more than it can avoid pressures from the political majority of the moment. It will be interesting to see how the balance between state control and commercial pressure develops in the coming years. Whatever happens, however, there remains a serious danger: squeezed between the politician and the businessman, both eager to exploit him, the citizen and his needs may easily be misunderstood or neglected. In France, as we shall see, this corner of the triangle has traditionally been the weakest.

CHAPTER FOUR

Broadcasting, Democracy and the Public

INFORMATION: 'THE GOVERNMENT IN THE DINING-ROOM'

Without the free access of citizens to adequate and impartially presented information, modern democracy can only be a cripple. France, of course, has a free press, which reflects the diversity of public opinion. But as in other countries, more and more people have come to rely on television as their major source of information on politics and current affairs. Nowhere more than in the political control of information programmes can the confusion between national television and organ of government prove so harmful.

A number of distinctions must first be made. In France, radio news, while hardly radical or free from pressures – Roger Gicquel, head of radio news from April 1973, was said to have been appointed after a personal telephone call from Alain Peyrefitte – has been generally recognized as freer and more impartial than television news. This has probably been due as much to the example and competition of the commercial stations on France's borders as to the general feeling in recent years that radio is not perhaps very closely attended to anyway. Television news has indeed been strictly controlled, but current affairs programmes in other formats – magazines, debates, documentaries – have often been allowed to be relatively more enterprising. Election and referendum campaigns constitute a special case, for during these periods the fair allocation of broadcasting time is controlled by an outside and independent commission. Finally, the long-standing controversy over a legally instituted right of access for parties and groups of various kinds, and a similar right of reply for persons or groupings slandered or misrepresented on the air, is a separate but related problem.

The control of television news dates back to the final years of the Fourth Republic, at a point when the expansion of the television audience coincided with the outbreak of war in Algeria.[1] From 1959, under de Gaulle, this tendency to interference became a general rule. It had its theory: television, according to the General and his ministers, must provide a political counterbalance to the hostility of the written press.[2] It also had its mechanisms: in particular, the Interministerial Information Liaison Service (*SLII*), set up by the Ministry of Information in 1963.

By 1961, political censorship was well-established, though it had as yet no official structures. Journalists had to be careful to use the right terms – *FLN* (National Liberation Front) rather than *GPRA* (Provisional Government of the Algerian Republic) for the Algerian nationalists, and to present news items in the right order – Georges Penchenier almost lost his job for putting news of a strike before an account of a presidential visit. The head of radio and TV news, André Gérard, was in direct contact with Michel Debré in the government, and there were already rumours of a 'news centre' to be set up at the Prime Minister's office in Avenue Matignon, which would sort out news for presentation on the air.[3] The following year, the role of television in the referendum (on the change in the Constitution to allow the election of the president by universal suffrage) caused a political storm, and after the strike in October that year three of TV's best journalists (Joseph Pasteur, Georges Penchenier and Michel Péricard) lost their jobs.[4] By 1963, Senator Édouard Bonnefous could write that 'freedom of expression and the right to objective information have disappeared from French broadcasting'.[5]

Political bias was not the only complaint concerning television news. What was not government propaganda was trivial anecdote, non-news.[6] Nor was the party line always put across with much subtlety. Official ceremonies, ministerial appearances monopolized the screen. Foreign news took the place of domestic news. The government expressed its views but made no attempt to convince. Even its own supporters might well be dissatisfied.[7]

Government control, however, remained the main focus of debate. The 1964 statute was presented by the Minister of Information, Alain Peyrefitte, as a step towards independence and credibility. It would, he said, eliminate the regrettable confusion in the public mind between *RTF* and its political leaders, the 'government in the dining-room'.[8] But this reform, like the later reorganization of TV news in 1967, only led to greater centralization and even more control.[9] 1965 was a particularly bad year for TV news, if it could still be called 'news'.[10] A number of politicians, asked their views in 1966, spoke strongly in condemnation of the system: 'a scandalous monopoly', a 'permanent scandal', 'one of the stains on the Fifth Republic', and so on.[11] Political skirmishing continued at regular intervals. In January 1968, the Minister of Information replied to a question from an Independent Republican member: between 1 January and 5 December 1967, major political figures from the government parties had appeared on television for a total of 3 hours 57 minutes and 23 seconds, while the opposition had appeared for 1 hour 58 minutes and 36 seconds. This was misleading, claimed the left, for those in power were allowed to address the viewer directly: the opposition viewpoint was usually put in the form of extracts and often deformed by commentators.[12] The pettiness of this exchange is perhaps an indication of the tensions involved.

The long and bitter strike at *ORTF* in May and June 1968 had as its primary impetus the failure of TV news and information programmes to give adequate coverage (and explanation) of the student riots. The subject was not only kept out of the news for as long as possible, but was presented with bias: thus, for example, of the several available press agency estimates of the size of a large union demonstration, the chief editor (J.-L. Guillaud) ordered the news reader to use the smallest.[13] And as the strike went on, the demand for free and impartial information and the structures to guarantee it remained at the centre of the *ORTF* journalists' conflict.[14]

At about the same time, the Senate special Commission of Control revealed in its report what had long been half-known and suspected about television news. Its analysis, free from political rhetoric or *parti pris*, provided the *ORTF* strikers with a complete justification after the fact. The information sector at *ORTF* was neither independent nor a reflection of the diversity of political opinion in France. The promises made by the government in 1964 had certainly not been honoured; indeed, the situation appeared to have got worse.

The structures of the *Office* – tutelage of the Information Ministry, inadequate powers of the government-appointed Administrative Council, personal relations between the Minister and the Director General – were the major culprits. Article 5 of the statute, which laid down that government communiqués must be clearly announced as such, had been applied in neither spirit nor letter. In pre-election periods bias was peculiarly in evidence, but even in periods of political calm the government point of view appeared to be the underlying preoccupation of those responsible for TV news. Foreign policy was a particularly notable example.

Within the news service itself, journalists were encompassed by a well-established hierarchy leading up to the Director General himself. The latter had the power not only to appoint to all posts, but to sign or veto permits to set out on a news mission (*ordres de mission*), to choose political commentators for personal 15-minute 'journals' and to preview news sequences if he desired. He was the final arbiter of any conflict between directors of news and their editors, and could impose his own bias on the overall information policy. In these circumstances, journalists were utterly devoid of protection against political pressures from outside, and indeed were required to subject themselves to the bias imposed from within. Sacking, transfer to less important or prestigious sectors (such as the regional or overseas stations), were used to punish too great a show of independence.[15]

Perhaps the most shocking revelation of 1967–68 was the disclosure by two sources (neither particularly anti-government) of the workings of the Interministerial Information Liaison Service (*SLII*). Set up in 1963 as a government information office, the *SLII* exercized an extraordinary degree of control over television news:

> Every morning, at about eleven o'clock, a dozen or so civil servants got together and asked themselves:
> (i) what television ought not to mention;
> (ii) which official ceremonies should be given ample coverage ...[16]

The *Diligent Report* confirmed some long-standing suspicions about the role of the *SLII* in controlling TV news. It had, for example, drawn up a list of towns to be reported on shortly before the municipal elections of March 1965. It had banned from the screen certain towns and certain personalities. It sent out 'blue notes' to journalists, Civil Servants and politicians, which described and defended government positions and policies. It appeared to act totally behind the backs of the Administrative Council and its President; and it had little dealings with the rest of the national press.[17]

The violence of May 1968 brought its reward. Although over 100 *ORTF* journalists lost their jobs or were transferred elsewhere, TV news was indeed reformed and the *SLII* disbanded. The latter was replaced by a more innocuous body, the Committee for Interministerial Information, run by Pierre Hunt, who had no inclination to interfere with news. Until 1974, when the Messmer government set up a new, enlarged information office (shortly before the death of President Pompidou), there was no attempt to recreate an official structure for ministerial control.

After the strike was over, however, television news gradually returned to its old habits. Government ministers continued to appear very frequently. Georges Pompidou, in disgrace, disappeared from the screen altogether for ten months. As the referendum on Senate and regional reform drew near, bias became more apparent. Then after de Gaulle's resignation, the interim President, Alain Poher, publicly reminded the President of the Administrative Council of his duty. For a few days, TV news was a model of impartiality, clear, precise, with interviews from all parties.[18] Whether this could continue would depend on the outcome of the presidential election.

Although no independent council of 'wise men' was created to ensure impartiality (as the strikers had demanded), in the event, the reform of TV news which was announced by the Prime Minister, Jacques Chaban-Delmas, in late 1969 was a genuine attempt to free information from the one-party stranglehold. A new statute was promised for the near future. Instead of the single hierarchical system criticized by the Senate commission, two entirely separate news teams were created, one for each channel. The heads of news would have considerable independence in the use of the means at their disposal. Though the heads themselves were of course appointed by the government, they were at least given a specific term of office and could only be sacked in the case of serious professional misconduct.[19] The appointments themselves were also proof of a new liberalism: on Channel One, Pierre Desgraupes, a TV journalist and by no means an unconditional supporter of the Pompidou régime (though not the leftist the UDR party pretended); on Channel Two, Jacqueline Baudrier, an experienced broadcaster and a moderate Gaullist. Their responsibilities included not only news bulletins as such, but also magazines and political programmes of various kinds.

Most observers are agreed that there was a real improvement in the credibility and quality of television news after 1969. But problems remained. On the political front, the right wing of the UDR party attacked the new system from the start: why should those journalists sacked in 1968 for endangering the security of the Republic now be taken on again at higher salaries? Why should Channel One be given over to leftists?[20] From the opposition benches and from the journalists' unions there were complaints that not enough of the sacked journalists had been re-employed; their action had after all been justified by the present reforms.[21] In fact, very few of those who had been sacked were given back their jobs. To do so on a large scale would probably have precipitated disaster, especially for Desgraupes.

Not all the problems were political. The audience which had fallen off badly during 1968 – Channel Two news had a listening figure of between 4 and 6 per cent in November 1969[22] – had to be recaptured. Personnel and equipment were insufficient to cope with the changes the directors intended. Each news team had only one outside-broadcast van, and on Sundays they had to share one between them.[23] Autonomy extended only to the frontier of the technical sector: large spending on equipment still required prior consent from the authorities.[24]

After a year's trial, the two directors assessed the experience. For Desgraupes, progress had been made, both in financial independence and in credibility. Only one news sequence had been shown in preview, even to the Administrative Council, who had the right to safeguard objectivity in this way. This was a great novelty for anyone who had known the old system. Listening figures had gone up by 15–20 per cent, and by even more for magazine programmes. Jacqueline Baudrier too was positive, and her listening figures also showed an increase. Relations with the government (hers was thought of as the government channel) were no different from those of the press, and were not felt as any constraint.[25]

In October 1971, the *ORTF* budget for the following year revealed the possibility of a threat to TV news. Channel Two news programmes were to be reduced by 87 hours in the year, and its finances were cut. Channel One news was also to have its budget pruned. Even worse, perhaps, the director of Channel Two, Pierre Sabbagh, whose task was to attract a larger audience to the second, colour channel, was planning to programme a game or a popular serial against Channel One news at 7.30 p.m. and a Maigret-type detective series against the political debate programme 'A armes égales' on Monday evenings.[26]

By the summer of 1972 in any case, the experiment was over. The government had, it was rumoured, been angered by both news teams' treatment of the Common Market referendum earlier that year. While Desgraupes' news, realistic as it was, had never been 'reassuring', Baudrier's team had on this occasion televised a report from other EEC countries which revealed their indifference to the result of the French referendum.[27] The overall balance between the two channels – the anti-government *Monsieur Tant-Pis* on One, and the pro-government *Madame Tant-Mieux* on Two[27a] – was ended by the new statute, which reattached the news teams to their respective heads of channels. Pierre Desgraupes did not renew his contract. His departure, linked appropriately with that of the Prime Minister who had appointed him, was a considerable victory for the right wing of the *UDR* party.

A number of well-known TV journalists left with Pierre Desgraupes. The new régime, under Arthur Conte as President-Director General, began in some bitterness for TV news. Jacqueline Baudrier, however, promoted to head Channel One, took her news team with her. It inherited Desgraupes' 40–45 per cent audience for the evening news, a figure in reality more connected with ownership of old, black-and-white, Channel One-only television sets than with the nation's political sympathies. The head of Channel One news and the head of its political service were both convinced 'Pompidolians'. On Channel Two, Jean Lefevre, from the Strasbourg regional station, took over news programmes. Pierre Sabbagh, director of the channel, proved his new powers by sacking and transferring large numbers of journalists and cameramen – as many as 200, according to the unions.[28]

Television news did not seem to have been much improved by the changes made in 1972. During the last week of July 1972, out of nearly three hours' news, about a quarter was devoted to the government and the *UDR* party and their achievements, another 19·5 per cent to foreign news and only 6·5 per cent to the opposition. The rest was general news: road accidents, pollution, fashion, sport, etc., presented on the level of a popular newspaper. Current affairs within France were treated either by rapid enumeration of facts and declarations, or with detailed exposés if the government was involved.[29] Later that year, President Pompidou repeated his conviction that the television journalist was 'the voice of France'. Between 2 and 23 January 1973, a viewers' association, 'Télé-Liberté', calculated that the party in power had allotted itself nine times as much broadcasting time as the opposition.[30]

By August 1973, the audience for Channel One news had dropped to less than 30 per cent; it had been nearer 50 per cent under Desgraupes. Channel Two news had increased its audience from 8–9 per cent to about 15 per cent (partly a reflection of the increased use of colour television), and Channel Three news at 10 p.m., and still in its infancy, had about 1–5 per cent. Financial difficulties exacerbated the problems: to retain two separate news teams was expensive and indeed wasteful, for even on foreign news stories, two teams might be sent out separately. Any suppression of the dual system, however, presented a clearcut danger to an already fragile independence.[31]

The unfortunate politicization of the whole question of television news in France can be illustrated by the experiment attempted in April 1973 by Arthur Conte and the Director of Harmonization, J.-P. Angrémy. Channel Two news was to go out much later, at 10 p.m. instead of at 8 p.m. This would mean a better differentiation of each channel's news; a more reflective atmosphere, since viewers would be away from the family dining-table; and the extra two hours' preparation time would enable more pictures to be shown and a greater use made of the contributions of the regional stations.[32] Whatever the real motives behind this change were, viewers certainly perceived it as a deliberate manœuvre. The more thoughtful and critical news on

Two (the 'Opposition Channel') was to be placed out of reach of the working man, whose bedtime in France is traditionally around 10 p.m.[33] The 8 p.m. news on One was to be for the masses, the 10 p.m. news on Two for the informed élite. In the event, the change was made clumsily, and the 'crossroads' earlier in the evening, when a viewer could switch channels without breaking up a programme, was lost. Complaints from the public forced Conte to return Channel Two news to its original site earlier in the evening.

If the national television news was often biased or prudently silent, regional news had long been an unadulterated government organ of the most blatant kind. The 23 regional news stations had been set up from 1963 onwards by Alain Peyrefitte, Minister of Information. It was felt that they would provide a political counterweight to the regional press, which was largely in opposition. Almost all the early directors had been loyal Gaullists.[34] M. Goulet for example, in 1964, was moved directly from the Ministry of Information to be Assistant to the Director General with responsibility for regional programmes.[35] Since then political control had never shown signs of loosening. In 1971, the Nancy delegate lost his post because he wanted to give broadcasting time to Jean-Jacques Servan-Schreiber, the local opposition deputy and general secretary of the Radical party.[36] Several regional stations were later given to journalists who had refused to strike in 1968: Finaltéri (Paris-Ile-de-France), Griveau (Rennes), Roubaud (Dijon).[37]

Regional news – 20 minutes daily in all regions and a weekly news magazine in some others – was controlled in a number of ways. Political appointments were one method, as we have seen. The small numbers of journalists involved (three or four per station) facilitated government control. Other pressures worked through the central office at Paris (the *délégation aux stations régionales*) which kept its eye on what the regions were up to. This system lasted until 1972 when the regions were placed under the aegis of Channel Three and its director J.-L. Guillaud (whose political sympathies have been mentioned earlier). Thirdly, at a local level, the influence of local figures such as the prefect (the government's representative at departmental level) and the *UDR* deputy has frequently been a pervasive one. No official structures for this sort of interference exist, of course. In Lyons, it is said that M. Chanet, the UDR deputy, has for years telephoned every morning to the regional news station to control and even dictate the day's news.[38] In other places this kind of pressure does not exist to the same extent, but the journalists themselves provide a prudent and pro-government news service. Prefects and ministers monopolize the screen. A viewer from the Midi-Pyrenees region complained that between 1 January and 20 October 1972, Doctor Bernard Pons, a UDR deputy and Under-Secretary of State for Agriculture, appeared 217 times (sometimes three times a day), and that his name had been mentioned a further 368 times.[39]

National and regional television news have always been closely controlled by the government in power. Current affairs programmes on the other hand have at various times, and depending on the political climate, been allowed a relative freedom. Paradoxically perhaps, de Gaulle's régime was capable of encouraging some of the finest magazine and documentary programmes as well as of suppressing them when they went too far.

The reasons for the discrepancy between these programmes and the regular news bulletins are complex and confused. For one thing, current affairs programmes naturally attract a smaller audience than the national news. Moreover, some of the main examples of this type of programme were created for Channel Two, which had started broadcasting in 1964 but which by 1971 still had only about one-third of the audience of Channel One.[40] Timing and programming are also important. Political programmes must be allowed to exist, if only for the sake of the liberal image a government wishes to project. But their audience can easily be depleted by timing them after 10 p.m. or by putting on a popular variety show or a big match on the other channel. Another factor – both cause and effect – has been the use of journalists from 'outside' to present or chair certain political programmes: Alain Duhamel on 'A armes égales', for example. ORTF journalists complain that this makes a clear distinction in the public mind between the 'tamed' (conditionnés) and the 'free', the 'house journalist' at the government's beck and call and the man from the national newspaper who can afford to take risks.[41]

The history of current affairs programmes shows that there have been problems in this area too. Some programmes only survived by virtue of the protection against pressure afforded by a particularly strong personality: Pierre Lazareff, the producer, for

'Cinq colonnes à la une', a documentary programme which lasted from 1959 to 1968; Jean Faran for the political interview programme 'Face à face'.[42] Others were removed for political reasons. 'Faire face', in 1963, which attempted to treat problems such as racism, divorce, alcoholism, only lasted a few numbers.[43] The most famous example before 1968 is 'La caméra explore le temps', a series of historical reconstructions which investigated France's past, sometimes exploding cherished national myths in the process. In 1965, when the programme was still at the height of its popularity – indeed, it appears to have been at the top of the ratings[44] – it was dropped. The Director of Programmes claimed he wanted to prevent its going stale. The two professional historians involved in the series, however, revealed that they had been asked to continue without the producer, Stellio Lorenzi. The latter was a Communist, and an active worker in the producers' union, which happened at that time to be in the midst of a conflict with the management. Although the national press in its entirety took up the programme's defence, the Administrative Council, appealed to by the producers' union, came down on the side of the directors.[45]

The creation and repression of political and current affairs programmes has, like everything else in French television, been closely linked to political events outside. The lack of adequate and impartial information before 1965 had caused a 'boomerang effect' during the presidential elections of that year; as the President of the Administrative Council said, one cannot pass with impunity from a diet to an orgy.[46] This, it was widely believed, was the reason for the creation or encouragement of a whole galaxy of new programmes designed to give the public more balanced viewing: 'Face à face', on the lines of the American 'Meet the Press', and created at the request of the Minister of Information; 'Zoom', 'Caméra III', and so on. These programmes were especially encouraged by Jacques Thibau, Director of Television, later to be evicted on suspicion of Communist sympathies at the end of 1967.[47]

While they lasted, these programmes certainly provided some counter-balance to the heavily controlled news. In 1966, 'Face à face' brought before the public opposition politicians such as Guy Mollet, François Mitterrand, Waldeck Rochet; there was a television debate between Maurice Schumann and Pierre Mendès-

France.[48] 'Zoom' treated subjects as diverse as unemployment, housing, Algeria, and French Communists.[49] Some sequences used in this kind of programme, however, only went on the air after a considerable struggle on the part of the producers.[50] And Harris and de Sédouy, the producers of 'Zoom', were in trouble with the directors of ORTF well before May 1968 when the programme on the student riots all too effectively put paid to the series.[51] After May 1968, almost all the current affairs programmes created in 1966–67 were taken off. Jacques Thibau defends de Gaulle from the charge of having exercised a personal vengeance in the matter. According to him, the General was far more disappointed by the 'betrayal' of the news teams, whom he had thought he could trust. The disappearance of the documentary programmes was, rather, the product of the overenthusiasm of the Minister of Information and the Director General, aided by the personal jealousy and animosity of mediocre newsmen inside the *Office*.[52] The new Director of Television, André François, defended the repression: according to him, these magazines had enjoyed 'excessive freedom'.[53]

Some of the suppressed current affairs programmes were later resuscitated under other names. Lazareff, for example, managed to retain his team from 'Cinq colonnes à la une' (though some of them had been strikers) and was allowed to produce a similar programme called 'De nos envoyés spéciaux'.[54] But on the whole, there was no great improvement in current affairs programmes after 1969. Channel One seemed to be given over more and more to facile entertainment programmes, and Channel Two seemed only marginally better.[55]

Political censorship continued to be regularly exercised. Harris and de Sédouy's controversial film on the Occupation in France, 'Le chagrin et la pitié', could not be shown, though viewers in several other European countries had seen it and it later appeared in the French cinema. A programme on work in the factory, by the Communist producer Jacques Frémontier, was dropped from the series 'Vivre aujourd'hui'. Frémontier commented that left-wing ideas were acceptable to the authorities as long as they were 'intellectual': but 'the truth, said in everyday words by ordinary people, that frightens them'.[56] In June 1970, Olivier Todd resigned from 'Panorama' after a clip from the film 'Battle of Algiers' was cut from his programme. After the refusal to allow the writer Rezvani to appear on 'L'Invité du dimanche', the Gaullist Romain Gary appeared instead, and made no secret of his political views. Soon afterwards, the Administrative Council sent out its directive warning producers to keep politics out of documentaries, historical programmes and the like.[57]

Some examples of censorship are almost too petty to be credible. Marcel Bluwal, making Hugo's 'Les Misérables', was asked whether in the barricades scene a red flag was really necessary. A policeman in a serial was not allowed to be seen wiping his moustache. Feydeau's plays were shorn of their social satire, reduced to bedroom farce. But the mechanisms involved were hardly laughable. There was talk of daily control of programmes in course of production. Direct intervention by politicians was not infrequent. Prime Minister Messmer, for example, at the request of the Lorraine steel industrialists, had a programme on the redeployment of a worker suppressed, even though its producer was a well-known prize-winner.[58]

The arrival of Arthur Conte as President-Director General in the summer of 1972 could have been the opportunity for a new beginning. Indeed, Conte made some gestures towards liberalism right at the start. He decided, for example, to show two episodes, 'Danton' and 'Robespierre', from the popular series 'La caméra explore le temps', which as we have seen was taken off in 1965. A decision not to show a programme called 'Vive le Cinéma' in June 1972 was reversed in September, with the approval of the Administrative Council. However, these were isolated measures, and the overall standard of current affairs and information programmes generally did not appear to be much improved during Conte's régime. Controversial programmes continued to be kept in stock indefinitely: a programme on Rosa Luxembourg made in 1970 by Marcel Bluwal and Georges Hourdin was never shown; another on racism, made by Daniel Karlin, was not put on by Conte (and was still waiting to be shown a year later, in September 1974).[59]

It would be unjust to paint too harsh a picture of the *Office*'s information programmes in recent years. It is true that some of the major current affairs programmes present defects in format or in practice. 'Dossiers de l'écran', for example, one of the oldest and best-established of these programmes, consists of a cinema film, followed by a debate on the topic concerned. Some recent subjects have been cancer (September 1973), handicapped children (October 1973), nuclear arms (November 1973). The problem is both to find films of sufficiently good quality and to sustain viewers' interest in the debate which takes place, after $2\frac{1}{2}$ hours of film, at 10.30 p.m. And as with other debate programmes, there has been controversy over the guests invited, for example, in the programme on pollution in February 1974.[60]

There have, of course, been successes. In January 1974, a television film by Jacques Krier, broadcast at peak hour on Channel One, showed 48 hours in the life of an ordinary couple with their everyday problems: work, money, motherhood, the possibility of abortion. On Channel One, but after 10 p.m., the series 'Un certain regard', produced by the Research Service, dealt, in the autumn of 1973, with topics such as Ho Chi Minh, France in AD 2000, the anthropologist Margaret Mead. On Channel Two, 'MM. les jurés' was designed to instruct the public in the machinery of justice: actors played out a trial, and 12 viewers were asked to give their verdict. On Channel Three (whose audience is still very small), a serial about a doctor was intended as a mixture of instruction and entertainment. Early in 1974, the same channel put on a series of semi-documentary cinema-vérité programmes about ordinary people's lives: 'Chez Charlot. Un café de quartier', 'Un petit garage', etc. The excitement with which these programmes and other successes have been received by critics is however some indication of their rarity.

While the quantity and quality of information programmes dealing with social and political issues is, of course, a major concern, the access of politicians to the screen has always been a more central topic of debate in France. The principal criticism of television in the de Gaulle and Pompidou years was the constant presence of government ministers and majority party politicians and the virtual denial of access to the opposition and other figures hostile to those in power – trade unionists, for example. A corollary of Pompidou's 'disgrace' in 1968–69 was his disappearance from the TV screen for many months. Even pop singers with unorthodox political views suffered under this anathema – Jean Ferrat is the best-known example.[61]

Election campaigns are a special case, for the proper exercise of democracy is increasingly dependent on the fair access to all the media by all the possible candidates. (The important question of the effects of television on voting do not concern us here.) In France, considerable efforts have been made to ensure that campaign broadcasting is fairly distributed. However, these attempts have not always been successful, either because of the unfair use of the media in the immediate pre-campaign period, or because the system adopted was felt to favour certain parties at the expense of others.

France's first 'television election' was the October 1962 campaign for the referendum on the election of the president by universal suffrage. De Gaulle's television appearances had been gradually multiplying between 1958 and 1962. Shortly before the campaign, his use of the medium to influence the voters led to a protest strike by RTF journalists. Then in the campaign itself, political parties on the 'NO' side protested against the derisory ten minutes allotted them. Furthermore, their spokesmen were forced to broadcast live, although, unlike de Gaulle, most of them were inexperienced performers.[62] Already in this election, the commercial radio stations were providing the genuine public service which should have been RTF's.[63]

The 1964 statute had been claimed by the government as the beginning of a new independence and impartiality for ORTF. However, the local council elections in March 1965 showed that there was little improvement. Local elections have never been given television and radio coverage, mainly for practical reasons.[64] Thus it was all the more unfortunate that the government used its control of the media to bring its own party candidates into the limelight. It was during this campaign that the SLII drew up its list of towns to be reported on and towns to be ignored.[65]

The presidential election campaign later that same year was heralded by a series of programmes designed to 'prepare the population psychologically' for the right vote.[66] During the two-week official campaign itself, however, and in accordance with the Law of 6 November 1962, broadcasting time for candidates was shared out equally, two hours for each. Again there were complaints, about the live broadcasting rule and the refusal to allow opposition candidates to use certain filmed sequences in their support. For its later stages, a special control committee independent of both government and Office was set up to supervise the campaign. Its workings were generally felt to be satisfactory.[67]

Parliamentary election campaigns, because of the number of parties involved, are more difficult to regulate than presidential ones. A Bill adopted in 1966 for the campaign the following year is still in force. According to this Law, the majority party and the opposition may each have an hour and a half's broadcasting time, to be transmitted simultaneously on both media. Other parliamentary groups are requested to agree amicably amongst themselves, with the possibility of arbitration by the National Assembly *bureau* and the chairmen of the groups concerned. Non-parliamentary parties presenting at least 75 candidates are allotted seven minutes before the first ballot and five before the second.[68] The notion of equal time-sharing between the two major groups was widely criticized from the start.[69] In 1967, it would have given the two Gaullist parties the same time as the four main and several minor opposition parties. And on that occasion, de Gaulle's personal appeal to the nation on the eve of the election was heavily condemned.[70]

Later elections have followed similar patterns, with the media usually criticized for propaganda before the campaign and the latter itself carefully supervised by the independent committee of magistrates created in 1965. The referendum in 1969 on Senate and regional reform which led to de Gaulle's resignation was a peculiarly bad example. Alain Poher, the centre-party president of the Senate, pointed out the absurdity of a week's official equality for both sides preceded by two months of one-sided 'sledgehammering' (*matraquage*).[71] In the Senate (where the opposition were in the majority) members inveighed against constant references to regional reform. One 'independent' organization, the Centre for Civic Information, very frequently mentioned on television, even happened to have the same telephone number as the *ORTF* directors of regions.[72] Meanwhile, a survey showed that national television was the source of information the public most relied on concerning the proposed reforms.[73]

Faced with a presidential election almost immediately, and in the wake of such widespread dissatisfaction, Alain Poher, now interim President of the Republic, called the Administrative Council to order, and considered the possibility of turning the control commission for election campaigns into a permanent supervisory body for all political programmes. The Administrative Council then suspended all programmes likely to cause controversy, thus leaving the way open once more for the commercial stations to provide the political information the public needed.[74]

[141]

The parliamentary elections of 1973 were run on the same general lines as in 1967. Once again, certain parties were placed at a disadvantage by the law – the Reformers, in particular, who were a relatively recent political force and had few seats in Parliament. The special commission and the President-Director General of ORTF agreed in this case to bend the rules in the party's favour. Some other liberal measures were also taken: the Communist League was given a few minutes to present its case, though through some mistake its documents had not been received by the special committee. ORTF in any case felt it necessary to deny any responsibility for the broadcast campaign. The National Assembly itself drew up the list of parliamentary parties and allotted them time in proportion to the number of seats they held, while for the other groups a committee sat at the Ministry of the Interior. The *Office*'s role was merely to fix the times and details of programmes and to provide the technical means required.[75]

Election broadcasts went out on all three television channels and on the main radio network France-Inter at 8.30 p.m. There were three basic formats for programmes: the monologue or 'profession of faith'; the interview; and the dialogue between two party spokesmen.[76] This was more flexible than had previously been the case. However, the campaign could still be criticized for not properly informing the country about the real issues at stake.[77] And yet again, after the official campaign was closed, the President of the Republic made an *ex cathedra* appeal to the nation, to which no one was permitted to reply.

Further changes took place in 1974, with the presidential election following the death of Georges Pompidou. The control commission continued to supervise the campaign, under the general conditions laid down in 1962. Each candidate would have equal time before each ballot; the Minister for Information was responsible for deciding on the number, length and timing of programmes, and the order of appearance of candidates was to be decided by lot.[78] The commercial stations also announced that they would respect the rule of equality.[79] In practice, because of the number of candidates (12), each was allotted 65 minutes of both television and radio, instead of the two hours originally envisaged.

The official campaign was denounced as tedious, likely even to put voters off politics.[80] But this time the commercial stations succeeded in changing matters. Television debates between

François Mitterrand and Jacques Chaban-Delmas and between Mitterrand and Valéry Giscard d'Estaing were scheduled on Télé-Monte Carlo, to be broadcast simultaneously on the radio networks Europe 1 and Radio-Monte Carlo. After a personal struggle by the President of the *Office*, Marceau Long, the special commission agreed to the staging of a similar duel on national television, between the two remaining candidates for the second ballot. The 1½ hour debate was to count as 45 minutes out of each candidate's allocation.

In the event, on 10 May, Giscard d'Estaing and Mitterrand confronted each other, from 8.30 to 10 p.m., live, before an invited audience composed largely of journalists, control commission members and *ORTF* dignitaries. The chairpersons were Alain Duhamel, a freelance journalist and a regular chairman-interviewer on political programmes, and Jacqueline Baudrier, director of Channel One. Unlike the American television duels, in which journalists put questions, the two candidates debated directly with one another. The television audience was estimated at 23 million; the streets of Paris were deserted. Symbolic of the *Office*'s recapturing of a certain role from its commercial rivals, the presidential duel marked an important step forward. The campaign control committee, publishing its report for the first time, judged the media to have acted satisfactorily overall, and proclaimed the debate formula a success.[81]

Outside election campaigns, the access of politicians to the media has been a thorn in the side of government. The 1964 statute included a clause making it the duty of the Administrative Council to ensure that the major currents of thought and opinion were expressed on the air, and enjoining the government to label its own messages clearly as official communiqués. A Senate amendment which would have given other political parties the right to reply, based on the number of their parliamentary seats (as in Great Britain and other European countries) was rejected by the government as being an invitation to 'permanent contradiction'.[82] It was not until after the 1965 elections that interviews with political figures of all persuasions became a regular feature of French television.

In the absence of what the French call 'le fair-play', reform projects have consistently included calls for statutory guarantees: equal broadcasting time for all political parties and for trade

[143]

unions.[83] Until 1974, however, the government never included in its broadcasting Bills more than a general clause referring to freedom of expression. Whatever the motives of successive governments, it must be recognized that a legal right of access in a multiple-party system would indeed be difficult to organize. Nor would the allocation of a few minutes' 'party political broadcast' necessarily palliate the more important problem of overall fairness, especially in news and current affairs programmes.

General attempts have indeed been made to give regular broadcasting time to political spokesmen. After 1968, the government promised to make it easier for all politicians – including government ministers – to appear on television. To avoid the abuses of the past, ministers would now have to make their requests for television-time through the Secretary of State for Information and not directly to ORTF as previously.[84] A series of monthly debate programmes – 'Face à la presse', 'Face à face', 'Face au public', and 'Au fil de l'enquête' – were to be organized. There would also be a monthly programme of 20 minutes for political parties with seats in the National Assembly, and a three-monthly programme of 45 minutes for those socio-professional organizations represented on the Economic and Social Council.[85] However, these programmes were to be scheduled on Channel Two, which would exclude a large number of viewers.

Under Arthur Conte, political parties were given their own programme: 'La parole est aux grands partis politiques'. Originally a 15-minute programme every three months, for parties with at least 30 seats in Parliament, its rules were later revised to include parties with only 20 seats. Eight parties had qualified under the first ruling: the Democratic Centre, the National Independent Centre, the Communist Party, the Radical Socialists, the Socialist Party, the Progress and Modern Democracy Party, the Independent Republicans and the Union of Democrats for the Republic (UDR).[86] The programme was attacked by the opposition as a red-herring as long as news programmes proper went on being under government control; it would be yet another academic debate masking the real issues.[87]

Political debate programmes continued under Conte but with some changes. Conte, for example, took a more personal interest in such programmes, often inviting politicians himself without consulting producers.[88] And whereas formerly, when Desgraupes

had been head of news on One, the producers of the debate programme 'A armes égales' had had to inform the Prime Minister of
their projects, after Desgraupes' departure discussions took place
directly with Conte and with the director of the channel. Producers
wanted to have more freedom in the choice of participants: during
the pre-election period in 1973, the majority party more or less
chose whoever it wanted to send.[89] There were other problems,
too. In December 1972, President Pompidou is reputed to have
forbidden any more ministers to appear on 'A armes égales' after
Edgar Faure had performed badly against the Socialist Gaston
Defferre.[90] Maurice Clavel, a left-wing journalist, had caused a considerable stir in December 1971 by walking out of the studio during
the (live) discussion; this was in protest against the fact that the
producers had cut one important word from his film. Later, he
was not allowed to sell the film he had had made by *ORTF* as part
of the programme, but 21 copies of the films made for Peyrefitte
and Debré in similar circumstances had been sold by the *Office* to
the *UDR* party for use in the election capaign.[91] Quite apart from
these particular instances of unfair play, there was the general
danger of the debate formula: politics would come to be perceived as a duel between black and white, and, moreover, would
be presented as a purely parliamentary phenomenon, minister
against shadow minister, spokesman against spokesman. This was
even more true of 'La parole est aux grands partis politiques'.

Coupled with the demand for a right of access for all political
parties has been that of a right of reply for persons or groups who
consider themselves misrepresented on the air. Claiming that the
practical application of such a right would present insuperable
difficulties, governments for many years refused to extend to the
audiovisual media the Law of 29 July 1881 for the press. However,
other European countries – Italy and West Germany, for example
– had overcome the problems involved, as the *Diligent Report*
pointed out in 1968.[92] Indeed, by 1968, the Senate had already
made at least three attempts to introduce such a right in France.[93]
The *Paye Report* of 1970, while recognizing the practical difficulties – how to prove misrepresentation in the absence of written
documents, for example, how and when to present the reply, who
to judge the cases concerned – also called on the government to
act.[94] The combined influence of these reports (plus the *Le Tac
Report* in 1972), the example of foreign broadcasting systems, and

a number of incidents where such a right would have proved useful, eventually caused the government to change its mind.[95] A right of reply for 'physical persons' only was written into the 1972 statute. By 1974, the High Audiovisual Council had drawn up its text for an Act of Parliament.

At the same time, in 1974, the Council of Europe's Committee of Ministers gave its approval to a text which it was intended should serve as a basis for the right of reply to be separately organized by the 17 member states.[96] According to this ruling, any individual of whatever nationality or country of residence who claimed to have been misrepresented could demand to reply in the appropriate medium. This would provide effective recourse against publication of facts or opinions which constituted either an invasion of privacy or an attack on a person's dignity, honour or reputation. The rules could not be invoked to support an act of censorship. This decision is presumably binding on members and will lead to the institution of a right of reply in France before very long.

The effects of the reforms of 1974–75 on information programmes are as yet unknown. Obviously each separate programme company will now have its own news unit and its own current affairs programmes in competition with the others, and if the experience of 1969–72 is anything to go by this could lead to much greater independence. It is to be hoped that the two national channels do not polarize themselves completely into a 'right' and a 'left' channel, government and opposition. The heads of news so far appointed (in the autumn of 1974) show no great move away from the *status quo ante*. On radio, Michel Péricard, formerly on Channel One news, and a *UDR* supporter (criticized in March 1973 for the partisan manner in which he announced election results).[97] On *TF 1*, Henri Marque, former chief political editor of *RTL*, with, as chief news editor, Christian Bernadac, from Channel Three. On *Antenne 2*, Jacques Sallebert, ex-head of radio. On *FR 3* (which has only a 15-minute newscast at 10 p.m.), Claude Lefèvre, from the Regional Information Bureau at Nantes. Channel Three has already been announced as the 'films and free speech' channel, a formula which may represent an attempt to emulate the commercial stations, and which has already drawn ironic comments on its implications for the other two channels. The influence of the Ministry of the Interior (Home Office) has been remarked on in the choice of those to be responsible for news programmes.[98]

Some lessening of government control over news may be expected, if only because of the less stable political situation of the president with respect to Parliament. There is no longer a monolithic majority which can do as it likes with impunity. If this is true, and a 'depoliticization' of broadcast information were to take place, then French radio and television could turn its attention to those other problems of a news medium. What should be the balance between 'information' and 'entertainment', and can the two be separated? How can the public best be informed about and led to take an interest in politics? Are people underinformed about real issues and at the same time saturated with indigestible facts and opinions? Specialists have not neglected these issues, and the *Office* Research Service had sections working on them; but the central issue of political bias has forced such problems into the shadows of public debate in France.

PARTICIPATION

If democracy cannot survive without information, it also needs a sense of involvement. This can be active; that is, the genuine participation of citizens in decision-making or controls. Or – since not everyone can take an active part – it can be emotional, a sense that what is being done is for the citizen's benefit, by people like him who have him and the community, rather than their own interests, in mind. For a nation which tends to think of 'the State' as a distant and only partly benevolent force, broadcasting could provide a useful service, bringing men together and giving them some responsibility for the public service which affects their lives more profoundly than any other.

In France, this problem has three important facets. One is the active participation of ordinary citizens, viewers or listeners, in the shaping of broadcasting. It can, of course, be argued that the control of broadcasting institutions by a democratically-elected government is in itself sufficient guarantee of the 'democracy' of broadcasting. But, as we have seen, in France this control has generally meant exploitation by one political party, while Parliament has been ineffective to prevent this. To this onesidedness, the active involvement of viewers and listeners could provide a counterweight, as well as fostering a deeper sense of community in all concerned. A second aspect is regionalization. The extraordinary degree of centralization in the French apparatus of State has been both the latter's strength and its weakness. In broadcasting as in other fields, involvement is easier and more meaningful if it takes place at a regional or local level. And programmes must be provided which deal with regional problems and which call on talents from outside Paris. Thirdly, there have been a number of experiments with community television on a smaller, local scale, but, significantly perhaps, these have almost always been conducted outside the traditional structures of *ORTF*: by *OFRATEME*, for example, an offshoot of the Ministry of Education, and very recently by the new local cable television networks which are under the control of local town councils.

The active involvement of the viewer and listener in the workings of broadcasting institutions has been particularly weak in France, at least since the war. Indeed, the experience of the immediate prewar period is peculiarly instructive from this point of view. In the infant years of radio, listeners' associations flourished as early as 1924. Groups such as the *Fédération électrique de la Tour Eiffel*, the *Association des amis de la radiodiffusion de France*, used the money from membership fees to produce their own programmes.[99] In 1935, the pioneering Minister Georges Mandel promulgated two decrees giving listeners real powers of control over radio stations. First, associations were empowered to meet annually in order to elect ten representatives to the management councils: the latter administered the stations, recruited staff and organized programmes. At the same time, there was set up a central Higher Broadcasting Council composed of distinguished personalities from various fields. This was much more representative than any similar body created since.[100]

Unfortunately, this democratic system did not last. On the one hand, the State increasingly took control of radio, reducing the powers of the listeners almost to nothing by 1938. On the other hand, the listeners' associations became more and more politicized. In 1937, the two major groupings *Radio-Liberté*, which supported the Popular Front government, and *Radio-Famille*, in opposition, waged an entirely political struggle for control of the management councils. Early in 1938, the listeners' representatives on the Management Council of *Paris-PTT* station complained of cavalier treatment by the minister responsible for radio. The latter had not convoked the council until August, and it had met regularly only from September, although they had been elected the previous February for a one-year term of office. They also complained that control of programmes had been unlawfully removed from their jurisdiction.[101] Certainly the extraordinary tensions of the late 1930s were to some extent to blame. None the less, the unwillingness of French governments to delegate real power to the citizen, and the excessively political flavour attaching to the involvement of listeners, were more than temporary phenomena in a country 'where people believe they have no choice except between the State and control by political and union groupings, a synonym for misappropriation, irresponsibility, and incompetence'.[102]

It was not until 1964 that any further attempt was made to give the public a voice in the organization of broadcasting. On the Administrative Council, created that year, one member was henceforth to represent viewers and listeners. He was appointed by the government from a short-list drawn up by the viewers' and listeners' associations. Under the statute of 1972, this representation was increased to two persons, to be chosen by the cultural affairs committees of the National Assembly and the Senate. In 1974, the next logical step was taken: the viewers and listeners are now represented by a Member of Parliament, one on each company's Council.

Within an institution as highly centralized as ORTF before 1974, the problem of giving viewers and listeners adequate representation was obviously a difficult one. The most democratic method in theory would, of course, be to hold elections involving all holders of radio and TV licences. But a similar system which had been in use for social security had had to be abandoned because of the clumsiness of the procedure and the lack of interest among the electors. As Paye pointed out in 1970, such elections would probably meet with indifference on the part of those concerned and at the same time give rise to political squabbles unconnected with the real problems of broadcasting.[103]

Certainly the system as it existed before 1974 was unsatisfactory. One culprit was the government, which used its power to appoint the delegate concerned largely to its own advantage. Between 1964 and 1974, it constantly chose as viewers' representative Jean

Cazeneuve, a supporter of its policies, and a sociologist who has published several works on the media. In 1967, the viewers' association *Télé-Liberté* succeeded in removing Cazeneuve, but this was quite exceptional,[104] and in any case, Cazeneuve merely moved on to the Programme Committee instead. In 1972, the Cultural Affairs Committee of the National Assembly appointed Cazeneuve once more, though only 14 members out of 100 were present, and the new statute had not even officially yet been made law.[105]

The problem of representation also arises. The second viewers' delegate chosen in 1972 was a (right-wing) journalist, Georges Riond. And while no one could dispute Professor Cazeneuve's knowledge of the problems of the media, it is debatable whether a professional university sociologist could be regarded as a genuine representative of the general public. Indeed, Cazeneuve's 'official', non-ordinary status was consecrated in 1974 when he was appointed president of the new broadcasting company replacing TV Channel One. Nor did the viewers' delegates apparently make much attempt to involve in their task those they purported to represent. When in early 1973, Georges Riond announced his intention to call together representatives from various viewers' and listeners' groups to discuss broadcasting policy with them, this was the first time that even such a modest step had been taken.[106]

The failure has not only been the government's. The viewers' and listeners' associations have been mostly feeble and always unrepresentative. The only group of any size, *Télé-Liberté*, was founded in 1964. In 1967, it had 15,000 local members and 880,000 collective members through its connections with the unions and the Communist Party.[107] Because of its political affiliations, it has always been studiously ignored by government and *Office*. The other associations are mostly Catholic, and their membership and activities are often mysterious. Too frequently, their aims are political. An association entitled *Radio-Télé-Vérité*, founded in July 1972 by René Tomasini, a *UDR* member, announced its intention of 'grouping together those viewers and listeners favourable to the presidential majority'.[108]

ORTF made no attempt to encourage viewers' and listeners' associations. Arthur Conte, President-Director General, referring to the Administrative Council, is reputed to have said, 'I am the public.'[109] A recent Director of Public Relations at the *Office* dismissed the associations with a sneer. Georges Riond, writing in the *ORTF* handbook for 1973, calls for the associations to play a larger role, but the publication gives no membership figures nor addresses to which the reader could write if he wished to join.[110]

The only other organ within *ORTF* which gave some share of decision-making to the public was the programme committees. These were in fact composed of professionals from various spheres, but two from each committee (one for radio and one for television) were to belong to the central office of a viewers' and listeners' association. In 1971, three of these four were chosen from *Téléspectateurs et auditeurs de France*, a pro-government organization.[111] In practice, in any case, the programme committees, which the *Paye Report* saw as the descendants of the prewar listeners' councils, had by 1970 lost most of their power to influence programme policy.[112] And quite apart from the specific representation of viewers and listeners, neither the Administrative Council nor the programme committees could be said to reflect the diversity of the nation as a whole. Donald R. Browne assessed the situation in 1973:

> In sum, the administrative council of the *ORTF* appears to be of little significance where citizen involvement is concerned. It is doubtful whether many French citizens even know of its existence, since its activities are essentially private...its members are Parisians, and most of them appear to share the same political views...control of the *ORTF* appears to remain squarely in the hands of its Director General and a few French Cabinet officials.[113]

This contrasted unfavourably with the situation in Holland, West Germany and Great Britain.[114]

A number of reforms have been proposed in recent years by various groups hoping to make the Administrative Council a more representative body. The journalists on strike in 1968 wanted the council elected by a larger national council of 50 or 60 members, representing the press, viewers and the personnel, as well as the many political, economic, religious and cultural 'families' of the nation. The *Diligent Report* that same year wanted increased representation of viewers, of press and of personnel, and new representatives of categories such as journalists, producers, men from the world of the arts, and the university.[115] In

1970 the Communist Party proposed a Bill which would create a national society of radio and television with a 'democratic statute'; its council would include government delegates and 'authentic representatives' of Parliament, of viewers and listeners and of personnel.[116] René Schaefer, a member of the Programme Committee, writing in *Droit Social* in 1970, set out a more radical reform. Control of regional transmitters should be given to people in the regions concerned. Responsibility should be shared mainly between creators and users, and the latter would elect their representatives. Even if *ORTF* were not thus decentralized, the Administrative Council should be given back to creators and users. Representatives of the public could be elected in two stages, first regional election by all users and then election of council members by those chosen in the first ballot.[117]

Even with government support for such proposals, it would need some fundamental changes in public attitudes for them to take effect. The general public has been notably apathetic in its approach to broadcasting.[118] While it would be unjust to generalize too far, it does seem that there has been little of the grass-roots initiative which in Germany, Holland and North America, for example, has ensured a degree of public accountability. Not only in broadcasting but in other domains, local groups in France tend to divide and disunite rather than to meet together for a constructive purpose. At the same time, the professional and intellectual élites in France have long refused to take an interest in the new media: André Malraux as Minister of Culture is the most notorious example.[119] This has left the general public without leaders in the matter – or rather, with only politicians for leaders, the traditional objects of mistrust.

If there has been little progress towards public involvement in broadcasting structures, there has on the contrary been a considerable move towards regionalization. In this, broadcasting has been part of a wider initiative on the part of Fifth Republic governments to give increased powers to the regions, and to dam up the draining of talent into Paris which has been for centuries a feature of French political and cultural life. The setting up of regional economic advisory boards (*CODERS*), the priority given to the development of provincial cities, and the creation of the *Maisons de la Culture*, are all part of the same policy.

Early radio was, as we have seen, totally regional. Stations had names such as *Radio-Lyon, Radio-Toulouse, Radio-Normandie* and so on. In the regions, the management councils were genuinely regional bodies, composed of local representatives. The war put an end to all these stations. In 1945, the radio regions were reconstituted on the basis of the 1936 Ferrié plan, but with much less independence than previously.[120] Television, for obvious technical reasons, was from its beginnings much more centralized, and only very recently has any genuine regionalization taken place.

Encouragement of regional broadcasting has not always been pure of political intentions. When Alain Peyrefitte as Minister of Information expanded regional news services in 1963–65, creating 22 regional information offices (*Bureaux Régionaux d'Information*) under the central control of a delegate for the regions in Paris, his major and explicit aim was to provide de Gaulle and his government with a political counterweight to the regional press.[121] This now famous argument did not really hold water. On the one hand, the majority of the press was not hostile; indeed, a recent specialist has shown how increasing concentration of the press – in some cases reduced to one major daily per area – has led to a corresponding increase in political neutrality, especially on local issues.[122] On the other hand, while a man could choose whether or not to buy a newspaper, if he wanted the entertainment of television he had to pay his licence fee, whatever his politics. The use of regional news from 1963 onwards to serve the political aims of the party in power has been discussed earlier in this chapter. It remained one of the major scandals of the whole regionalization policy.

The *Diligent Report* in 1968 deplored this state of affairs and summed up regional development as basically unsatisfactory. Ten of the *BRIs* were located in the regional radio centres: Bordeaux, Dijon, Lille, Limoges, Lyons, Marseilles, Nancy, Rennes, Strasbourg and Toulouse. Twelve others were placed at Besançon, Amiens, Poitiers, Clermont-Ferrand, Nice, Rheims, Caen, Rouen, Orleans, Nantes, Le Mans and Montpellier. Each put out a 15-minute regional TV news bulletin six days a week at 7.40 p.m. Seven of these centres also put out half-hour weekly magazine programmes. At the regional radio centres, four radio news bulletins were broadcast daily; the other *BRIs* put out between one and three radio bulletins. Certain other local centres also broadcast news bulletins and there were 'artistic' programmes three evenings a week after 8.30 p.m. Each *BRI* had an average of nine journalists and cameramen.[123]

While recognizing that the *Office*'s financial difficulties had prevented it from carrying out its good intentions concerning regionalization, *Diligent* nevertheless made a series of recommendations and implied a number of criticisms. Regional stations must not become an exclusive tool of propaganda. The *Report* suggested that the stations have recourse to local newspapermen as political commentators. (This was unlikely to appeal to the authorities.) As far as culture was concerned, *Diligent* felt that better use should be made of existing local resources – provincial theatre groups, *Maisons de la Culture*, universities and so on – though they should beware of aiming only at a regional audience. Regional programme committees could be set up, and the *Report* noted that none of the members of the central *ORTF* programme committees was a provincial.[124] The present number of regional centres (ten) was probably too many. The *Report* suggested six or seven as the maximum which would ensure a proper use of resources. The organization of greater autonomy for the regions was a problem. *Diligent*'s solutions were hesitant, and involved the retention of a considerable degree of central control.[125]

The question of regional broadcasting became particularly topical in 1968–69. De Gaulle planned his referendum on regional administrative reform for April 1969. A working party was set up at the Ministry of Information to look into the development of regional language and culture programmes. There were calls for a third television channel, already technically possible in the Paris area, and the Secretary of State for Information promised one in the near future. A new *Maison de la Radio* was opened at Lyons in September 1968.[126] The lack of men and equipment in the regions became a subject for comment, and there was increasing awareness of competition from foreign television, for example in Alsace, where many viewers preferred the regional programmes provided by German TV.[127] In the regions themselves, there was dissatisfaction. On a visit to Brittany in February 1969, de Gaulle was met outside the *ORTF* building by demonstrators carrying slogans which attacked the *Office*. The Bretons also complained that the five-minute daily Breton-language programme on *Radio-Brest* was devoted for most of the week to a translation of *Robinson Crusoe*.[128] Meanwhile, the multiplication of official statements, and a sudden rush of new regional programmes (a series of regional 'days' on national radio, a Sunday afternoon television series on topics of regional interest, for example),[129] were denounced by the opposition as part of the government's propaganda for the April ballot.[130] Around the same time, regional news bulletins were increased to 20 minutes daily.[131]

While discussion continued around the technical possibilities and cultural purposes of a third television channel, the *Paye Report* in June 1970 came down heavily in favour of regionalization as the primary motive which should lie behind any extension of *ORTF* services. The *Report* deplored the progressive centralization of radio programmes and noted the BBC's recent development of local radio. It pointed out the disadvantages of the existing system, in which regional programmes cut into national programmes at specific times of the day. This had satisfied no one, neither the regional stations, nor the director of radio in Paris, nor the public. Regional radio and television were already working in close conjunction – they used the same journalists, for example – and *Paye* hoped this would be pursued even further rather than regional radio being joined more closely to radio in Paris.[132]

The major innovation, however, and the one which made the headlines, was *Paye*'s suggestion of a totally regional third television channel. A whole chapter of the *Report* was devoted to an examination of the various forms such a channel might take. The need for another channel was evident. It would provide greater choice in peak-hours, and thus end the 'cultural ghetto' – 'difficult' programmes put out after 10 p.m. It would solve the dilemma of whether channels should be competitive or complementary, and begin a new era in which a multiplicity of publics could be catered for rather than the 'average viewer' at whom programmes were at present aimed. It would parry competition from foreign television and from the commercial television stations such as Télé-Monte Carlo. It would give a welcome boost to the development and sales of colour television in France and to the electronics industry as a whole.[133]

All those questioned by the commission had been in agreement: the third channel must be regional. Not only did France need cultural decentralization at all levels, but a new national channel could well prove a failure. Five years after its beginnings, Channel Two had still only captured 20–30 per cent of the viewing audience.

Regionalization, furthermore, must mean regional production both for regional transmission and for broadcasting on the national networks, the latter not only for the sake of quality but also as a sound economic policy.[134]

There was no such unanimity when it came to the practical problem of organizing a regional channel. *Paye* considered in some detail four separate solutions. The first was the proposal agreed upon in February 1970 by the Transmissions Committee of the Sixth Plan, and already under consideration by *ORTF*. This project, which would create a third channel entirely within the existing structure, had the advantage of being relatively cheap, but would present serious problems of organization and perhaps act as an insufficient stimulus to competition between 'creative centres'. A second solution was, at the other extreme, a single commercial channel: *Paye* examined several such projects (*Canal 10* for example), and rejected them on the grounds of the commission's attachment to the monopoly.

Two other solutions were more in the nature of compromises between private and public systems. One, on the lines of ITV in Great Britain but incorporating the recommendations of the *Pilkington Report*, comprised a number of private regional companies held together by a national company with mixed private and public capital (*société d'économie mixte*). Again, *Paye* rejected this as incompatible with the monopoly. Finally it examined a federation of public-owned regional stations administered either independently from *ORTF* or as one affiliate among a number of such companies grouped under *ORTF* as a 'holding' company. *Paye* much preferred this last solution.[135] However, the government chose the first. Channel Three began broadcasting in 1973 as an integral part of *ORTF*, to be reconstituted as a separate company in 1975, in a system not identical with but much nearer to *Paye*'s.

It is perhaps worth looking at the situation of regional broadcasting in 1971, before the creation of the third channel, which was due to begin transmission on 31 December 1972. On television, there was a daily 20-minute evening news bulletin at 7 p.m., which went out (for technical reasons) simultaneously on both channels. The audience was estimated at ten million. Two evenings a week there were regional programmes: on Monday, a separate programme for each region – drama, music, poetry or varieties;

on Friday, one region's programme shown on all stations at once, or an inter-regional discussion. There were ten weekly regional magazine programmes put out at lunchtime on Saturdays, plus four weekly sports programmes. In the regional languages the achievement was unpromising: a total of ten hours in the whole year, made up of fortnightly magazine programmes of a quarter of an hour each in Alsatian, Breton and Basque.

The total volume of regional television production in 1971 was 2,617 hours, about the same volume as Channel Two. On radio, 13,645 hours' programmes were composed of a variety of productions designed for both the regional and national audience. During most of 1971 there were three daily news bulletins totalling 80 minutes; an extra ten minutes of 'practical' news – weather, road conditions, situations vacant – was added in October at 6.20 p.m., and the midday bulletin was extended. In some areas there were regional language broadcasts: a weekly hour and a daily ten minutes of Breton; a weekly hour of Occitan; a weekly half-hour and a daily five minutes of Basque; a considerable amount in the Alsatian dialect, spread throughout that region's local programmes.[136]

Regional broadcasting, though it had increased in volume over the years, was still felt to be largely unsatisfactory. In the Alsace region in particular, French programmes had nothing like the success of German ones (which most of the population were able to receive). Both the French government and the local councils of towns such as Strasbourg, Colmar and Mulhouse were felt to be to blame for this neglect of local culture. But in all the regional stations, lack of money, and hence lack of staff and equipment, frustrated efforts to improve the programmes. News bulletins suffered not only from political pressures but from practical limitations. Thus, in the absence of newsfilm agencies and with inadequate equipment for outside video-recording, only the most predictable of events could be covered. This was another reason for the preponderance of speechdays, official openings and so on. Nor were programmes put out at hours which might have ensured them a good audience.

Meanwhile, continuing administrative centralization – the overall responsibility for the regions still lay in Paris – was naturally a hindrance to the development of any real feeling that the regional programmes belonged to the regions themselves. The stations were felt as offshoots from Paris. Even worse, for journalists and producers, they were places one might be apprenticed to before promotion to the capital, retired to when too old to be of use in Paris, or exiled to in cases of unorthodoxy.[137]

Between 1971 and the beginning of 1975, when the regions were reorganized along with everything else, two major innovations took place. One was Channel Three, which as *Paye* had suggested was given a largely regional flavour. The other was the creation of new radio programmes in urban centres; one hesitates to describe the result as 'local radio'.

After a number of years of 'Holiday Radio' (*Radio-Vacances*) from tourist centres in the summer months, and motorists' radio (*radioguidage*) on Sundays, it was decided to set up a full-time local radio service on medium-wave in the Paris region. Known as *FIP 514* (*France-Inter-Paris* plus the wavelength), the programme began in January 1971, with a catchment area of about 45 miles' radius. The formula proved successful. As *France-Inter-Vacances*, it was given five weeks' trial on a national scale that summer. Throughout 1972, new local radios were created on the same model: at Marseilles in April, Rheims and Nancy in May, Bordeaux in October and Lyons a month later.[138] Further stations were planned at Dijon, Limoges, Grenoble, Rouen-Le Havre, Rennes and Montpellier-Nîmes.[139]

Designed to 'make easier the daily life of an essentially urban public', *FIP* is in direct contact with local services such as the prefect's offices, traffic control, leisure facilities and so on. Its formula has been carefully concocted to create 'a climate of intimacy and a holiday atmosphere'. Briefly, this means three minutes of news and practical information, presented in a 'pleassantly cynical' manner, or with 'sophisticated irony', over a background of 60 minutes of music. Each hour contains 45 per cent jazz, blues and varieties, 20 per cent classical music, 12 per cent 'foreign songs', 10 per cent folk music and 8 per cent 'French songs'.[140] It is true that *FIP* and its provincial cousins were not just imitations of the commercial radio stations, and that one could (at a pinch) indeed describe their function as that of a 'town-crier'.[141] However, far from fostering any new consciousness of community, their role seems more one of lulling the citizen through his daily struggle with traffic jams, small ads and cinema queues. The *ORTF* handbook presents this as a virtue:

FIP, a radio one hears but doesn't listen to, a radio which 'allows you to do something else', as its inventors define it. Moreover, motorists apart, most of its audience is made up of students, managers and executives. 'You can work with *FIP* on', they say.[142]

According to one commentator, *FIP* is the radio of tomorrow, functional, concerned mainly with trivia.[143] For others, it is a betrayal of the cultural role of radio.[144] When *FIB* (*FIB*ordeaux) replaced France-Culture on VHF in the Bordeaux area, the Director of Radio discounted protests as the reaction of the 'intellectual ghetto'. According to him, *FIB* provided essential competition against the local commercial stations, Sud-Radio and Atlantique 2000. He was, none the less, obliged to let France-Culture continue, on a different transmitter. Similar protests were heard at Rheims and Nancy.[145] In spite of its popular success[146] and its usefulness as a vehicle for practical information, one has only to reflect on the possibilities of local radio as a catalyst for community life to find the *FIP* formula rather a saddening one.

The creation of a third television channel involved regionalization on quite a different scale. This was not, however, the only motive on the part of the government. Sales of television sets had stopped increasing as early as 1965, before the normal point of saturation and earlier than is usual in developed countries.[147] Colour television sets were not selling as well as had been hoped. In this context, a third channel was to do for television what colour had failed to achieve and what the introduction of VHF normally does for radio: provide a boost to public interest and to the industries concerned. National prestige was also involved. France would be the only country to run three national public service channels, while the third channel would, more specifically, fight off foreign competitors on the nation's borders.[148] However, the project was an expensive one. Technically possible as early as 1968, and originally planned to begin in October 1970,[149] Channel Three had to be postponed until December 1972 for lack of funds.

At its beginning on New Year's Eve 1972, Channel Three covered the Paris region, the north, the east, and Alsace, about 26 per cent of the population. By January 1974, this figure was to be increased to 50 per cent and by December 1975 to 80 per cent, by a series of steps: the Marseilles-Avignon region in July 1973,

Lyons in September 1973, Bordeaux-Toulouse in November 1973, Rennes and Nantes in January and February 1974. Whereas Channel One had taken twelve years to cover the territory and Channel Two eight, Channel Three would be finished in five.[150] Its programmes go out in colour on 625 lines, and many viewers in the right areas who can already receive Channel Two can receive Three without set-adjustment. To begin with, programmes are concentrated in the peak-hours between about 6.30 p.m. and about 10 p.m., which is the time when more choice was felt to be needed, and the evening's viewing starts slightly earlier than on the other channels, since in the provinces people come home from work more quickly.[151]

The regional radio and TV news stations were, as we have seen, badly underequipped. For Channel Three, TV production centres had to be created in the regions more or less from scratch. The first of these were Lille and Marseilles, followed by Lyons in 1973. Other centres were to follow gradually – Toulouse, Bordeaux, Nantes and so on.[152] In 1973, the regional stations produced about one-third of Channel Three's total programme output; the rest was made up of 30 per cent *ORTF* production from Paris and 40 per cent external production (purchases and co-productions).[153] There were no commercials, and no lady announcers (*speakerines*): this helped to give the channel a new look. News programmes were, in the beginning at least, to be produced in conjunction with the France-Inter radio network, but 60 per cent of the newsfilm used was shot by the regional news centres themselves.[154]

After only two years in operation, Channel Three's achievement, or contribution to regional development, cannot be fairly assessed. Some of the problems faced by the regional production centres, however, became clear fairly soon. Lille had been chosen as one of the first regional centres: the region was flat, heavily populated, and exposed to competition from Belgian television and *RTL*. The introduction of Channel Three gave the city and its surroundings a welcome intellectual stimulus: television men succeeded in making contact with local actors, journalists, authors and so on. On the other hand, it was difficult to persuade staff to move to Lille. In December 1972, shortly before the centre's programmes were to go on the air, several dozen out of a total of 115 technical and production posts were still vacant. Furthermore, equipment promised by Paris did not always arrive. There were not really enough qualified people in the area, and although the whole process of production from conception to finished programme took place at Lille, men often had to be borrowed from Paris.[155]

More money, more equipment, and (most important) a greater degree of autonomy: these are what Channel Three needs in order to fulfil its task as a truly regional channel. Clearly the new channel was launched at a time when ORTF could ill afford such a grandiose venture.[156] And the centralizing force of Paris remained a heavy burden on regional staff. The head of Channel Three had his offices in Paris. For the official opening of the Marseilles centre, Paris sent its own journalists down to read the evening news on Three. The regional stations had no programme committees, reading committees or administrative councils of their own.[157] Indeed, a parliamentary report in 1973 claimed that Channel Three had decreased the powers of regional directors even further. The latter had lost control of news services in 1963, and now had their financial, technical and administrative responsibilities removed as well.[158] Thus while it is true that regional programmes had been much improved and increased, and that the regions were now far more directly involved with production, the ideal of regionalization advocated by the *Paye Report* in 1970 was far from being attained. If about half the population could receive Channel Three in January 1974, only about one-twelfth were regular viewers.[159]

Apart from Channel Three, there had been some other improvements in regional broadcasting since 1971. According to the 1973 handbook, the volume of programme hours had increased from 2,615 to 2,856 for television (excluding Three) and from 12,291 to 16,431 for radio.[160] Regional languages had been given more time on the air, though in some cases the increase was negligible. There were only 16 hours of television in Breton in 1973. In February 1974, Breton nationalists blew up a television transmitter, partly to call attention to the lack of Breton-language programmes.[161] In the Alsatian dialect, there was one hour on radio and two hours' bilingual programme weekly, plus a monthly 45-minute television programme on Channel Three. In Basque, there was 5 minutes daily and a 30-minute weekly magazine programme, both on radio (no increase since 1971). In Occitan, there were two weekly radio programmes of 16 minutes and one hour each from Toulouse and Montpellier. New languages had been added: there was now 5 minutes daily and 15 minutes weekly of Catalan (on radio) from Perpignan and Montpellier; 5 minutes daily and 30 minutes weekly in Provençal (on radio) from Marseilles; thrice-weekly 5-minute radio bulletins in Corsican and some sequences in Corsican in the weekly regional TV magazine programme; a weekly 5-minute radio bulletin in Béarnais from Pau.[162]

The reorganization of 1974–75 will make some difference to regional broadcasting. Channel Three and the regional radio stations (plus the overseas stations on French territories) are now combined into one new programme company, FR 3. This has already been earmarked as the channel for 'free speech and the cinema'. The new statute set up advisory regional committees in each regional centre. These were to include representatives of the main currents of thought and the principal social, cultural and economic forces of the particular region. One-third of the members were to be locally-elected officials (mayors or councillors) chosen by the local councils. An amendment which would have given these committees independent resources was quashed at the Bill's second reading.

In 1975, the regions were to produce an estimated 2,839 hours of programmes, to be televised on FR 3. The 23 regional TV news bulletins would continue as before to go out at 7.20 p.m. on all networks. There would be regional magazine programmes, produced in the 11 regional centres, every Monday, Wednesday and Friday on FR 3 from 8 to 8.30 p.m. The regions in which these programmes would be seen were to be redrawn into seven areas, some larger than before: North-Picardy, Paris-Normandy-Centre, Rennes-Brittany-Loire Valley, Marseilles-Provence-Côte d'Azur, Nancy-Strasbourg, and two new regions, Limoges-Toulouse (the south-west) and Lyons-Dijon (Burgundy). The regional television production centres, created for what was Channel Three, at Lille, Lyons, Marseilles, and so on, would be used either for the production of the regional magazines, or for FR 3's own internal production, or as a 'supplier', in competition with the national production company in Paris.[163]

National broadcasting in France has been criticized for its 'Parisianized', middle-class view of culture, its neglect of certain sections of the public, and its virtual denial of access to those outside the charmed circles of the intellectual or entertainment élites. With the development of the new audiovisual technology – cheap, light video cameras, simpler methods of playback and above all, video-cassettes and the multiple-channel cable TV systems – all this cannot but change. Apart from its research service, *ORTF* itself, clinging like a barnacle to its monopolies of transmission and programme planning, has not, by and large, done much to foster this transformation. Other agencies, some government-backed, some private, with or without commercial motives, have shown a lot more initiative. However, the French situation presents its own particular difficulties, and in general, France's audiovisual revolution still lags behind that of other developed countries.

One of the earliest examples of the use of television both to reach a specific public and to foster changes of attitude through information and debate was the scheme known as *Télépromotion rurale*, begun in 1966 in the west of France. Launched by a government agency, the *Délégation générale à la promotion sociale* (General Delegation for Social Advancement) with the help of *ORTF* and the Ministry of Agriculture, *TPR* was planned to help French farmers adjust to the modernization of agriculture as well as to a modern world which had to some extent left them behind. The television programmes, broadcast by *ORTF* on both channels, but produced by special groups helped by farmers' organizations, were often watched collectively in a rural centre where they could be followed by debate and discussion. Printed materials were used to back up the programmes. The scheme eventually spread to the rest of France and is still in operation. However, it appears to have lost some of its impetus. This may be due to the simple fact of having fulfilled at least part of its mission: the agricultural world has perhaps outgrown its need. The growth of TV ownership has been, paradoxically, a handicap, for farmers are no longer so willing to turn out for a discussion when they can see the programme at home. More significantly, and a lesson perhaps for later experiments, farmers feel they have not been sufficiently involved in the production of programmes, nor in the administration of the scheme, which retained a certain 'night-school' flavour.[164]

Since 1968, there has been a growing trend towards experiment in the use of video techniques in various social contexts. Many of these experiments have been extremely short-lived – a week, perhaps, during a festival or local crisis – and not all have been equally successful. Initiatives have come from all possible sources: the Ministry of Cultural Affairs, which encouraged a travelling theatre company to expand into the Communications Techniques Workshop; the French League of Education; political organizations and notably the trade unions, with *CREPAC* (Research Centre for Permanent Education and Cultural Action), which in 1969 formed its own production company, *Scopcolor*; *ORTF*'s research service; small groups of private persons interested in video for political action; and local town councils such as Chatou, near Paris, which in April 1973 produced a town video-magazine, recorded on video-cassettes and financed entirely by local commercial interests rather like a kind of local newspaper.[165]

Among the most ambitious experiments in social action through video have been those of the *ORTF* research service. Some involved communication between warring groups, or groups that rarely confront one another. At Rheims, for example, in conjunction with the local cultural centre, architects and public were brought together by means of interviews recorded in front of certain groups of buildings: these interviews and a film made at the same time formed the starting-point of a public debate. At Carpentras near Avignon in 1972 a number of different experiments took place: the inhabitants of a new housing complex were recorded in groups discussing their views, on the basis of an *ORTF* programme dealing with public administration; there was an attempt to solve a conflict between a local village council and its cultural centre, by enabling each side to make a film expressing its viewpoint and then showing it to the opposition; the research service also attempted (with limited results) to televise a meeting of the municipal council; and local groups were given the opportunity to make their own films and reportages. The research service drew a number of lessons from these experiments. On the one hand, the latter were novelties, and caused too much disturbance in the town; this led to a certain lack of perspective. On the other hand, the population of Carpentras did not really become very involved in what was happening. The reasons suggested were complex: the atmosphere of the festival during

which the experiments took place; the refusal of the middle classes
to be stirred out of their peaceful existence; the habits of passivity
fostered by traditional television; the fear of being guineapigs;
the uneasiness of the local authorities when faced with the prospect
of an increase in 'citizen power'; the absence of a permanent
audio-visual centre; and the presence of 'outsiders', that is, the
ORTF researchers and the community workers involved in the
experiment. A longer experiment – three weeks in all – in a housing estate in the suburbs of Toulon, where the residents were
encouraged to record and talk out the problems of living in a
complex without shops, cafés or parks, was more successful,
probably because of its length.[166] However, these and other
experiments are extremely valuable, for the research service has
been constructively self-critical, and careful in drawing its conclusions.

It seems clear from these and other experiences that only a
permanent audiovisual centre can have long-lasting or significant
effects within a community. For this purpose, the cabling of a
whole town or residential quarter is essential. Cable television networks already exist in France in places where traditional reception
is poor, but community television on the lines of certain Canadian
experiences, for example, is still very much in its infancy. In
March 1972, the government set up the *Société française de télédistribution* (*SFT*: French Cable Television Company), owned
jointly by ORTF and the Ministry of Posts. This company was
given overall responsibility for the early development of cable
television in France. In November that year, a report made by
Maurice Bujon, a newspaper director, for the ORTF Administrative Council made a number of recommendations. ORTF alone
could not take on financial responsibility for the proposed new
networks. The government should issue decrees specifying the
composition of the local companies empowered to run cable
systems, and the length of the breach of the ORTF monopoly to
be envisaged (Bujon suggested 15 years). It should also regulate
the financial and technical aspects of the new technology. So far,
no legal texts have been issued; in January 1974, the Pompidou
government intended to follow the progress of the experimental
systems for about two years before committing itself to legislation.[167]

The names of the seven towns selected as pioneers for cable

television were announced in 1973 with the creation of the High Audiovisual Council. The choice of towns was directed by several motives. Grenoble and Créteil have large new housing developments in which cables can be laid from the start. Cergy-Pontoise is a new town in the Paris area. Nice and Chamonix were chosen as international tourist centres. Rennes already has the Centre for Television and Telecommunications Studies, while Metz is a frontier town in which cable TV would provide foreign television as well as possible local programmes.[168]

At Grenoble, in a large new housing complex known as La Villeneuve, an experimental audiovisual centre has been in operation since October 1972. This scheme was financed jointly by the local authorities and the national Fund for Cultural Aid (*Fonds d'Intervention Culturelle*); its aim was to provide the facilities for an experiment in genuine community television. The major activity so far has been the production of a half-hour-long video news magazine which appears twice monthly. The residents suggest topics, usually of local interest, and it was hoped that they would also make the recordings: so far, however, most of the filming and montage has been done by the small team of professionals. The magazine was shown on a communal screen in the community centre as well as (collectively) in separate apartment blocks. The cable system at La Villeneuve has not yet got under way. Indeed, at the end of the experimental phase of the Audiovisual Centre, in the summer of 1974, the future of the latter was still unclear. About 2½ million francs' worth of equipment, paid for by the Cultural Affairs Ministry and the Grenoble city council, with some help from the Ministry of Education, was expected to be provided, though not all of this would be for the use of the video magazine or for community action. For the cable system, there were legal and administrative problems, as well as financial ones: the annual budget, estimated at 1 million francs, could not be found from subsidies alone, and it was feared that the introduction of private capital might interfere with the centre's objectives.

Whatever the problems, the experiment has again been a valuable one. In particular, it forced *ORTF* to define its position on cable television. Furthermore, it brought into the open the problem, common to most similar projects, of striking a balance between the work of a small activating group with independent resources, and the needs of a local television system, which requires a considerable budget and hence runs the risk of either becoming institutionalized or of being taken over by private finance.[169]

Créteil, a new town of 40,000 people added to an old one, has also had its problems. A 16-channel cable network is being laid in the new housing developments. This will be run by a mixed economy company (*société d'économie mixte*) composed of SFT (34 per cent), local councils (33 per cent) and certain private companies (33 per cent). There may later be shares for the Paris and local press. Each household will pay 150 francs to be connected to the network and an annual rental of 160 francs: these figures have been described as unrealistically low.[170] Three kinds of programmes are planned, lasting from 4 to 14 hours daily: a 'background', FIP-style, with local news and small ads, etc.; reportages on the town and its institutions; and more traditional programmes but with a local flavour. Channels may also be hired out to other producers, such as the university or the labour exchange, at a charge of between 75 and 130 francs an hour.[171] In early 1974, ORTF programmes were already being transmitted, but the local programme, scheduled to begin in the autumn of that year, ran into financial problems and consequent delays.[172]

At Nice, in June 1974, the cable system was waiting to be installed. Viewers – 55,000 eventually – would be given not only much better reception than in the past, but a choice between three ORTF channels, Télé-Monte Carlo, two Italian channels, six VHF radio programmes and their local television. The connection fee would be 100 or 200 francs and the annual rental 300 francs. The main problems are financial and administrative. A mixed economy company was set up by the town council, SFT, and the local daily paper, *Nice-Matin*. Under existing regulations, the network reverts to the Minister of Posts after 15 years; hence some reluctance on the part of the financial partners. Furthermore, the network can only succeed with good local programmes and local advertising, and this needs the co-operation of the local newspaper; the latter, however, is afraid of losing money. The local council fears it may have to underwrite more than 50 per cent of the capital of the new company.[173]

The possibilities of cable television appear to be enormous: a new forum, a direct dialogue between citizen and citizen, a remedy for all the ills of an over-urbanized society. In France, however, a long tradition of centralized government and State-controlled broadcasting adds to the legal, administrative, financial and political problems found elsewhere. Some observers are already pessimistic. Who will run the networks? Who will pay for them or reap the profits? Will the local political machine be less tempted than the national one to abuse its powers? Will the rich, who can afford the rental, once more be favoured at the expense of the poor? Or the towns, to the detriment of the country-side? Will everyone eventually drown in a flood of meaningless audiovisual stimuli?[174] For the moment, cable TV in France awaits its legal statute; it is to be hoped that government and local authorities will give the new technology the careful consideration it deserves.

Conclusion

Any summing-up of the effects of the reform of broadcasting which took place in January 1975 can still only be tentative. Political pressures seem to be much eased under the new regime; however, major problems exist in other areas, and there are fears that in some ways the quality of broadcasting is suffering.

From the early days of the new system, President Giscard d'Estaing stressed his intention to guarantee the independence of broadcasting from government control. In an interview on national radio, for example, he deliberately rejected the Pompidolian concept of broadcast journalism. Journalists working in radio and television were henceforth to be considered as no different from their colleagues in the press: the successors of *ORTF* were not to be thought of as the 'voice of France'. Giscard wanted 'independence' and 'quality' to be the keywords of the new networks. There was to be no censorship. A few days later, in mid-January, the new presidents of the programme companies received a letter from the head of state: the government would interfere neither in their management nor in their treatment of news. The companies were to think of themselves as similar to newspapers. Their presidents were confirmed in office until the end of 1977 in the first instance.[1]

News programmes are generally considered to be much improved since January 1975. More politicians and public figures of all persuasions appear on debate and discussion programmes than ever before. The fifteen-minute soapbox programme (at 7.40 p.m. each weekday on *FR 3*) in which groups of all kinds – political parties, religious and intellectual 'sects' – present their case appears to have proved successful, though its impact is reduced by the channel's small audience and the meagreness of the technical resources put at the groups' disposal. (A special independent committee composed largely of judges and magistrates was set up to assist the channel's Administrative Council in drawing up lists of suitable groups and to advise on format and on possible legal problems.) A decree setting up a right of reply for persons who consider themselves slandered or misrepresented by the media seems at last to be emerging from a long gestation.[2] This right will be confined to 'physical persons' (i.e. not groups or parties) and to national broadcasting (i.e. not the commercial stations). Furthermore, sensitive topics such as abortion, contraception, homosexuality and race relations have been discussed more freely and in more depth.

Even in this much improved area, there remain some reasons for dissatisfaction. Opposition politicians would like the right to reply with equal time to the President's frequent television addresses to the nation. Certainly it can be argued that in this case only the style – intimate fireside chats as opposed to the formal speeches of De Gaulle – has changed. Again, new government instructions regarding the 'minimum programme' to be broadcast in times of strike have increased that minimum to the point of almost completely neutralizing the effect of any strike action. The Council of State has further ruled that not only news but 'entertainment' and 'culture' must also be provided, in accordance with the functions of national broadcasting as set out in its statute.[3]

The most serious problem is, however, financial. None of the programme companies was given what it considered it needed to balance its budget in 1975. TF 1 has had to obtain a bank loan of eight million francs; FR 3 has announced reductions in output for the summer of 1975 and increased use of repeats. There have even been rumours that these two channels might be obliged to merge. According to the president of the SNRT union, the programme companies' total deficit in 1975 could be as much as 400 million francs – three times the amount of the 'hole' which led ostensibly to the reform in the first place.[4] In any case, the *cahiers des charges*, which define each company's obligations and resources, though promised for mid-December 1974, were not finally made public until the end of the following April. This meant that not only could no definite budgets be drawn up, but also that the programme companies were for some months unable to place firm orders with the national production company. Meanwhile the transmission company has its own problems: changing TF 1 over to colour will involve, as a temporary measure, the reduplication of all its programmes and their simultaneous transmission in both colour and black and white. This project alone could cost 400 million francs.

These financial difficulties have a number of repercussions. For reasons of economy, channels are putting out an ever-increasing volume of cinema films, imported serials and live talk shows. This has caused not only an outcry from the ailing cinema industry, but serious difficulties for production staff trained to work in television. Half of the three hundred or so regular TV producers are out of work (in March 1975) and the position of actors and musicians is if anything worse: this in spite of an enormous increase in the volume of programmes transmitted. Television drama was drastically reduced in comparison with 1974. The conditions of work in the production sector had deteriorated. According to the *SFRT* union, the number of days allotted for the making of a major documentary was 77 days in 1971, 50 days in 1973 and only 26 in early 1975. Teams had been reduced in size and in some cases the 'producer' completely eliminated. In the last week of January 1975 (admittedly part of a difficult, transitional period for the new system), $17\frac{1}{2}$ out of 21 peak viewing hours was composed of American material. The unions, in short, fear that the new system means the death-knell of a creative and truly national broadcasting service.[5]

There remains, too, the fear of going commercial. With their budgets now partly dependent on the ratings (the 'applaudimeter'), the companies have already indulged in some skirmishing over audience figures. A plan put forward in early 1975 by the head of *Antenne 2* to sell morning viewing time to various professional, administrative and commercial organizations for the purposes of public information or staff training was vetoed by the government: it was felt that clandestine advertising was too obvious a danger. For the moment, a fourth television network is impossible, since the only available channel is to be used for TF 1's colour programme. However, the difficulties of the national production company could prove insuperable. And if the latter were to go private, the programme companies would indeed – as the unions claim is already happening – become no more than transmission agencies, choosing the cheapest and most popular programmes from a totally private production sector.

The outlook, then, is still unsettled. One can only hope that habits of independent reporting and free discussion will establish themselves too firmly to be given up for a mere change of President, and that the financial crisis can somehow be resolved without further damage to France's national networks.

Notes

CHAPTER ONE

1. *Loi du 30 juin 1923.*
2. *Décret du 24 novembre 1923; décret-loi du 28 décembre 1926.*
3. Philippe Amaury, *Les deux premières expériences d'un 'Ministère de l'Information' en France* (1969), pp. 397–398.
4. *La radio a 50 ans* (1972), p. 62; B. Favreau, *Georges Mandel, un clémenciste en Gironde* (1969), pp. 189–190.
5. Benjamin Huc and François Robin, *Histoire et dessous de la radio en France et dans le monde* (1938), pp. 168ff.
   Amaury, op. cit., p. 398, gives the proportion of elected representatives as one-third. The official texts are the *décrets du 12 octobre 1934* and *du 13 février 1935.*
6. *Décret du 13 octobre 1938.*
7. *Décrets-lois du 29 juillet 1939* and *du 1er septembre 1939.*
8. For all this section on the Vichy years, see Amaury, op. cit., pp. 409ff.
9. *Actes dits lois du 1er octobre 1941* and *du 7 novembre 1942.*
10. *Ordonnance du 23 mars 1945.*
11. Robert Chapuis, *L'Information* (1959), p. 189.
12. Jacques Thibau, *Une télévision pour tous les Français* (1970), p. 77.
13. Chapuis, op. cit., p. 118; André Roche and René Bailly, *Le Dictionnaire de la télévision* (1967), p. 91.
14. Jean Thévenot and Jean Queval, *T.V.* (1957), p. 163.
15. Ibid., pp. 154ff.
16. Ibid. pp. 178ff.
17. René Blanckeman, *Le roman vécu de la télévision française* (1961), p. 117.

18. Jean-Guy Moreau, *Le règne de la télévision* (1967), p. 35.
19. Étienne Lalou, *Regards neufs sur la télévision* (1957), p. 164.
20. Thomas Cadett, in *The Listener*, 20 February 1958, p. 309.
21. George A. Codding Jnr., *La radiodiffusion dans le monde* (1959), p. 45.
22. Cf. Gérard Rateau, 'L'autonomie financière et la publicité', in *Droit Social*, No. 12, December 1970, p. 106.
23. Lalou, op. cit., p. 162.
24. Cadett, in *The Listener*, loc. cit.
25. Chapuis, op. cit., p. 104, note 1.
26. Ibid., p. 103.
27. Ibid., p. 104. Cf. Jean Montaldo, *Tous coupables* (1974), pp. 19–118, on control of broadcasting in the Fourth Republic.
28. Henri Spade, *Histoire d'amour de la télévision française* (1968), pp. 127–128.
29. Chapuis, op. cit., p. 103, note 2; Thibau, op. cit., p. 84.
30. 'L'information, clef de la démocratie', in *Revue française de science politique*, No. 1, January–July 1951, p. 35.
31. Spade, op. cit., p. 74. However, in 1959, 'news' and 'entertainment' each constituted 29 per cent of a 53-hour week's viewing (Joffre Dumazedier, in *Vers une civilisation du loisir?* (1962), pp. 153ff.)
32. Cadett, in *The Listener*, loc. cit.
33. René Bernard, 'Comment fonctionne cette inconnue, la RTF?', in *La Nef*, No. 8, October–December 1961, pp. 27–33. The advertising agent referred to is Marcel Bleustein-Blanchet, director of *Publicis*.
34. *Économie et Politique*, No. 151, February 1967, p. 34.
35. *Ordonnance No. 59–273 du 4 février 1959.*
36. *L'Année politique 1964*, p. 399. The Watchdog Committee was set up by the 1961 Finance Act (*loi du 23 décembre 1960*) (*Diligent Report* 1968, I, p. 70).
37. Marcel Pellenc, commenting on a report by the *Cour des Comptes*, in *Cahiers de la télévision*, No. 8, August 1963, p. 79.
38. 'RTF: si vous avez besoin d'un pot de colle...' in *Cahiers de la télévision*, No. 7, July 1963, p. 68.
39. Roland Nungesser, deputy and spokesman for the RTF budget in the National Assembly, in *Cahiers de la télévision*, No. 8, August 1963, p. 80.
40. Philip M. Williams, *Wars, Plots and Scandals in Post-war France* (1970) pp. 167–168 (from a section first published in *Encounter*, January 1961).
41. P. Viansson-Ponté, *Histoire de la république gaullienne* (1970), I, p. 311.

42. Philip M. Williams and Martin Harrison, *De Gaulle's Republic* (1960), p. 92.
43. *L'Année politique 1962*, pp. 113ff., 243ff.; A. Morice, quoted in G. Dupuis and J. Raux, *L'ORTF* (1970), pp. 6–7.
44. *L'Année politique 1962*, p. 199; Thibau, *Une télévision pour tous les Français* (1970), p. 101; *Économie et politique*, No. 151, February 1967, p. 23.
45. Thibau, op. cit., pp. 99ff.
46. Quoted in René Bernard, 'La censure au journal télévisé', *La Nef*, No. 8, October–December 1961, pp. 65–67.
47. 'Their Master's Voice', *The Economist*, 2 March 1963, p. 785.
48. Pierre Viansson-Ponté, *Les Gaullistes, rituel et annuaire* (1963), p. 52.
49. E.g. his speech on Algeria, 4 November 1960.
50. Philip M. Williams, *The French Parliament 1958–1967* (1968), p. 78.
51. Cf. René Bernard, 'Comment fonctionne cette inconnue, la RTF?', in *La Nef*, No. 8, October–December 1961, pp. 30–31.
52. R. Rémond and C. Neuschwander, 'Télévision et comportement politique', in *Revue française de science politique*, Vol. 13, No. 2, June 1963, p. 326.
53. Moreau, op. cit., p. 121.
54. Charles Debbasch, *Le droit de la radio et de la télévision* (1969), p. 19.
55. E.g. Maurice Duverger, 'Sociologie du statut de la télévision', in *Cahiers de la télévision*, No. 3, March 1963, pp. 4–8.
Édouard Bonnefous, 'Présent et avenir de la radiotélévision française', in *Revue politique et parlementaire*, No. 734, May 1963, pp. 22ff.
56. *L'Année politique 1963*, p. 165.
57. Philip M. Williams and Martin Harrison, *Politics and Society in De Gaulle's Republic* (1972), p. 217.
58. *JO, Débats A.N., 14 juin 1963*, 15/6/63, pp. 3408ff.
59. Philip M. Williams, *The French Parliament*, p. 91; Debbasch, op. cit., p. 19.
60. Williams, op. cit., pp. 91–93 for detailed discussion; *L'Année politique 1964*, pp. 51–53, 57–59.
61. Alain Peyrefitte, Minister of Information, in *JO, Débats A.N., 26 mai 1964*, 27/5/64, pp. 1376ff.
62. *JO, Débats A.N., 26, 27, 28 mai, 18, 23, 25 juin 1964, Débats Sénat, 11, 12, 18, 23 juin 1964*.
63. *Loi No. 64–261 du 27 juin 1964*. (Text in Dupuis and Raux, *L'ORTF*, 1970, pp. 28–30).
64. *Décrets Nos. 64–737, 64–738, 64–739 du 22 juillet 1964*.

65. *Décret No. 64–736.*
66. *Décret No. 64–740.*
67. Alain Peyrefitte, speaking in 1964, quoted by *Diligent Report* (1968), I, p. 51.
68. Quoted by Peyrefitte, *JO, Débats A.N., 26 mai 1964*, 27/5/64, p. 1376.
69. *JO, Débats A.N., 30 avril 1965*, 1–2/5/65, p. 1059.
70. J. P. Manel and Alomée Planel, *La crise de l'ORTF* (1968), Chapter 1.
71. Jacques Thibau, *Une télévision pour tous les Français* (1970), Appendix 5.
72. Cf. p. 136 below.
73. Sanche de Gramont, *The French: Portrait of a People* (1970), p. 236; Roger Errera, *Les libertés à l'abandon* (1968), p. 65.
74. J.-F. Revel, *En France. La fin de l'opposition* (1965), p. 156.
75. *Diligent Report* (1968), II, p. 163.
76. Moreau, op. cit., p. 106; Revel, op. cit., pp. 133ff.
77. Revel, op. cit., pp. 146–147.
78. *L'Année politique 1965*, p. 92.
79. National Control Commission, set up by *Décrets No. 64–231 du 14 mars 1964* and *No. 65–909 du 28 octobre 1965*.
80. Moreau, op. cit., pp. 97ff; Burton Paulu, *Radio and Television Broadcasting on the European Continent* (1967), pp. 153ff.
81. Manel and Planel, op. cit., p. 36; *Diligent Report* (1968), I, p. 97.
82. Moreau, op. cit., p. 101.
83. Quoted in *Diligent Report* (1968), I, p. 95.
84. Paulu, op. cit., p. 154.
85. Errera, op. cit., p. 64.
86. Paulu, op. cit., p. 155.
87. Debbasch, op. cit., pp. 28–29.
88. *L'Année politique 1966*, p. 182 (strike in June), p. 207 (strike in December).
89. *Diligent Report* (1968), I, pp. 14–21.
90. *Diligent* I, pp. 298–306, 352–355.
91. *Diligent* I, pp. 103–106.
92. *Le Monde*, 24/7/64; *Le Monde* in 1967, quoted by Errera, p. 63.
93. Errera, op. cit., pp. 61–62; *Diligent*, I, pp. 362, 370.
94. *Diligent Report* (1968), I, pp. 355–360.
95. *Diligent*, I, p. 361.
96. *Diligent*, I, p. 362.
97. Jacques Thibau, *Une télévision pour tous les Français* (1970), p. 150.
98. *Le Monde*, 23/2/68.
99. *Diligent Report* (1968), II, p. 217, Appendix 82; p. 226, Appendix 83; *Le Monde*, 11/4/68; 12/4/68.

100. *Le Monde*, 19/4/68.
101. A number of books have been devoted to relating the chronology and significance of the 'events of May' at ORTF. So far, most have been written in the heat of combat. The present account is only intended as a summary. For more details, see Roger Louis, *L'ORTF, un combat* (1968); J.-P. Manel and Alomée Planel, *La crise de l'ORTF* (1968). Cf. also (more general) Adrien Dansette, *Mai 1968* (1971); and the *Chronologie des événements de mai-juin 1968*, published by the Documentation Française, Notes et Etudes Documentaires, Nos. 3722–23, 28 septembre 1970.
102. Sanche de Gramont, op. cit., p. 237.
103. *Le Monde*, 1/6/68.
104. `Le Monde, 29/5/68.
105. *Le Monde*, 1/6/68.
106. *Le Monde*, 5/6/68.
107. Cf. Pierre Schaeffer, *Machines à communiquer. 2. Pouvoir et communication* (1972), p. 80.
108. *L'Année politique 1968*, p. 371.
109. *Le Monde*, 22/6/68.
110. *Le Monde*, 28/6/68.
111. *Le Monde*, 14–15/7/68.
112. *Télé-7 jours*, reported in *Le Monde*, 31/7/68.
113. *Le Monde*, 1/8/68.
114. Jacques Garat, in *Le Monde*, 14/8/68 (q.v. for unofficial list of those sacked, transferred, etc.).
115. André Diligent, in *Le Monde*, 7/8/68.
116. *Union des journalistes de télévision* press conference, in *Le Monde*, 7/8/68.
117. P. Viansson-Ponté, 'La télévision retourne lentement à son insignifiance truquée', 'Mai cinq ans après', *Le Monde*, 3/5/73.
118. *Décret No. 68–755 du 20 août 1968; arrêté du 28 août 1968.*
119. *Le Monde*, 13/2/71.
120. Cf. Wladimir d'Ormesson (President of the Administrative Council from 1964 to 1968) in *Revue de Paris*, No. 76, July–August 1969, pp. 79–87.
121. J. le Theule, in National Assembly debate on ORTF budget (*Le Monde*, 21/11/68).
122. *Le Monde*, 17/4/69.
123. Jacques Thibau, *La télévision, le pouvoir et l'argent* (1973), p. 17.
124. *Le Monde*, 27/6/69.
125. *L'Année politique 1969*, p. 71.
126. *Le Monde*, 18/9/69.
127. *Le Monde*, 1/11/69; 23–24/11/69.

128. J. Favard and J. Rocchi, *Scandales à l'ORTF* (1972), p. 60.
129. Interview with Baudrier and Desgraupes, *Le Monde*, 22/4/70.
130. *Le Monde*, 26/11/69; 8/12/70; Jacques Chevallier, 'L'ORTF face aux pouvoirs publics', *Droit Social*, No. 12, December 1970, p. 83.
131. *Le Monde*, 20/11/69.
132. *Décret No. 68–1235 du 26 décembre 1968; arrêté du 30 décembre 1968. Décret No. 69–1222 du 24 décembre 1969; arrêté du 24 décembre 1969.* (Texts in *ORTF grande entreprise nationale*).
133. *Le Monde*, 3/1/69; 23–24/11/69 (National Assembly budget debate).
134. *Le Monde*, 9/12/69.
135. *Rapport de la commission d'étude du statut de l'ORTF, le 30 juin 1970,* La Documentation Française, 1970.
136. Henri Mercillon, 'Quelques réflexions sur le monopole de l'ORTF', *Droit Social*, No. 12, December 1970, p. 77, and 'Avant-propos', by A. Diligent and J. Chevallier, Ibid., pp. 3–4.
137. *Paye Report* (1970), pp. 278–283.
138. Cf. P. Drouin, 'Mai cinq ans après,' *Le Monde*, 3/5/73.
139. Its main clauses involved the completion of the second TV channel's technical network, the creation of a third channel, extension of local radio and of the foreign service. ORTF agreed to cut down its expenditure on administration and production, while its revenue from brand advertising was to be limited to 25 per cent of its total resources. The licence fee would be allowed to increase by 3–5 per cent per annum, to keep pace with the cost of living. For details see ORTF, *Rapport d'activité 1971*, pp. 122–126. See also pp. 84–86 below.
    Note that the concept of *tutelle* in French law implies that the tutee is a minor.
140. Georges Pompidou, press conference of 2 July 1970, in *L'Année politique 1970*, p. 430.
141. Cf. Jacques Thibau, *La télévision, le pouvoir et l'argent* (1973), pp. 61–68.
142. *Le Monde*, 14–15/6/70; 26/6/70; 9–10/5/71; 26/3/72; Favard and Rocchi, op. cit., p. 83; Thibau, *La télévision, le pouvoir et l'argent* (1973), pp. 64–65.
143. J. Siclier, in *Le Monde*, 25–26/7/71; C. Durieux, in *Le Monde*, 1/1/72; *Journal de l'année 1971–1972*, pp. 269–275.
144. *Journal de l'année 1971–1972*, p. 271.
145. Thibau, op. cit., pp. 148–149, quoting *IFOP* survey published in *Le Nouvel Observateur*, 2/11/70.
146. 'L'Opinion de juillet 1971 à juillet 1972 (ii)', in *Sondages*, 1972, No. 4, p. 173.

147. *ORTF Rapport d'activité 1971*, p. 134; *Le Monde*, 18/9/69; 19/9/69; 19/11/69.
148. *ORTF Rapport d'activité 1971*, pp. 18–19. Concise official account of the reforms in *EBU Review*, B, No. 126, March 1971, p. 20.
149. C. Durieux, 'L'ORTF à la croisée des chemins', *Le Monde*, 20/3/71; 21–22/3/71; 23/3/71.
150. *Le Monde*, 9/11/71; 31/12/71; 1/1/72.
151. Quoted in Favard and Rocchi, op. cit., p. 91.
152. *Le Monde*, 30/1/70; 31/10/70; 7–8/11/71 (manifesto of producers and directors); 19–20/3/72. Cf. Pierre Schaeffer, op. cit., pp. 287ff. for attack on the concept of message as product and its implications.
153. See pp. 117–118 below.
154. *Le Monde*, 19/7/72.
155. *Loi No. 72–553 du 3 juillet 1972 portant statut de la radiodiffusion-télévision française; décret No. 72–569 du 5 juillet 1972; arrêté du 5 juillet 1972; arrêté du 24–25 juillet 1972.*
156. Jacques Thibau, *La télévision, le pouvoir et l'argent* (1973), pp. 20–21.
157. *JO, Documents A.N., No, 2410, Projet de loi portant statut de la radiodiffusion-télévision française. Annexe au procès-verbal de la séance du 8 juin 1972*, pp. 2–4.
158. *JO, Documents A.N., No. 2416, Rapport fait au nom de la commission des affaires culturelles...sur le projet de loi portant statut de la radiodiffusion-télévision française. Annexe au procès-verbal de la séance du 14 juin 1972*, p. 27.
159. *Décret No. 72–569 du 5 juillet 1972; arrêté du 5 juillet 1972.*
160. 'Délibère son budget' (1964) becomes 'vote le budget' (1972).
161. *Décret No. 72–569*, Art. 5.
162. *Le Monde*, 27/6/72.
163. *JO, Documents A.N., No. 2416* cit. p. 18.
164. *Le Monde*, 27/6/72; Michel Lemerle (an ORTF journalist), in *Le Monde*, 12/7/72.
165. *Le Monde*, 10/6/72.
166. Article 17 was concerned with the technical aspects of the relationship between ORTF and the Posts and Telecommunications Ministry; Article 18 abrogated the previous statute.
167. Cf. *Entreprise*, 19–25/4/73.
168. Maurice Denuzière, 'L'ORTF que voilà ... ', *Le Monde*, 14/6/72. Union reactions, *Le Monde*, 11–12/6/72; 14/6/72 and following.
169. L.-A. Delmas for the National Assembly Finance Committee, *JO, Documents A.N., No. 2416* cit., p. 34.
170. 'Une loi-cadre qui au milieu présente un vide extraordinaire', reported in *Le Monde*, 1/7/72.
171. Quoted in *Le Nouvel Observateur*, 24–30/7/72.

172. *Le Monde*, 13/7/72; 15/7/72.
173. *Le Nouvel Observateur*, 24–30/7/72; Arthur Conte, *Hommes libres...* (1973), pp. 22–25.
174. *Le Monde*, 14/7/72.
175. *JO*, 24–25/7/72 (*Le Monde*, 26/7/72).
176. 'Une information politique loyale' (reported in *Le Monde*, 27/7/72); 'assurer une information libre'... 'plus important encore [de] développer les forces de la joie et de la distraction' (*Le Monde*, 14/7/72); 'faire chanter la France' (*Paris-Match*, 12/8/72); 'tous ces spectacles pseudo-intellectuels qui sont censés diffuser ce qu'on appelle des messages' (*Le Nouvel Observateur*, 24–30/7/72); cf. too, Conte, op. cit., pp. 41–42.
177. *Le Monde*, 27/7/72; *Le Nouvel Observateur*, 24–30/7/72; *L'Express*, 31/7–6/8/72.
178. *Le Monde*, 11/8/72.
179. *Le Monde*, 9/9/72.
180. *Le Monde*, 18/7/72; 19/7/72.
181. *Le Monde*, 10/8/72; 1/9/72.
182. *Le Monde*, 25/11/72.
183. Claude Durieux, '*Monsieur ORTF un an après...*', *Le Monde*, 5/7/73; 6/7/73.
184. For this mechanism, see p. 94 below.
185. *Le Monde*, 19/10/73; 24/10/73.
186. Extracts in *Le Monde*, 19/10/73.
187. Interviews with *Télé-7 jours* (*Le Monde*, 8/2/73) and *Télémagazine* (*Le Monde*, 3/8/73).
188. Maurice Duverger, 'La France sans lois', *Le Monde*, 14/11/73.
189. 17/12/73 (*Le Monde*, 19/12/73).
190. Arthur Conte, *Hommes libres...*(1973).
191. *Le Monde*, 27/10/73; *Le Point*, 11/2/74.
192. *Le Monde*, 27/10/73; 2/11/73.
193. *Le Monde*, 28–29/10/73; 1/11/73; 15/11/73; 22/2/74; 11/5/74.
194. *Le Monde*, 23–24/12/73; 25/12/73.
195. Further details of negotiations in *Le Point*, 11/2/74.
196. *Le Monde*, 17/1/74; 1/3/74; *Le Point*, 11/2/74.
197. *Programme commun de gouvernement du parti communiste et du parti socialiste...27 juin 1972*; *Le Monde*, 19–20/5/74.
198. *Le Monde*, 3/5/74.
199. Jacques Sallebert, head of radio, to the strikers (*Le Monde*, 25/6/74).
200. In *Le Figaro*, 24/6/74.
201. *Le Monde*, 26/7/74.

CHAPTER TWO

1. *ORTF 73*, p. 36.
2. Maurice Duverger, *Droit public* (1963), pp. 236–240; Pierre du Pont, *L'État industriel* (1961), p. 27.
3. *Loi No. 72–553 du 3 juillet 1972*, Articles 6, 9.
4. E.g. *ORTF 73*: 'Le président-directeur général dirige et gère l'Office selon les orientations générales définies par le conseil d'administration...' (p. 53); '...il appartient au président de préparer une politique générale, de définir les objectifs à long terme et de rendre les arbitrages importants' (pp. 53–54).
5. *ORTF 73*, p. 89.
6. Ibid., p. 53.
7. Ibid., pp. 70–73.
8. Ibid., loc. cit.
9. *Diligent Report* (1968), I, p. 223; *Chinaud Report* (1974), I, p. 81. Donald R. Browne, 'Citizen involvement in broadcasting: some European experiences', *Public Telecommunications Review*, Vol. 1, No. 2, October 1973, pp. 24–26.
10. This information is taken from an internal memorandum, 'Instruction No. 33 du 15 février 1973 sur l'organisation générale de l'Office de Radiodiffusion-Télévision Française', unless otherwise stated.
11. See pp. 83–4 below.
12. *ORTF 73*, p. 305.
13. Ibid., pp. 116–121.
14. Ibid., pp. 54–55; *arrêté du 21 juillet 1972*, ibid., p. 68.
15. *ORTF grande entreprise nationale*, 'Statut et organisation', unpag.
16. *Le Monde*, 30/9/72.
17. *ORTF 73*, pp. 600, 625.
18. *Le Tac Report* (1972), I, p. 314.
19. *ORTF 73*, pp. 49, 586–588.
20. Charles Debbasch, *Le droit de la radio et de la télévision* (1969), pp. 57–60.
21. *ORTF 73*, pp. 595–599.
22. Ibid., pp. 595–596, 'Les personnels artistiques'.
23. Jacques Thibau, *La télévision, le pouvoir et l'argent* (1973), pp. 88–90.
24. *ORTF 73*, pp. 596–597; 'Radiographie de la gestion de l'ORTF', *Entreprise*, 19–25 April 1973.
25. *Entreprise*, article cited; *Chinaud Report* (1974), II, pp. 162–169.
26. *ORTF 73*, p. 597; *Le Monde*, 4/10/72.
27. ORTF *Statut des journalistes*, JO, *Décret No. 64–739 du 22 juillet*

1964, modifié par les décrets No. 69–1024 du 12 novembre 1969 et No. 69–1188 du 24 décembre 1969. The *SNJ* sees this document as foisted onto it by the government.

28. See p. 35.
29. *ORTF 73*, p. 590.
30. See p. 93.
31. *ORTF 73*, p. 590; *Le Monde*, 18/1/73.
32. *Le Monde*, 23/8/73.
33. *Le Monde*, 23/8/74.
34. E.g. from 1/1/71 to 3/2/71, 53 partial strikes and a general one announced for 9/2/71 (*Le Tac Report*, 1972, II, ii, Annexe 76, 'Note du directeur général sur les mouvements de grève', p. 428).
35. Pierre Schaeffer, *Machines à communiquer. 2. Pouvoir et communication* (1972), p. 80 (my translation).
36. According to union leaders. C. Bretagne, *Chère Télévision* (1972), p. 133, gives a figure of 5,000 for union membership.
37. *ORTF 73*, pp. 605–609.
38. *Le Tac Report* (1972), I, p. 319; Thibau, op. cit., p. 91.
39. André Rossi, government spokesman on information (*Le Monde*, 23/7/74).
40. Prime Minister Jacques Chirac, reported in *Le Monde*, 25/7/74.
41. E.g. *Le Monde*, 8/10/74.
42. *Loi No. 74–696 du 7 août 1974.*
43. Article 1. See pp. 39–43 above for purposes of comparison.
44. *Loi du 7 août 1974*, Article 3; *Décret No. 74–946 du 14 novembre 1974.*
45. *Loi du 7 août 1974*, Articles 5 and 6; *Décret No. 74–795 du 24 septembre 1974.*
46. *Loi du 7 août 1974*, Articles 7 to 11; *Décret No. 74–791 du 24 septembre 1974.*
47. *Loi du 7 août 1974*, Article 13; *Le Monde*, 27–28/10/74.
48. *Loi du 7 août 1974*, Articles 14 and 15.
49. André Rossi, government spokesman on information, in *Le Monde*, 9/11/74.
50. Gérard Ducaux-Rupp, acting President of the Higher Council of the French Cinema Industry, *Le Monde*, 17–18/11/74.
51. *Le Monde*, 18/12/74.
52. *Loi du 7 août 1974*, Article 16.
53. Ibid., Articles 25 and 26.
54. *Le Monde*, 28/9/74.
55. *Le Monde*, 9/10/74.
56. *Le Monde*, 8/10/74; 23/11/74; 5/12/74.
57. *ORTF 73*, pp. 96–97.

58. Francis Balle, *Institutions et publics des moyens d'information* (1973), pp. 450–451; *Chinaud Report* (1974), I, pp. 59–62.

59. *JO, Documents, No. 682. Avis présenté au nom de la commission des affaires culturelles, familiales et sociales sur le projet de loi de finances pour 1974, Tome XVIII, Office de Radiodiffusion-Télévision Française. Annexe au procès-verbal de la séance du 10 octobre 1973*, pp. 11–12.

60. *JO, Documents, No. 681. Rapport fait au nom de la commission des finances, de l'économie générale et du plan sur le projet de loi de finances pour 1974. Annexe No. 44, Office de Radiodiffusion-Télévision Française. Annexe au procès-verbal de la séance du 10 octobre 1973*, p. 5.

61. *Chinaud Report* (1974), I, pp. 61–62.

62. *JO, Documents, No. 682*, cit., p. 13.

63. *Chinaud Report* (1974), I, pp. 74–76.

64. *JO, Documents, No. 682*, cit., pp. 13–14.

65. *Chinaud Report* (1974), I, p. 70.

66. Ibid., I, pp. 72–74.

67. Ibid., I, p. 165.

68. See pp. 110–117 for further details.

69. *Chinaud*, I, pp. 151–154.

70. Ibid., I, p. 151.

71. *JO, Documents, No. 681* cit., pp. 49–50.

72. *ORTF 73*, pp. 96–97.

73. *JO, Documents, No. 681* cit., pp. 5–6 (which points out that most of the figures put out by *ORTF* are inaccurate).

74. *ORTF 73*, pp. 578–579, 'Fiscalité'; *Chinaud Report* (1974), I, p. 52, which gives 71 million francs as the sum to be paid to the Treasury in 1969.

75. *Chinaud*, I, p. 54; text of the Constitutional Council's decision in G. Dupuis and J. Raux, *L'ORTF* (1970), pp. 78–79.

76. See pp. 94–95 below.

77. *ORTF 73*, pp. 619–622, 'Les Contrôles'.

78. *ORTF 73*, pp. 76–78, 622–623.

79. *Chinaud Report* (1974), I, pp. 11–13.

80. Ibid., I, p. 13.

81. Ibid., loc. cit; *Le Monde*, 11/5/74.

82. *Chinaud*, I, pp. 15–28.

83. Ibid., I, pp. 29–39.

84. Ibid., I, pp. 59–86.

85. Ibid., I, pp. 132–150, 171–173.

86. Ibid., I, pp. 91–102.

87. *Le Monde*, 14/2/74.

88. Cf. André Astoux, ex-Assistant Director General of *ORTF* (1964–68), in *Le Monde*, 17/7/74.

89. René Jannelle, General Secretary of the National Federation of Spectacle (*CGT*), in *Le Monde*, 27/6/74.
90. According to the National Union of Radio and Television (*CGT*), in *Le Monde*, 3/7/74.
91. *Chinaud Report* (1974), I, pp. 49–51.
92. *JO, Documents, No. 681* cit., p. 5.
93. *Chinaud Report* (1974), I, p. 50.
94. René Jannelle, in *Le Monde*, 27/6/74.
95. Budget debate in the National Assembly (*JO, Débats A.N., 15 novembre 1974*, 16/11/74, p. 6497).
96. *Le Monde*, 3–4/11/74.
97. For this mathematical formula, see *Le Monde*, 24–25/11/74.
98. Budget debate cited, p. 6497.
99. Cf. J.-L. Guillaud, Director General of *TF 1*, in *France-Soir*, 18/12/74.
100. Budget debate cited, pp. 6498, 6512.
101. *Le Monde*, 3–4/11/74; 17–18/11/74.
102. Budget debate cited, p. 6491.
103. Budget debate cited, pp. 6497–98.
104. *Le Monde*, 17–18/11/74.
105. *Le Monde*, 8–9/12/74, commenting on the Senate budget debate. The estimates of needs were supplied by the new presidents.
106. Budget debate cited, p. 6492.
107. Senate budget debate, *Le Monde*, 8–9/12/74.
108. Prime Minister Jacques Chirac, *Le Monde*, 4/7/74.
109. Senate budget debate, *Le Monde*, 8–9/12/74.
110. *Le Monde*, 8/10/74.
111. Jobs (not all these mean sacking): A. Rossi, government spokesman, in Senate budget debate, *Le Monde*, 12/12/74; reductions in foreign service: *Le Monde*, 26/10/74.

CHAPTER THREE

1. *ORTF 73*, pp. 35–36.
2. *Le Monde*, 24/4/73.
3. Joël le Theule, in National Assembly, 19 November 1968 (*Le Monde*, 26/12/68).
4. *Le Monde*, 28/2/74.
5. *Diligent Report* (1968), I, p. 106; *Paye Report* (1970), p. 226.
6. *ORTF 73*, p. 40.
7. Cf. Philippe Malaud, Minister of Information, attacking 'all these pseudo-intellectual spectacles...' (*Le Nouvel Observateur*, 24–30/7/72).
8. *Diligent Report*, loc. cit; *Paye Report*, loc. cit; Pierre Emmanuel, *Pour une politique de la culture* (1971), pp. 200–202.

9. See *Le Nouvel Observateur*, 1/10/73, for a strong implication that a cultural programme 'Chefs-d'œuvre en péril' had been dropped at the suggestion of the Minister of Culture, Maurice Druon, who had been criticized on the programme.
10. For Parliament's powers of control, see pp. 93–99.
11. *Décret No. 69–1222 du 24 décembre 1969*, Art. 2.
12. *Décret No. 68–1235 du 26 décembre 1968*, Art. 16.
13. '...a person of some importance, the State Controller, whose office is only yards away from the President's [of the *Office*]', *Entreprise*, 19–25/4/73.
14. *Arrêté du 24 décembre 1969*.
15. *Chinaud Report* (1974), I, pp. 106–107.
16. *Décret No. 64–737 du 22 juillet 1964*.
17. Jacques Chevallier, 'L'ORTF face aux pouvoirs publics', *Droit Social*, No. 12, December 1970, pp. 82–95.
18. For further details, see *ORTF Rapport d'activité 1971*, pp. 122–126; *ORTF 73*, pp. 37–39, 539–542.
19. Cf. L.-A. Delmas, in National Assembly debate, 8 November 1971 (*JO, Débats A.N., 8 novembre 1971*, 9/11/71, p. 5494).
20. 'Convention de coopération...' in *ORTF 73*, pp. 153–158.
21. *Le Monde*, 16/3/72.
22. *Le Monde*, 23–24/1/72; 26/6/73.
23. *Le Monde*, 5/2/72.
24. J. Favard and J. Rocchi, *Scandales à l'ORTF* (1972), p. 52; *Le Monde*, 14–15/11/71.
25. *Chinaud Report* (1974), I, pp. 78–79, 187–188.
26. According to André Rossi, Secretary of State for Information, responsible for the 1974 Bill (*Le Monde*, 23/7/74).
27. Charles Debbasch, *Le droit de la radio et de la télévision* (1969), pp. 28–29.
28. *Le Monde*, 12–13/5/74.
29. *Le Tac Report* (1972), I, pp. 189ff., 'La crise du commandement'.
30. Interviewed in *Le Monde*, 28/11/73.
31. *Le Monde*, 5/1/73.
32. *Le Monde*, 9/12/72.
33. Arthur Conte, *Hommes Libres...*(1973), p. 149.
34. Alain Peyrefitte, Minister of Information, in National Assembly debates on the reform of the statute (*JO, Débats A.N., 26 mai 1964*, 27/5/64, p. 1378).
35. Composition of Administrative Council 1964–68: *Décret No. 64–736 du 22 juillet 1964*.
36. 'Une radio-télévision démocratique' (special number), *Économie et politique*, No. 151, February 1967, pp. 34–35.

37. Composition of Administrative Council 1968–72: *Décret No. 68–755 du 20 août 1968*; *arrêté du 28 août 1968*.
38. Jacques Chevallier, art. cit. pp. 91–94; *Le Monde*, 14/9/71.
39. Composition of Administrative Council 1972–74: *Décret No. 72–569 du 5 juillet 1972: arrêté du 5 juillet 1972*.
40. Roland Cayrol, *La presse écrite et audio-visuelle* (1973), pp. 332–333.
41. Cf. Wladimir d'Ormesson, President of the Administrative Council 1964–68, interviewed in *Le Figaro* (*Le Monde*, 9/8/68); *Le Monde*, 13–14/7/69; 7–8/5/72.
42. Suggested by Jean Cazeneuve to Donald R. Browne, 'Citizen involvement in broadcasting: some European experiences', *Public Telecommunications Review*, Vol. 1, No. 2, October 1973, p. 28, note 35.
43. Composition of Administrative Councils from 1974: *loi du 7 août 1974; Décret No. 74–791 du 24 septembre 1974*.
44. *Décret No. 64–740 du 22 juillet 1964*.
45. *Le Monde*, 6–7/6/71.
46. *Décret No. 64–740; ORTF 73*, pp. 116–121, 'Les comités de programmes'.
47. For examples of government appointments before 1964 (Contamine, Riou), see *JO, Débats A.N., 27 mai 1964*, 28/5/64, p. 1416.
   For Jacques Thibau, see his *Une télévision pour tous les Français* (1970), Appendix 5, pp. 273–277.
48. *Le Monde*, 1/8/68; 21–22/9/69; 20/9/74.
49. Cf. Gabriel de Broglie, General Secretary of *ORTF*, quoted in *Entreprise*, 19–25/4/73.
50. *JO, Rapport fait au nom de la commission des finances...sur le projet de loi de finances pour 1973, A.N., No. 2585, Annexe 44. Annexe au procès-verbal de la séance du 12 octobre 1972*, p. 6; *Chinaud Report* (1974) I, p. 80.
51. *Le Monde, 28–29/10/73; Chinaud Report* (1974), pp. 80, 183.
52. *Le Monde*, 9/12/69.
53. Henri Mercillon, 'La télévision, l'ORTF et le public', *Le Monde*, 19/2/72; 20–21/2/72.
54. *Le Monde*, 23–24/11/69.
55. *Loi du 7 août 1974*, Art. 4.
56. *Loi du 3 juillet 1972*, Art. 13.
57. *Loi du 7 août 1974*, Arts. 4, 15, 20.
58. Cf. *Diligent Report* (1968), I, pp. 69–71, on the limitations of this kind of body. For membership in June 1973, *Le Monde*, 16/6/73; for 1974–75, *Le Monde*, 3–4/11/74.
59. *Ordonnance No. 58–1100 du 17 novembre 1958*, quoted in *Le Tac Report* (1972), II, p. 5; for further details, *Diligent Report* (1968), I, pp. 72–74.

60. Philip M. Williams, *The French Parliament* (1968), p. 51.
61. According to Étienne Dailly, Vice-President of the Senate, in *Le Monde*, 7/7/73.
62. Summary of a memoire on the parliamentary commissions of enquiry in the Fifth Republic (no title given) by Michel Ceoara, in *Le Monde*, 7/7/73.
63. See p. 22 earlier.
64. See John S. Ambler, *The Government and Politics of France* (1971), pp. 149ff., for summary of ways in which the government can control the legislative process in the Fifth Republic.
65. Roger Errera, *Les libertés à l'abandon* (1968), p. 75.
66. Errera, op. cit., p. 76 (my translation).
67. Errera, op. cit., pp. 67–69.
68. *Loi du 3 juillet* 1972, Art. 8; *Le Monde*, 1/8/73; 16/1/74. See pp. 145–146 below.
69. *L'Année politique 1972*, pp. 49–51.
70. *Décret No. 73–325 du 21 mars 1973* (*JO, Lois et décrets, 23/3/73*).
71. *Loi du 3 juillet 1972*, Art. 16.
72. Names and party affiliations in *Le Monde*, 15/6/73 and 16/6/73.
73. *Le Monde*, 1–2/7/73; *Who's Who in France 1973–74*.
74. Based on a count which excludes André Audinot, Jean-Paul Parayre, Pierre Simonetti and Gérard Thurnauer.
75. *Le Monde*, 1/8/73; 16/1/74.
76. *Loi du 7 août 1974*, Arts. 10 and 20.
77. On the commercial stations, see Burton Paulu, *Radio and Television Broadcasting on the European Continent* (1967), pp. 85ff; Walter B. Emery, *National and International Systems of Broadcasting...* (1969), pp. 158–169; Roland Cayrol, *La presse écrite et audiovisuelle* (1973), pp. 348–359.
78. *Le Monde*, 9/10/74.
79. Bernard Voyenne, *L'Information en France* (1972), p. 133.
80. *Le Monde*, 12/2/74; 11/4/74; 8/10/74; 9/10/74.
81. *Le Monde*, 9/10/74. On Europe 1 in general, see Pierre Laforêt, *La prodigieuse aventure d'Europe No. 1* (1960).
82. *JO, Documents A.N., No. 681, Rapport fait...sur le projet de loi de finances pour 1974, Annexe 26, Information,* p. 11.
83. *Paye Report* (1970), p. 52. Radio-Andorre is indirectly controlled by the Spanish Ministry of Information (Voyenne, op. cit. p. 134). Its capital is mostly Spanish and its advertising resources mostly French (*Paye*, loc. cit.).
84. Cayrol, op. cit., p. 356.
85. Voyenne, op. cit., p. 134.
86. Cayrol, op. cit., pp. 356–357.
87. *Le Monde*, 13/2/70.

88. *JO, Documents A.N., No. 2582, Rapport fait au nom de la commission des finances...sur le projet de loi de finances pour 1973. Annexe 44. Annexe au procès-verbal de la séance du 12 octobre 1972*, p. 25.
89. Georges Verpraet, *La télévision et ses métiers* (1972), pp. 229–230; *Le Monde*, 2–3/12/73.
90. *Le Monde*, 17/4/71.
91. Charles Debbasch, *Le droit de la radio et de la télévision* (1969), p. 115.
92. *Le Monde*, 12/10/74 (information budget).
93. Verpraet, op. cit., p. 224.
94. *Le Monde*, 3/10/73; *Le Nouvel Observateur*, 26/3/73.
95. *Paye Report* (1970), p. 51.
96. *JO, Documents A.N., No. 681, Rapport...*, p. 11.
97. Verpraet, op. cit., p. 229 (q.v. for financial interests in Télé-Monte Carlo).
98. *Le Monde*, 23/1/74.
99. *Le Monde*, 18/5/72; 23/1/74.
100. Henri Mercillon, 'La France, son système d'information, sa télévision', in *Direction*, No. 166, November 1969, p. 1139.
101. *Le Monde*, 26/10/74; 30/10/74.
102. *JO, Documents A.N., No. 681, Rapport...*, p. 11.
103. *Le Monde*, 20–21/6/71.
104. Voyenne, op. cit., p. 133.
105. *Le Monde*, 27–28/2/72; *JO, Documents A.N., No. 2582*, p. 25.
106. *L'Année politique 1965*, pp. 100–101.
107. *Le Monde*, 19/12/73 (does not remark on the choice of station).
108. Jacques Thibau, *La télévision, le pouvoir et l'argent* (1973), pp. 54–55.
109. *Programme commun de gouvernement...27 juin 1972*, Part 3, Chapter 5.
110. Charles Debbasch, *Le droit de la radio et de la télévision* (1969), p. 37: the Law of 31 December 1953 set up a sort of monopoly of production. According to *Économie et Politique*, No. 151, February 1967, p. 69, this disappeared in 1964.
111. *ORTF grande entreprise nationale*, 1973, unpagin. The *Chinaud Report* (1974), II, p. 40 gives 29·5 per cent in October 1973.
112. *Chinaud*, loc. cit; *ORTF 73*, p. 293.
113. *Le Monde*, 21–22/7/74.
114. Jacques Thibau, *Une télévision pour tous les Français* (1970), pp. 97–98.
115. *ORTF 73*, pp. 446–448.
116. *Paye Report* (1970), pp. 157–158.
117. *Le Tac Report* (1972), I, pp. 149–155.
118. *Chinaud Report* (1974), I, p. 176, interview with a producer, Guy Seligmann, in *Le Monde*, 24/7/74.

119. Verpraet, op. cit., pp. 53ff.
120. *Le Monde*, 21–22/7/74.
121. *Économie et Politique*, No. 151, February 1967, pp. 69–70.
122. *Chinaud*, I, pp. 56–57 and II, pp. 79–83.
123. Jacqueline Grapin, in *Le Monde*, 3/7/74.
124. '...et faire consommer' (quoted in Errera, *Les libertés à l'abandon*, 1968, p. 72).
125. The law in question refers specifically to the government's policy of economic expansion (*Loi No. 51–601 du 24 mai 1951*, in *Diligent Report* (1968), II, p. 144).
126. *L'Année politique 1964*, p. 402.
127. Cf. Prime Minister Georges Pompidou, in the National Assembly debate of 24 April 1968 (*JO, Débats A.N., 24 avril 1968*, 25/4/68, p. 1306).

 The top six advertisers in 1967 were: perfume, the National Lottery, chicory, the Crédit Agricole Bank, French Gas, and coffee (*Diligent Report*, 1968, II, p. 147).
128. Figures from *L'Année politique 1964*, p. 402. By 1968, this had increased to about 50 million francs for 30 hours of advertising per annum (*Le Monde*, 9/2/68).
129. *JO, Débats A.N., 24 avril 1968*, 25/4/68, p. 1306.
130. *Le Monde*, 2/2/68; IFOP survey in *Le Monde*, 31/10/67, quoted by Deputy Bernard Pieds in the National Assembly debate (*JO, Débats A.N., 24 avril 1968*, 25/4/68, p. 1300).
131. *L'Année politique 1967*, pp. 83, 88, 130–131.
132. *Le Monde*, 28–29/1/68.
133. For further information on this aspect, see *Étude spéciale de certains problèmes posés par l'introduction de la publicité de marques à l'ORTF*, Documents d'Études No. 8, La Documentation Française, April 1970, pp. 22–24.
134. *JO, Débats A.N., 24 avril 1968*, 25/4/68, pp. 1299ff.
135. Ibid., p. 1306.
136. *Diligent Report* (1968), I, p. 234. See pp. 210–256 of the *Report* for the whole question of advertising.
137. Ibid., p. 254.
138. *ORTF 73*, pp. 637–638. In late 1974, *ORTF*'s shares were taken over by the French Government.
139. Cf. *Le Tac Report* (1972), I, p. 284.
140. *Le Monde*, 4–5/7/71.
141. *Le Monde*, 15/11/72 (information budget in the National Assembly).
142. *Le Monde*, 3/4/73.
143. 'Tarifs de la publicité de marques televisée', document issued by the *RFP*, dated 11 May 1973.

144. *ORTF 73*, pp. 559–561 (p. 561 gives a table showing the daily volume of commercials of both kinds from 1968 to 1972).
145. 'Tarifs...'; *ORTF 73*, p. 639.
146. *ORTF 73*, p. 560.
147. *Le Tac Report* (1972), II, ii (Annexes et documents), p. 365.
148. *Le Monde*, 15/11/72 (information budget).
149. *Chinaud Report* (1974), I, p. 154.
150. J.-L. Servan-Schreiber, in *Le Monde*, 1/10/74.
151. 'Règlement de la publicité radiophonique et télévisée', document issued by the RFP, dated 1 January 1973 (and cf. *ORTF 73*, pp. 559–610).
152. *Le Monde*, 3/4/73.
153. 'La publicité à la télévision', in 'L'Opinion de juillet 1971 à juillet 1972 (ii)', *Sondages*, 1972, No. 4, pp. 152–153.
154. *Le Tac Report* (1972), I, p. 290.
155. *Le Monde*, 7/6/69; *Programme commun de gouvernement...27 juin 1972*, Part 3, Chapter 5.
156. *Chinaud Report* (1974), I, p. 151; *Le Monde*, 19/7/74.
157. *Le Monde*, 18/7/74.
158. *Le Monde*, 5/7/74.
159. *Loi du 7 août 1974*, Art. 22.
160. *Le Monde*, 30/7/74.
161. Jacques Thibau, *La télévision, le pouvoir et l'argent* (1973), pp. 117ff. J. Favard et J. Rocchi, *Scandales à l'ORTF* (1972). pp. 105ff.
162. Concise account of the affair in *Journal de l'année 1971–72*, pp. 348–349.
163. *Le Tac Report* (1972); *Diligent Report* (1972).
164. *Le Monde*, 28/4/72.
165. *Journal de l'année 1971–72*, p. 349.
166. *Le Monde*, 11–12/11/73. Cf. Jean Montaldo, *Tous coupables* (1974), pp. 254ff.
167. *Chinaud Report* (1974), I, pp. 156–158.
168. Henri Mercillon, in *Le Monde*, 19/2/72 and 21/2/73; Bernard Voyenne, *Le droit à l'information* (1970), pp. 195ff; Pierre Desgraupes in *L'Express*, 6–12/7/70.
169. *Le Monde*, 19/2/72; 24/11/73 (58 per cent in favour).
170. Thibau, *Une télévision pour tous les Français* (1970), pp. 141–143. Mercillon, loc. cit.
171. Desgraupes, loc. cit.; Voyenne, loc. cit.
172. Roberto Rossellini, 'Plaidoyer pour la télévision d'État', in *Le Monde*, 10/5/72.
173. Charles de Fréminville, Director of Financial Control at *ORTF*, 'Avenir de l'audio-visuel, aspects économiques', in *Projet*, March 1973, pp. 265–278.

174. *JO, Documents A.N., Proposition de loi...Annexe 109, No. 110. Annexe au procès-verbal de la séance du 19 juillet 1968.* Full text in *Le Tac Report* (1972), II (ii), pp. 598–609; summary in *Le Tac*, I, pp. 352–353.
175. *Le Tac Report* (1972), I, pp. 354–356; *Paye Report* (1970), pp. 179–184; 'L'Affaire de la télévision privée', in *L'Express*, 8–14 June 1970.
176. *Le Monde*, 9/6/70.
177. *Le Monde*, 19/2/72; 21/2/72.
178. Fréminville, article cit.
179. *Le Monde*, 22/6/73.
180. According to Sanche de Gramont, however, in 1969, both Pompidou and Alain Poher (the presidential candidates) were privately in favour of a commercial channel on the English model (*The French*, 1970, pp. 237–238).
181. *L'Année politique 1972*, p. 50.
182. *Le Monde*, 13/6/74; 14/6/74.
183. *Le Monde*, 25/6/74.
184. Maurice Duverger, in *Le Monde*, 3/7/74.
185. *Le Monde*, 25/7/74.
186. *Le Monde*, 5/7/74.
187. *Le Monde*, 20/9/74; 21/9/74.
188. Francis Balle, *Institutions et publics des moyens d'information* (1973), p. 405.
189. *Le Monde*, 6/6/74; *ORTF 73*, p. 649 for *SFT*.
190. André Diligent (*Le Monde*, 5–6/3/72).
191. Joseph Rovan, general secretary of 'Culture et Télévision' (*Le Monde*, 23–24/1/72).
192. *Le Monde*, 5–6/3/72; 1–2/10/72.
193. *Le Monde*, 5–6/3/72; *ORTF 73*, pp. 645–648.
194. *Chinaud Report* (1974), II, Annexe XIV, pp. 88–89, for details of financial holdings. *Le Monde*, 6/7/73; 19/9/73; 3/10/73.

CHAPTER FOUR

1. See pp. 9–10 above.
2. De Gaulle before June 1963, mentioned in R. Rémond and C. Neuschwander, 'Télévision et comportement politique', *Revue française de science politique*, Vol. 13, No. 2, June 1963, p. 327.
   Alain Peyrefitte in the National Assembly, *JO, Débats A.N., 30 avril 1965*, 1–2/5/65, p. 1059.
3. René Bernard, 'La censure au journal télévisé', *La Nef*, No. 8, October-December 1961, pp. 65–67.

4. *L'Année politique 1962*, pp. 113ff., 223ff; Jacques Thibau, *Une télévision pour tous les Français* (1970), p. 101.
5. 'Présent et avenir de la radiotélévision française', *Revue politique et parlementaire*, May 1963, p. 22.
6. J.-F. Revel, *En France. La fin de l'opposition* (1965), pp. 146–148.
7. Thibau, op. cit., p. 119; André Brincourt, *André Malraux ou le temps du silence* (1966), pp. 72–77.
8. *JO, Débats A.N., 26 mai 1964*, 27/5/64, p. 1378.
9. Claude Frédéric, *Libérer l'ORTF* (1968), p. 26.
10. Jean-Guy Moreau, *Le Règne de la télévision* (1967), pp. 40, 101, 105–107.
11. Jean Lecanuet, Waldeck-Rochet, Maurice Faure, in 'L'opinion de douze hommes politiques', *La Nef*, No. 27, May-July 1966, pp. 152–161.
12. *Le Monde*, 24/1/68; 13/2/68.
13. Roger Louis, *L'ORTF, un combat* (1968), p. 28.
14. *Le Monde*, 11/6/68.
15. *Diligent Report* (1968), I, pp. 90–133.
16. Jacques Thibau, in *Notre République*, 22/12/67, reprinted in Thibau, *Une télévision pour tous les Français* (1970), pp. 278–279.
17. *Diligent*, I, p. 97, pp. 122ff.
18. *Le Monde*, 3/5/69; 23/5/69. Sometime between July 1968 and June 1969, Jean Montaldo, a journalist, managed to 'cut' the end of 'Panorama' by ringing up ORTF and pretending to be the Minister of Information (Jean Montaldo, *Tous coupables*, 1974, p. 168).
19. Prime Minister Chaban-Delmas, in the National Assembly, 16 September 1969 (*Le Monde*, 18/9/69).
20. M. Tomasini, *UDR* deputy (*Le Monde*, 16–17/11/69); MM. Vendroux and Pasqua (*UDR*), in the budget debate (*Le Monde*, 23–24/11/69).
21. *Le Monde*, 28/11/69; 9/12/69.
22. *Le Monde*, 7/11/69.
23. *Le Monde*, 25–26/1/70; P. Desgraupes, interviewed in *L'Express*, 6–12/7/70.
24. *Le Monde*, 22/4/70.
25. *Le Monde*, 8/12/70; 12/12/70.
26. *Le Monde*, 24–25/10/71.
27. *Le Monde*, 19/7/72.
27a. Cf. Arthur Conte, *Hommes Libres...*(1973), p. 16.
28. *Le Monde*, 9/9/72.
29. P. Viansson-Ponté, in *Le Monde*, 6–7/8/72.
30. *Le Nouvel Observateur*, 12–18/2/73.
31. *Le Monde*, 23/8/73; 15/9/73; 21/11/73.

32. *Le Monde*, 24/3/73; *ORTF 73*, p. 263.
33. *Le Monde*, 15–16/4/73.
34. Claude Frédéric, *Libérer l'ORTF* (1968), p. 21.
35. *JO, Débats A.N.*, *27 mai 1964*, 28/5/64, p. 1417.
36. *Le Monde*, 26–27/12/71.
37. *Le Monde*, 19/8/72.
38. *Le Nouvel Observateur*, 12–18/2/73.
39. Letter in *Le Monde*, 5–6/11/72.
40. *ORTF Rapport d'activité 1971*, p. 200.
41. Cf. *SNJ Résolution finale, Assemblée générale du 8 mai 1973*.
42. Thibau, op. cit., p. 113; Louis, op. cit., p. 14.
43. Moreau, op. cit., pp. 65–66.
44. Ibid., p. 14.
45. Ibid., pp. 66–67.
46. Interview in *Le Figaro*, March 1966, quoted in *Diligent Report* (1968), I, p. 100.
47. *Diligent*, I, p. 100; Moreau, op. cit., pp. 100–101; Thibau, op. cit., p. 110.
48. Thibau, op. cit., p. 122.
49. Thibau, op. cit., p. 112 (lists subjects treated).
50. Louis, op. cit., p. 14.
51. *Le Monde*, 16/5/68.
52. Thibau, op. cit., pp. 160–162.
53. *Le Monde*, 12/7/68.
54. *Le Monde*, 12/9/68.
55. *Le Monde*, 6/2/70; 3–4/5/70; 3/7/70; Thibau, op. cit., p. 112 and *passim*.
56. In *Le Monde*, 2/5/70.
57. *Le Monde*, 14–15/6/70; 8–9/11/70; 17/11/70; 13/2/71.
58. J. Favard and J. Rocchi, *Scandales à l'ORTF* (1972), pp. 79–101.
59. *Le Monde*, 20–21/8/72; 16/9/72; 15–16/4/73; 25/5/73; 15–16/9/74.
60. *Le Monde*, 27–28/1/74; 25/2/74.
61. Favard and Rocchi, op. cit., p. 82.
62. Burton Paulu, *Radio and Television Broadcasting on the European Continent* (1967), p. 59; Rémond and Neuschwander, article cited, pp. 343–344; *L'Année politique 1962*, pp. 113ff.
63. Maurice Duverger, 'Sociologie du statut de la télévision', *Les cahiers de la télévision*, No. 3, March 1963, p. 8.
64. Cf. *Le Monde*, 24/3/71, quoting *JO*, 20/3/71.
65. *Diligent Report* (1968), I, pp. 97–98.
66. Ibid., p. 99.
67. Paulu, op. cit., pp. 153–154; *Diligent*, I, p. 100; Roger Errera, *Les libertés à l'abandon* (1968), pp. 63–64.
68. *Loi No. 66–1022 du 29 décembre 1966.*

69. *L'Année politique 1966*, p. 97.
70. Paulu, op. cit., pp. 154–155.
71. *Le Monde*, 27/3/69; 4/4/69; 10/4/69.
72. According to Senator Roger Carcassonne (Socialist) in Senate debate 8 April 1969 (*Le Monde*, 10/4/69).
73. IFOP survey (*Le Monde*, 13–14/4/69).
74. *Le Monde*, 2/5/69; 23/5/69.
75. *Le Monde*, 2/2/73; 21/2/73.
76. *Le Monde*, 15/2/73.
77. Claude Sarraute, in *Le Monde*, 13/3/73.
78. *Le Monde*, 4/4/74.
79. *Le Monde*, 12/4/74.
80. *Le Monde*, 28–29/4/74.
81. *Le Monde*, 3/5/74; 8/5/74; 10/5/74; 11/5/74; 12–13/5/74; 26/7/74.
82. *Diligent Report* (1968), I, pp. 127–128.
83. E.g. Jacques Duclos, Communist Party candidate for the presidency (*Le Monde*, 25–26/5/69); *Programme commun de gouvernement du parti communiste et du parti socialiste...27 juin 1972*, Part 3, Chapter 5.
84. *Le Monde*, 18/12/68.
85. *Le Monde*, 9/1/69; 28–29/9/69.
86. *Le Monde*, 10/8/72; 20/9/72; 23/12/72.
87. Radicals and Socialists, in *Le Monde*, 1/9/72.
88. According to Guy Claisse, one of the producers of 'A armes égales' (*Le Monde*, 9/2/73).
89. Alain Duhamel, one of the producers of 'A armes égales', interview with the author, and in *Le Monde*, 11/4/73.
90. *Le Monde*, 30/12/72; Arthur Conte, *Hommes libres...*(1973), p. 141.
91. *Le Monde*, 15/12/72.
92. *Diligent*, I, pp. 130–133 (gives examples of reforms proposed in Parliament).
93. Errera, op. cit., pp. 67–69.
94. *Paye Report* (1970), pp. 104–107.
95. Roger Errera, in *Le Monde*, 25–26/2/73.
96. *Le Monde*, 30/7/74.
97. *Le Monde*, 9/3/73. (See, however, p. 13 above).
98. *Le Monde*, 24–25/11/74; 20/12/74.
99. Benjamin Huc and François Robin, *Histoire et dessous de la radio en France et dans le monde* (1938), pp. 97–98.
100. Ibid., pp. 101–104; Pierre Paraf, *L'information hier, aujour'hui, demain* (1946), pp. 69–70; B. Favreau, *Georges Mandel, un clémenciste en Gironde* (1969), p. 189.
101. Huc and Robin, pp. 98, 168–178.
102. Roger Errera, *Les libertés à l'abandon* (1968), pp. 60–61. ('où

l'on *croit* n'avoir de choix qu'entre l'État et la mainmise des groupes politiques et syndicaux, synonyme d'accaparement, d'irresponsabilité et d'incompétence'.)

103. Cf. *Paye Report* (1970), pp. 214–215.
104. Donald R. Browne, 'Citizen involvement in broadcasting: some European experiences', *Public Telecommunications Review*, Vol. 1, No. 2, October 1973, p. 25, note 31.
105. *Le Monde*, 9–10/7/72.
106. Browne, article cited, p. 28, note 36.
107. *Le Monde*, 28/2/69.
108. *Le Monde*, 12/7/72.
109. Browne, article cited, p. 25.
110. *ORTF 73*, pp. 671–674.
111. *Le Monde*, 6–7/6/71.
112. *Paye Report* (1970), pp. 218–219.
113. Article cited, pp. 25–26.
114. Ibid., p. 26.
115. Jacques Chevallier, 'L'*ORTF* face aux pouvoirs publics', *Droit Social*, No. 12, December 1970, p. 93.
116. Text in J. Favard and J. Rocchi, *Scandales à l'ORTF* (1972), pp. 165–182, in particular, p. 169.
117. 'Faut-il – et pourquoi – "décentraliser" l'*ORTF* ou le "régionaliser"?' *Droit Social*, No. 12, December 1970, pp. 103–104.
118. Cf. Bernard Voyenne, *Le droit à l'information* (1970), pp. 220–221, who also remarks that 'The example of viewers' associations, which cannot even manage to make us believe in their existence, does not incite to optimism' (my translation).
119. Cf. André Brincourt, *André Malraux ou le temps du silence* (1966), *passim*.
120. *Le Monde*, 26/1/68.
121. Cf. p. 191, Note 2.
122. *Diligent Report* (1968), I, p. 98; Francis Balle, *Institutions et publics des moyens d'information* (1973), p. 309.
123. *Diligent*, II, p. 159, Annexe 55, 'Bilan de la régionalisation'.
124. *Diligent*, I, p. 194.
125. *Diligent*, I, p. 209, pp. 285–288.
126. *Le Monde*, 10–11/3/68; 18/9/68; 19/10/68; 12/12/68.
127. *Le Monde*, 26/1/68; 20/11/68.
128. *Le Monde*, 2–3/2/69; 18/3/69.
129. *Le Monde*, 16–17/2/69; 28/3/69.
130. *Le Monde*, 23–24/2/69; 13–14/4/69.
131. *Le Monde*, 28/3/69.
132. *Paye Report* (1970), pp. 89–91.
133. *Paye*, pp. 170–172.

134. *Paye*, pp. 172–174.
135. *Paye*, pp. 174–200.
136. *ORTF Rapport d'activité 1971*, pp. 92–94.
137. *Le Monde*, 7/11/70; 17/4/71; 24–25/10/71.
138. *ORTF 73*, pp. 195–196.
139. *Le Monde*, 27/9/73.
140. *ORTF 73*, p. 195.
141. Martin Even, *Le Monde*, 30/1/71; 2–3/5/71.
142. *ORTF 73*, p. 195.
143. Martin Even, *Le Monde*, 2–3/5/71.
144. *Le Monde*, 16–17/4/72.
145. *Le Monde*, 19–20/11/72; 26–27/11/72; 27/12/72.
146. *Journal de l'année 1971–72*, pp. 274–275.
147. Francis Balle, *Institutions et publics des moyens d'information* (1973), pp. 450ff.
148. *Le Monde*, 19/10/68; 23/12/72.
149. *Le Monde*, 19/10/68; 11–12/5/69.
150. *ORTF 73*, pp. 270–273 (with diagrams).
151. Ibid., pp. 277–278; *Le Monde*, 11–12/2/73.
152. *ORTF 73*, p. 268; *Le Monde*, 3–4/6/73.
153. *ORTF 73*, p. 268.
154. Ibid., pp. 280–281.
155. *Le Monde*, 10–11/12/72; 2–3/9/73.
156. André Astoux, former Assistant Director General of *ORTF*, in *Le Monde*, 17/7/74.
157. *Le Monde*, 1–2/7/73.
158. *JO, Documents A.N., No. 681, Rapport fait au nom de la commission des finances...sur le projet de loi de finances pour 1974, Annexe No. 44, ORTF, Annexe au procès-verbal de la séance du 10 octobre 1973*, pp. 32–33.
159. *Le Monde*, 20–21/1/74. The *Report* just cited gives an audience figure of 0–1 per cent (p. 33).
160. *ORTF 73*, p. 293. These figures do not correspond exactly to those given in the handbook for 1971.
161. *Le Monde*, 15/2/74.
162. *Le Monde*, 17–18/2/74.
163. *Loi du 7 août 1974*, Art. 10; *Le Monde*, 3/8/74; 19/12/74.
164 *Télédistribution et vidéo animation: la situation française. Janvier 1974*, La Documentation Française (1974), pp. 17–19; Brian Groombridge, *Television and the People* (1972), pp. 191ff.
165. *Télédistribution et vidéo animation...*(1974), pp. 27–43; *Le Monde*, 7/4/73.
166. *Télédistribution et vidéo animation...*(1974), pp. 29–36.
167. Ibid., pp. 106–108; *Le Monde*, 3/7/73; 6/2/74.

168. Ibid., pp. 45–46.
169. Ibid., pp. 55–58.
170. Ibid., pp. 47–48.
171. *Le Monde*, 6/2/74.
172. *Télédistribution et vidéo animation*...(1974), p. 48, note 2.
173. *Le Monde*, 6/6/74.
174. G. Suffert and J. Rovan, in *Télévision et éducation*, No. 32, quoted in *Télédistribution et vidéo animation* ... , p. 85. Cf. André Holleaux, 'La télédistribution: vers une télévision communautaire?', *Revue politique et parlementaire*, No. 842, May 1973, pp. 40–59.

CONCLUSION

1. *Le Monde*, 8/1/75; 18/1/75.
2. Details in *Le Monde*, 28/3/75.
3. *Le Monde*, 16/1/75; 23/1/75.
4. Press conference, reported in *Le Monde*, 22/3/75.
5. *Le Monde*, 22/3/75; 29/4/75.

Appendix

HEADS OF BROADCASTING SINCE 1944

Radiodiffusion Française
- 1944 Jean Guignebert
- 1945 Claude Bourdet
- 1946 Wladimir Porché

RTF
- 1949 Wladimir Porché
- 1957 Gabriel Delaunay
- 1958 Christian Chavanon
- 1960 Raymond Janot
- 1962 Robert Bordaz

ORTF
- 1964 J.-B. Dupont
- 1968 J.-J. de Bresson
- 1972 Arthur Conte
- 1973 Marceau Long

National Broadcasting Companies
- 1975 J. Autin (transmission); Jacqueline Baudrier (radio); J. Cazeneuve (*TF 1*); Claude Contamine (*FR 3*); J.-C. Edeline (production); Pierre Emmanuel (Audio-visual Institute); Marcel Jullian (*Antenne 2*).

Bibliography

1. BOOKS AND ARTICLES CONSULTED

AMAURY, PHILIPPE. *Les deux premières expériences d'un 'Ministère de l'Information' en France*. Pichon. Paris. 1969.

AMBLER, JOHN S. *The Government and Politics of France*. Houghton Mifflin. Boston. 1971.

Après-demain. 'L'ORTF', 107, October 1968.

BALLE, FRANCIS. *Institutions et publics des moyens d'information. Presse. Radiodiffusion. Télévision*. Éditions Montchrestien, Collection Université Nouvelle. Paris. 1973.

BLANCKEMAN, RENÉ. *Le roman vécu de la télévision française*. Éditions France-Empire. Paris. 1961.

BONNEFOUS, ÉDOUARD. *Présent et avenir de la radiotélévision française*. *Revue politique et parlementaire*, 734, May 1963.

BRETAGNE, CHRISTIAN. *Chère télévision*. Julliard. Paris. 1972.

BRINCOURT, ANDRÉ. *André Malraux ou le temps du silence*. La Table Ronde. Paris. 1966.

BROWNE, DONALD R. Citizen involvement in broadcasting: some European experiences. *Public Telecommunications Review*, 1, 2, October 1973. 16–28.

CAYROL, ROLAND. *La presse écrite et audio-visuelle*. P.U.F. Paris. 1973.

CHAPUIS, Robert. *L'Information*. Éditions de l'Épi. Paris. 1959.

CODDING, GEORGE A., JNR. *La radiodiffusion dans le monde*. UNESCO. Paris. 1959.

CONTE, ARTHUR. *Hommes libres...*Plon. Paris. 1973.

DANSETTE, ADRIEN. *Mai 1968*. Plon. Paris. 1971.

DEBBASCH, CHARLES. *Le droit de la radio et de la télévision.* P.U.F. Paris. Collection 'Que sais-je?' 1969.

DESCAVES, PIERRE. *Quand la radio s'appelait Tour Eiffel.* La Table Ronde. Paris. 1963.

DESCAVES, PIERRE and MARTIN, A. V. J. (ED.). *Un siècle de radio et de télévision.* ORTF et les Productions de Paris. Paris. 1965.

D'ORMESSON, WLADIMIR. L'ORTF libéré? *Revue de Paris,* July–August 1969. 79–87.

Droit Social. L'ORTF et ses problèmes, 12, December 1970.

DUMAZEDIER, JOFFRE. *Vers une civilisation du loisir?* Seuil. Paris. 1962.

DUPUIS, G. and RAUX, J. *L'ORTF.* Collection 'U2'. Armand Colin. Paris. 1970.

DUVERGER, MAURICE. *Droit Public.* 3rd edition. P.U.F. Paris. 1963.

Économie et Politique. Une radio-télévision démocratique, 151, February 1967.

EMERY, WALTER B. *National and International Systems of Broadcasting. Their History, Operation and Control.* Michigan State University Press. East Lansing. 1969.

EMMANUEL, PIERRE. *Pour une politique de la culture.* Seuil. Paris. 1971.

ERRERA, ROGER. *Les libertés à l'abandon.* Seuil. Paris. 1968.

FAVARD, J. and ROCCHI, J. *Scandales à l'ORTF.* Le Pavillon-Roger Maria Editions. Paris. 1972.

FAVREAU, B. *Georges Mandel, un clémenciste en Gironde.* Editions A. Pedone. Paris. 1969.

FRÉDÉRIC, CLAUDE. *Libérer ORTF. Documents et témoignages recueillies par Claude Frédéric.* Seuil. Paris. 1968.

GRAMONT, SANCHE DE. *The French: Portrait of a People.* Hodder and Stoughton. London. 1970.

GREEN, TIMOTHY. *The Universal Eye. The World of Television.* Stein and Day. New York. 1972.

GROOMBRIDGE, BRIAN. *Television and the People. A Programme for Democratic Participation.* Penguin. Harmondsworth. 1972.

HOLLEAUX, ANDRÉ. La télédistribution: vers une télévision communautaire? *Revue politique et parlementaire,* 842, May 1973. 40–59.

HUC, BENJAMIN and ROBIN, FRANÇOIS. *Histoire et dessous de la radio en France et dans le monde.* Les Éditions de France. Paris. 1938.

Journal de l'Année 1971–1972. Larousse. Paris. 1972.

LAFORET, PIERRE. *La prodigieuse aventure d'Europe No. 1.* Pierre Horay. Paris. 1960.

LALOU, ÉTIENNE. *Regards neufs sur la télévision.* Seuil. Paris. 1957.

L'Année politique, économique, sociale et diplomatique en France. P.U.F. Paris. 1944–.

La Nef. La télévision, 8, October 1961.

La Nef. L'Information politique, 27, May 1966.

La Radio a 50 ans. ORTF. Paris. 1972.

Les Cahiers de la télévision. Julliard. Paris. 1961–1963.

LOUIS, ROGER. *L'ORTF, un combat.* Seuil. Paris. 1968.

MANEL, J.-P. and PLANEL, ALOMÉE (ps.). *La crise de l'ORTF.* J.-J. Pauvert. Paris. 1968.

MERCILLON, HENRI. La France, son système d'information, sa télévision. *Direction,* 166, November 1969.

MERLIN, LOUIS. *Le vrai dossier de la télévision.* Hachette. Paris. 1964.

MIQUEL, PIERRE. *Histoire de la radio et de la télévision.* Editions Richelieu. Paris. 1972.

MONTALDO, JEAN. *Dossier ORTF 1944–1974: Tous coupables.* Albin Michel. Paris. 1974.

MOREAU, JEAN-GUY. *Le Règne de la télévision.* Seuil. Paris. 1967.

ORTF Rapport d'activité 1971. Paris. 1971.

ORTF 73. Presses Pocket. Paris. 1973.

PARAF, PIERRE. *L'Information hier, aujourd'hui, demain.* Bourrelier. Paris. 1946.

PAULU, BURTON. *Radio and Television Broadcasting on the European Continent.* University of Minnesota Press. 1967.

PONT, PIERRE DU. *L'État industriel.* Sirey. Paris. 1961.

Programme commun de gouvernment du parti communiste et du parti socialiste. 27 Juin 1972. Éditions Sociales. Paris. 1972. (Each party published the identical text with a preface by its own leader.)

RÉMOND, R. and NEUSCHWANDER, CLAUDE. Télévision et comportement politique. *Revue française de science politique,* 13, 2, June 1963.

REVEL, JEAN-FRANÇOIS. *En France: la fin de l'opposition.* Julliard. Paris. 1965.

ROCHE, ANDRÉ and BAILLY, RENÉ. *Le Dictionnaire de la télévision.* Larousse. Paris. 1967.

SCHAEFFER, PIERRE. *Machines à communiquer. 1. Genèse des simulacres. 2. Pouvoir et communication.* Seuil. Paris. 1972.

SCHAEFFER, PIERRE. *Une charte pour la télévision*. *Preuves*, 14, 2e. trimestre 1973. 116–144.

Sondages. IFOP. L'Opinion de juillet 1971 à juillet 1972 (i) et (ii), 3–4, 1972.

SPADE, HENRI. *Histoire d'amour de la télévision française*. Éditions France–Empire. Paris. 1968.

Télédistribution et vidéo-animation. La situation française. Janvier 1974. La Documentation Française. Paris. 1974.

THÉVENOT, JEAN and QUEVAL, JEAN. *T.V.* Gallimard. Paris. 1957.

THIBAU, JACQUES. *Une télévision pour tous les Français*. Seuil. Paris. 1970.

THIBAU, JACQUES. *La télévision, le pouvoir et l'argent*. Calmann-Levy. Paris. 1973.

VERPRAET, GEORGES. *La télévision et ses métiers*. Bordas. Paris. 1972.

VIANSSON-PONTÉ, PIERRE. *Histoire de la république gaullienne*. 2 vols. Fayard. Paris. 1970.

VIANSSON-PONTÉ, PIERRE. *Les Gaullistes, rituel et annuaire*. Seuil. Paris. 1963.

VOYENNE, BERNARD. *Le droit à l'information*. Aubier-Éditions Montaigne. Paris. 1970.

VOYENNE, BERNARD. *La presse dans la société contemporaine*. Collection 'U', 4th edition. Armand Colin. Paris. 1971.

VOYENNE, BERNARD. *L'Information en France*. McGraw-Hill. London. 1972.

WILLIAMS, PHILIP M. *The French Parliament, 1958–1967*. Studies in Political Science. George Allen and Unwin. London. 1968.

WILLIAMS, PHILIP M. *Wars, Plots and Scandals in Post-War France*. Cambridge University Press. 1970.

WILLIAMS, PHILIP M. and HARRISON, MARTIN. *Politics and Society in de Gaulle's Republic*. Longmans. London. 1971. Doubleday. New York. 1972. (Revised and continued from *De Gaulle's Republic*. Longmans. London. 1960).

2. DOCUMENTS

(i) *Journal Officiel de la République Française* (*JO*): *Débats Assemblée Nationale; Débats Sénat; Documents Assemblée Nationale; Documents Sénat: Lois et décrets.*

(Full details are given in Notes.)

(ii) *Special parliamentary reports on broadcasting*
  (a) *Diligent Report* (1968): JO, *Documents Sénat, No. 118, Rapport fait en conclusion des travaux de la Commission de Contrôle...chargée d'examiner les problèmes posés par l'accomplissement des missions propres à l'Office de radiodiffusion-télévision française, par M. André Diligent...Déposé le 13 avril 1968. Rattaché, pour ordre, au procès-verbal de la séance du 2 avril 1968. Tomes I et II.*
  (b) *Diligent Report* (1972): JO, *Documents Sénat, No. 165, Rapport d'information, par M André Diligent, présenté au nom de la mission commune d'information désignée par la commission des affaires culturelles, par la commission des affaires économiques et du Plan, par la commission des lois constitutionelles,...par la commission des finances,...et chargée d'examiner la régularité de la gestion de l'Office de radiodiffusion-télévision française et des relations que cet organisme entretient avec diverses entreprises nationales, etablissements publics, sociétés d'economie mixte ou autres, notamment dans le domaine de la publicité. Mis en distribution le 27 avril 1972.*
  (c) *Le Tac Report* (1972): JO, *Documents A.N., No. 2291, Rapport fait au nom de la Commission de Contrôle de la gestion de l'Office de radiodiffusion-télévision française. Par M. Le Tac...Annexe au procès-verbal de la séance du 28 avril 1972. Tomes I et II (i) et (ii).*
  (d) *Chinaud Report* (1974): JO, *Documents A.N., No. 1072, Rapport fait au nom de la Commission de Contrôle de la gestion financière de l'Office de radiodiffusion et télévision française. Par M. Chinaud...Annexe au procès-verbal de la séance du 20 juin 1974.*
(iii) *Independent enquiry*
  Paye Report (1970): *Rapport de la commission d'étude du statut de l'ORTF, 30 juin 1970.* La Documentation Française. 1970.
(iv) *Other documents*
  Étude spéciale de certains problèmes posés par l'introduction de la publicité de marques à l'ORTF, in *Les Articles 34, 37 et 38 de la Constitution de 1958*, Droit Constitutionnel et Institutions Politiques, Documents d'Etudes No. 8. La Documentation Française. April 1970.
  ORTF: 'ORTF grande entreprise nationale' (1973), a

dossier of information and statistics distributed by the ORTF *Service des relations avec la presse.*

'Instruction No. 33 du 15 février 1973 sur l'organisation générale de l'Office de Radiodiffusion-Télévision Française' (internal memo).

Régie française de publicité: 'Conditions générales de vente et conditions techniques applicables à la publicité de marque', including 'Règlement de la publicité radiophonique et télévisée'; 'Tarifs de la publicité de marques télévisée 1973'; 'Conditions générales de vente et conditions techniques applicables à la publicité collective (Télévision)' including 'Tarifs de la publicité collective'; 'Frais techniques de production'. Both folders dated 1 January 1973.

Syndicat national des journalistes ORTF: 'Mémoire revendicatif du SNJ-ORTF,' 15 September 1972; 'Résolution finale, Assemblée générale du 8 mai 1973'. The chaotic conditions surrounding the reorganization of ORTF in the autumn of 1974 made it impossible to obtain the *SNJ*'s *Livre blanc sur les problèmes de l'information.*

3. FURTHER READING

EBU REVIEW. Periodical of the European Broadcasting Union (French version *Revue de l'union européenne de radiodiffusion*). Published in Geneva.

HARWOOD, KENNETH. A world bibliography of selected periodicals on broadcasting. *Journal of Broadcasting*, 16, 2, 1972. 131–146.

Presse-Actualité. Periodical devoted to the press and audiovisual media.

SALDICH, ANNE. 'Politique et télévision sous de Gaulle'. Unpublished thesis, *École pratique des hautes études.* University of Paris. 1971.

Name Index

Subject Index